ANCIENT EGYPT
IN THE
AFRICAN CONTEXT

RECASTING ANCIENT EGYPT IN THE AFRICAN CONTEXT:

TOWARD A MODEL CURRICULUM USING ART AND LANGUAGE

CLINTON CRAWFORD

Africa World Press, Inc.

P.O. Box 1892

Trenton, NJ 08607

P.O. Box 48

Asmara, ERITREA

Africa World Press, Inc.

P.O. Box 1892
Trenton, NJ 08607

P.O. Box 48
Asmara, ERITREA

Copyright © 1996   Clinton Crawford

First Printing 1996

Book Design: Jonathan Gullery
Book Cover: Linda Nickens
Cover Art, Illustrations: Reba Ashton-Crawford

Library of Congress Cataloging-in-Publication Data

Crawford, Clinton
      Recasting ancient Egypt in the African context : toward a model curriculum using art and language / Clinton Crawford.
         p. cm.
      Includes bibliographical references and index.
      ISBN 0-86543-380-1 (cloth : alk.paper). -- ISBN 0-86543-381-X (pbk. : alk. paper)
         1. Egypt--Civilization--To 332 B.C. 2. Art, Egyptian.
      3. Egyptian language. 4. Egypt--Civilization--African influences.
      5. Egypt--Civilization--Study and teaching--United States.
      6. Curriculum change--United States. 7. Multiculturalism--United States. I. Title.
      DT61.C74   1996
      932--dc20   95-51262
                                                                      CIP

*To the memories of
the late Dr. Cheikh Anta Diop
and the late Dr. Chancellor Williams,
who charged my generation to continue the enormous task
of building a civilization as great as — or even greater than—
the mouthpiece of ancient Alkebu-lan,
Kemet*

The Meaning of the Adinkra Symbol:
Sankofa

Sankofa ("Go back to fetch it") -- symbol of the wisdom in the learning from the past in building for the future. Prov.: *"Se wo were fi na wo sankofa a yenkyi"* ("It is not a taboo to go back and retrieve if you forget").

CONTENTS

ILLUSTRATIONS
(following page 124)

*Drawings by Reba Ashton-Crawford
† Courtesy of the Museum of Fine Arts, Boston, Mass.
‡ Courtesy of the Cairo Museum, Cairo, Egypt

§ Courtesy of the Metropolitan Museum of Art, New York, N.Y.

17: Rogers Fund, 1918

20: Harris Brisbane Dick Fund, 1962

26: Rogers Fund, 1908

28. (a)Rogers Fund, 1907; (b-c) Rogers Fund, 1910;(d)Rogers Fund, 1929; (e) Rogers Fund, 1938; (f) Purchase, Fletcher Fund and the Guide Foundation, Inc. Gift, 1966;(g) Theodore M. Davis Collection, bequest of Theodore M. Davis, 1915; (h) Gift of Mrs. Frederick F. Thompson, 1915.

37: Gift of J. Pierpont Morgan, 1912 (upper panel): Rogers Fund, 1908 (lower panel).

Courtesy of the Oriental Institute, University of Chicago, Chicago, Ill.

PROLOGUE

Many have asked why there is a field of study called "Black History." If there is a "Black" history, they say, then that implies that there is a "White" history. Shouldn't there only be "History" — pure and simple?

Yes, but there isn't, because what is labeled "History Pure & Simple" is neither pure nor simple. Rather, it is a version of recorded events systematically denuded of significant contributions of peoples of color. This is just as true of other disciplines as well.

This book is an example of how we can begin the process of obviating the need to emphasize ethnic studies. Here is a unique guide for infusing multi-cultural facts — and perspectives — into the heart of the American educational system.

Dr. Crawford cites chapter and verse as to how we can most naturally fashion the curriculum to reflect all of the diverse legacies and contributions to our society and, in so doing, render diverse and sundry individual subject areas genuinely interdisciplinary.

I sincerely hope that this fine work gets the broad airing it deserves. If enough educators are exposed to it, I am certain it will play an important part in energizing the studies that take place in schools across the nation.

Dr. Arthur Lewin, Chair
Black & Hispanic Studies
Baruch College
City University of New York

FOREWORD

What are we to do after we accept the challenge to diversify school curricula so that they can brightly reflect the many-splendoured contributions of America's many peoples to American civilization? The author of *Recasting Ancient Egypt in the African Context:Toward a Model Curriculum Using Art and Language* suggests a course of action that is both well-conceived and supported by voluminous research. Blending the "science" of archaeology with the "art" of progressive educational philosophy, Clinton Crawford argues that the "curricularization" of the already popular subject of Egyptology (especially if focused on the art and language of that ancient society) would prove an indispensible and empowering course of study for contemporary American schoolchildren—not only African American, but those from other ethnic backgrounds as well. In other words, Professor Crawford is saying, *all students* need multicultural studies, in order to inform and improve the quality of their insights, decisions, and actions in a (post-) modern and increasingly complex society. Even students in the so-called "main stream," Crawford maintains, would benefit immensely from the proper (i.e., "africanized") study of Egyptology as the cornerstone of a transcultural liberal arts education.

Crawford does a service in re-opening a stalled debate on Egyptian history (particularly that of the first six dynasties). Even though the historical importance of ancient Egypt is not disputed today, his insistence that the dynastic Egyptians were Black Africans (the "recasting" referred to in the title) is still quite controversial in our society at large. He is therefore careful, in his opening salvos, to be accurate and detailed, for his main concern—and what is at stake here—is the self-esteem of African American students *and* the ability of others to appreciate that the seminal cultural achievements of our civilization were attained by the forebears of their Black fellow-students. He knows that there can be no nationalistic boost for Africans in America (such as every other ethnic group here already enjoys), nor any general increase in respect for the historical contributions of Black Africans, if the dynastic Egyptians continue to be regarded as other than Africoid. Crawford is on solid ground, however, thanks to the pioneering work of formidable scholars like Cheikh Anta Diop and Ivan Van Sertima, who have solidly established that the early Egyptians were indeed Black.

Dr. Crawford painstakingly and patiently educates his readers on the impressive innovations made by the Egyptians in art, language, and literature. Moreover, in contrast to the conventional view that Egyptian art is too narrowly conceptualized and overly religious, he stresses its versatility and openness. Of particular interest and irony, especially for those who like me are fascinated by the relationship between language and education, is the fact that the African *literate* tradition is the oldest known to humankind. (This, apparently, is why Thoth, the god of writing and wisdom, was so highly revered.) Such facts should not be lost sight of, even as we continue to celebrate the enormously rich African *oral* tradition; rather, teachers of African American students need to stress the *multiple* nature of our communicative heritage and actively resist the pernicious notion that African Americans shouldn't be expected to excel in *writing* because they are, "after all, primarily an *oral* people." In other words, *"We been some serious oral **and** literate people, and **that's** what the present and future generations need to git wit."*

This book should also provoke other teacherly moves. The ample historical information, combined with the author's strong pronouncements on intellectual rigor, critical thinking, and interdisciplinarity can generate a variety of important units and courses. If educators—formal and informal alike—are serious about education, they can certainly use the present text to justify and implement curricular initiatives.

As befits a work that strives "toward a model curriculum," this book is more *descriptive* than *prescriptive*. Happily, Dr. Crawford plans to publish a teacher's guide, specifying how a three-course sequence he envisions for high school and college students may actually unfold. While we eagerly await that welcome work, let us begin reaping the benefits of the equally valuable one now at hand.

Prof. Keith Gilyard
Director of The Writing Program
Syracuse University

PREFACE

This work is an attempt at a cross-disciplinary analysis of the language, art, and culture of ancient Egypt—specifically, as African in origin—in order to provide new areas of content for multicultural curricula. These new areas of curricular content will also add to the existing national debate on multicultural studies, which I view as a step towards improving the American educational system. The call for multicultural studies is raised by the demographic reality that nearly fifty percent of the youth under eighteen in this country are "people of color." Given this reality, curriculum planners must address the interests of the diversified student population.

Those who have already embraced multiculturalism are beginning to identify many valuable contributions this approach has to make to our declining education system.

One of these is the multidisciplinary method of learning and teaching. In the case of education in language and the arts, accessing other disciplines such as anthropology, linguistics, archaeology, history, and the sciences can provide a broader knowledge base. In employing an interdisciplinary model, the young student not only becomes familiar with the earliest known system of language and art, but also gains an understanding of these varied contemporary disciplines, as well. The student experiences how the data for the debate over the origin of an ancient civilization are culled from an examination of anthropological, archaeological, linguistic, and historical records as well as the architecture, sculpture, and painting of that culture. In turn, the hieroglyphics, architecture, sculpture, and painting reveal the politics, economics, and sociology (social order) of these peoples and those who came after them.

Hence this document is conceived to offer a balanced view of a culture, its language, and its arts that may well serve as a model for other endeavors of the same kind.

The study is organized as follows: (a) the origin and development of the Egyptians; (b) an examination of the complex culture of the people from the Nile Valley, which is crucial to our understanding of their arts and language; (c) summary examination of their artistic and linguistic achievements; and (d) specific proposals regarding a model curriculum. Thus we anticipate an education in the arts and language that not only benefits from multiculturalism, but which is informed by an interdisciplinary approach that broadens one's knowledge base about culture, language, and the arts and the means by which one can learn about them.

ACKNOWLEDGEMENTS

Assembling a work of this magnitude could not have been possible if the African spirit of cooperation were not present throughout the past four years. Although my signature is written all over this text, I am most grateful to many close friends.

For sound advice and strength during the trying moments of this work, I called on my brother, Dr. Arthur Lewin. He assured me that I was doing the work of our ancestors, whose spirits were evoked by this study, and that they would guide me throughout the journey. He was right. I am indebted. Our long walk from 18th Street on Fifth Avenue to 42nd Street on that warm spring day in 1992, while we talked about this work and other related subject matter, could not be captured in words. You had to be there.

To the students in my English classes at Hostos Community College, CUNY, Long Island University, Brooklyn Campus and at Medgar Evers College, CUNY, who always listened to me talk about my work and nudged me on with their assurance that I was doing a noble task, I say thank you for your kindred spirits.

To Dr. Edison O. Jackson, President of Medgar Evers College, City University of New York, I offer my thanks and appreciation for his leadership and commitment to the academic and intellectual project of excellence.

For helpful words of advice and brotherly support in the final stages of this work, I salute an outstanding scholar, Dr. Keith Gilyard.

To the untiring hands and pens of the editors at Africa World Press, I thank you.

And to my wife Reba, not the least at all, for her never-ending support not only as a companion during the lonely times as I tapped away on my word processor, but in moments of panic to meet my deadlines, researching and securing permission for illustrations from museums across America, Europe, and Egypt. She has contributed her fair share to the success of this work. Reba's illustrations that accompany this text testify to but one of her many talents. Hotep sister! You will be rewarded.

INTRODUCTION

Any serious discussion about ancient Egyptian art and language must also include a discussion of ancient Egyptian history and its place in the history of the world. In the African country that the Greeks called *"Aigyptos,"* art, language, and culture were developed to the point that they had become part of the everyday way of life of all the people. Good speech and fine art were not the exclusive domain of the privileged, but were matters of which all Egyptians strove to be part. And you, dear reader, by virtue of your interest in this book, *Recasting Ancient Egypt in the African Context: Toward a Model Curriculum Using Art and Language,* are a vital part of Professor Clinton Crawford's serious effort to examine the vital role played in Egyptian culture by Egyptian art and language. Before examining the substance of this book, therefore, we need to locate Egypt and its people on the map of human memory.

In a broader sense, what is under discussion here is Nile Valley Civilization and its contribution to world civilization. This necessarily means that we will be discussing the southern origins of this civilization because (as pointed out repeatedly by many scholars in this field*) there was no functioning "Europe" at the point in history that Egypt emerged.

Africa's academic adversaries and detractors have made every effort to avoid dealing with African people as thinkers whose social thought helped to lay the basis for much of the world's spiritual literature, including the Bible, and whose philosophical thought went into

---

*See: Gerald Massey's two-volume work, *Egypt: Light of the World* (Baltimore: Black Classic Press, 1992 [*1907]); Chancellor Williams, "Ethiopia's Oldest Daughter," [Chapter 2] in his *Destruction of Black Civilization* (Chicago: Third World Press, 1976); John G. Jackson, *Ethiopia and the Origin of Civilization* (Baltimore: Black Classic Press, 1985 [*1939]); George G. M. James, *Stolen Legacy* (Trenton: Africa World Press, 1992 [*1954]); and Theophile Obenga's *A Lost Tradition: African Philosophy in World History* (forthcoming).

the making of what some people think of as "Greek Philosophy." Even the most cursory information about these African contributions to the main stream of civilization is lacking in the standard history books. The works cited above, especially Obenga's *Lost Tradition,* have begun the task of replacing the missing pages and restoring Africa's proper place in the history of the world.

Every conqueror needs to make a conquered people forget how, before the arrival of the conqueror, they once ruled themselves politically, educationally, and philosophically. In Africa, European powers undertook massive efforts to prove (to themselves and to their "subjects") that Africans had nothing in their past worthy of being called "history." The late Caribbean writer and activist, Richard B. Moore, reminded us that no such massive effort would have been carried out in order to obscure and bury what was actually of little or no significance.

In actuality, ancient Egypt was a composite and a culmination of a number of African civilizations, mostly coming from the South via the world's first great cultural highway, the Nile River. The Nile cuts through 4,000 miles of the physical body of Africa, and the civilization accredited to the Egyptians was formed mainly by migrations of peoples along this river. When the vast area now called the Sahara dried up and became a desert, large numbers of people from this area migrated toward the Nile Valley and ultimately became contributors to the art, language, and culture of Egypt—making Egypt the beneficiary of the greatest assemblage of talent and skill in the history of its world. Egypt produced the world's first consistently organized agriculture, which enabled it to feed its large and growing number of people (and, eventually, those of its neighbors as well!). The true greatness of ancient Egypt, however, consists in the Egyptian people's acceptance of a society ruled by collective discipline and high morality. It was no accident that Egypt led the world of its day in "fine art and good speech"; it was because these two virtues were not left to chance. This is doubly demonstrated in the present work and in Professor Jacob Carruthers' new book, *Divine Speech,* which also calls our attention to the significance of both art *and* language in the development of Egypt. Indeed, no nation in history has left a better record of such twin achievements.

A serious *African* re-examination of the art, language, and culture of ancient Egypt and its place in the progression of human development did not really get underway until the twentieth century. With the appearance of Cheikh Anta Diop, and his magnum opus and crowning achievement, *Civilization or Barbarism,* our understanding of this ancient society took a monumental leap forward. Many areas previously ignored were now on the agenda. The disciples of Dr. Diop, such as Obenga, Ki-Zerbo, and Father Mvang joined in creating a new intellectual climate for information about the neglected history of African people before foreigners interfered with the intellectual struc-

ture of their societies. Professor Crawford, in his book, has convincingly shown that art and language are weapons in a nation's cultural survival. In preparing this book with the projected hope that it will be
used in a multicultural curriculum, he has opened a new educational
door by demonstrating the modern significance of ancient Egyptian art
and language.

John Henrik Clarke, Ph.D.
Professor Emeritus of African Studies
Hunter College, City College of New York

CHAPTER ONE

STATEMENT OF THE PROBLEM

It is unfortunate that our society, in its customary cultural products, has perpetuated ignorance and prejudice among its citizens through negative characterizations of people of various cultural extractions, to the point that such negative characterizations have now become institutionalized. In the canons of American art and literature, for instance, African-Americans, Asian-Americans, Latinos, and Native Americans are routinely depicted in such a way that their parent cultures are either marginalized, omitted, or distorted. This treatment has resulted in a noticeable lack of self-esteem among these so-called "minorities." In many current secondary school and collegiate textbooks, moreover, Euro-American culture clearly is the one most highly valued, judging by the emphasis placed on its history and its contribution to civilization.

According to the Task Force of the New York State Board of Education (1989), the general curriculum of many schools, by reflecting the Eurocentric view, has contributed to the "intellectual victimization and miseducation of Americans from all cultures" (p. 1). The curriculum, in the view of the Board of Education, is demeaning and alienating in its descriptions of so-called minorities' cultures, while representatives of the dominant, Euro-American culture are depicted in an exclusionary and flattering light.

More specifically with respect to art and language education, in many secondary schools and colleges the curriculum focuses almost exclusively on Euro-American languages, literatures, aesthetics, and art history. The lesser importance assigned to knowledge of other cultures, such as Native American or African, is accepted not only by local educators but also by those at the highest levels of educational policymaking.

If education in art, language, and literature is going to move beyond its present monocultural stage, it is of pivotal importance that we develop and ensure an accurate, comprehensive, and bias-free education with a balanced curriculum that meets the needs of impressionable young people in a pluralistic society. An important component of such an education generally (and especially so in art and language education) is to trace the history and aesthetics of ancient African art, language, and literature of the first six Egyptian dynasties.

The rationale for choosing this particular period of ancient African art, language and literature is based on the accepted and indisputable archaeological and cultural evidence. Over the last two centuries, excavations have shown that the art, language, and literature of the first six Egyptian dynasties constituted the high point of that civilization. The art, architecture, science, religion, literature, and medicine of that earliest era were unsurpassed in the succeeding periods of Egyptian and Indo-European cultures. Moreover, it is necessary to clearly define the impact of the ancient period of African art and literature upon later African, African-American, and European culture. Even a general understanding of ancient Africa and early dynastic Egyptian art and language will contribute to a person's liberal education.

All of the above are central concerns in my work. Given that people of African ancestry constitute an important and sizable group in America, and that African civilizations, ancient and medieval, have left a rich legacy of sophisticated works of art and literature, it seems appropriate to promote as one of the goals of American education an awareness of the history, literature, and aesthetics of African art and language. I want to enable young African-Americans to participate more fully in programs of art and literary education. Mindful of the overall objective of including all cultures—which, in this context, means including that of ancient Africa—the present work is designed to (a) provide background material and analysis of ancient Egyptian culture, language, literature, art, and aesthetics, and (b) compile material for a curriculum model for secondary-school and college students. Further, the curriculum model will incorporate an interdisciplinary approach to education in art and language. For example, to foster a better understanding of a given culture's artwork, the disciplines of anthropology, archaeology, and history will be utilized to lay a foundation for understanding the world-view that has influenced the making of art within that culture. These particular disciplines are selected because in modern times archaeological excavations and anthropological findings have been among the most reliable sources of historical information. Thus, even in the teaching of art the student will discover the usefulness of anthropology and archaeology as essential sources of reliable historical information. In this way, a broad methodologic perspective is taught as well as new content conveyed. For example, the technique of excavation allows the archaeologist to secure concrete and non-subjective information. In fact, the integrity of the discipline requires that the archaeologist assume the role of chronicler, continually verifying and updating "historical" information.

On the other hand, anthropology helps us see a culture as an integrated whole rather than merely as the sum of its parts. Anthropology, states Colin Turnbull (1983), is a necessary discipline because of its analytical division of social organization into such categories as domestic life, economic life, political life, and religious life. Thus one not only understands the ethnographic origins and descriptions of a people, but also seeks "to understand the concepts, to look for the regularities and relationships that can be seen through all spheres of social organization" (Turnbull, p. 20).

Ultimately, an interdisciplinary approach to education in art and language reinforces such sharing of information among related fields of study, thereby integrating distinct disciplines within a single educational experience.

Limitations

It would be beyond the scope of this work to trace in detail the entire history of Ancient African art, language, and literature. I will therefore restrict myself to documenting the major historical developments in "Black" art and literature which evolved in the northern reaches of the Nile Valley. The foremost ancient civilization of this region is Egypt, originally named Kemet. According to W. B. Emery (1961), Cheikh Anta Diop (1974), and other students of Nile Valley civilizations, pharaonic Egypt received a long history and tradition of dispersed predynastic peoples who lived in enclaves in Lower and Upper Egypt and Ethiopia. Furthermore, some historians—such as Yosef ben-Jochannan (1989), John Jackson (1970), and Chancellor Williams (1976)—argue that the roots of the ancient Egyptian culture are displayed on the Narmer-Menes palettes of 3100 B.C. These palettes illustrate events leading up to the unification of Egypt from the once-scattered peoples of the north and south. One of the illustrations on the Narmer palettes shows that Menes was the first pharaoh, and that the crystallization of a great Egyptian civilization started with his reign.

Most importantly, this study will be limited to the following parameters: examination of the early era of pharaonic Egypt; determination of the needs of students at the secondary-school and college level; consideration of a model curriculum which includes a multicultural and an interdisciplinary approach; and a redefinition of art and language education that will encompass art history, aesthetics, criticism, language development, and the literary texts that illustrate many aspects of Egyptian daily life.

The analysis of the ancient roots of African art and language is intended to form the literary base for the instruction of adolescents at high-school level and at the college level. Although the primary ethnic group to be addressed is of African ancestry, the course content will make an effort to include the interests of students from other ethnic groups. One of the objectives will be to engage students from all socio-economic classes, since most students, African-Americans or otherwise, simply have no understanding of ancient African art and literature. The proposed model curriculum will encourage the study of ancient African art and language in terms of their histories and their aesthetics. Such study will broaden the knowledge base of students who are normally curious about, and receptive to, learning about other cultures.

The specific artistic and literary forms from ancient Egyptian culture to be examined are architecture, murals, bas-relief, freestanding sculpture, pottery, jewelry, the linguistic history of the hieroglyph, and the common literature of hymns, stories, mythology, and philosophical texts. Indeed, the aforementioned geographical area is well known for these specific artistic and literary expressions. For example, ancient Egypt is famous for its elaborate architecture of temples, tombs, and pyramids. In particular, the pyramids—the burial places of the pharaohs—are important sites for the examination of numerous artistic and literary objects of ancient Egyptian civilization. Attention will also be focused on their technical achievement of stonework (i.e., pyramids, temples, and vases), which are grounded in advanced mathematical principles of great precision. (A detailed use of mathematics in the science of architectural construction will be offered later.) In addition, an examination of the inner walls of the pyramids' chambers, with their elaborate murals and written texts chronicling the life of each pharaoh, will be an area for in-depth investigation of painting techniques, the depiction of ideas, and the manipulation of materials.

Equally important, examples of freestanding portraiture made from stone and wood will not be omitted. In fact, ancient Egyptian art is dominated by such immortalized images of royalty. With the concept of portraiture so well documented in Egyptian art, some special attention to the phenomenon of three-dimensional portraiture is in order. An examination of the magnificent jewelry found at Tut-ankh-Amen's tomb will complete the students' study of Egyptian art. Of equal importance is the development of writing, from pictograms and ideograms to the sophisticated fruition of the hieroglyph, with its many unparalleled language features which served as a model for language development beyond Egypt. The voluminous literary works—which include mythology, hymns, poetry, master literary epics, philosophy, and recorded scientific findings in medicine, mathematical formulae, and astronomy—will also be highlighted.

Method of Analysis

The method of analysis in this work falls into three broad categories: the background information on ancient Egypt, the needs of adolescents and young adults in the United States, and related curriculum development. Each category will employ a different approach to distilling and interpreting data and then integrating the appropriate information.

The background information on ancient Egypt draws upon sources such as history, anthropology, archaeology, and linguistics, which function in various ways. First, the primary historical data about ancient Egypt derives from sources such as the historiographic sketches by a Hellenistic-period Egyptian priest and chronicler named Manetho; the second-millenium-B.C. "pyramid texts" known as *The Book of the Dead;* and the writings of the classical Greek historians Herodotus, and Diodorus Siculus. Second, modern historical sources will include works by Ivan Van Sertima, Yosef ben-Jochannan, Basil Davidson, Cyril Aldred, and others. Third, both classical and modern archaeological findings, as presented by Count Volney, Sir Flinders Petrie, Peter Tompkins, and Cheikh Anta Diop are used to buttress the claims of history. Fourth, the linguistic findings of Gerald Massey, Anta Diop, Theophile Obenga, Weidemann, and Wallis Budge will serve as the core resources for my investigation into the language and literature of ancient Egypt.

Finally, the anthropological investigations of moderns like Anta Diop, ben-Jochannan, James Brunson, Martin Bernal, Van Sertima, and others who have elucidated the history and archaeology of ancient Egypt will couch and buttress my own argument.

The Needs of the Adolescents and Young Adults

The needs of adolescents and young adults are the real reason why this work is important. According to the report on Equity and Excellence, the Task Force for the New York State Board of Education's proposal *A Curriculum of Inclusion* (1989), upholds that the curriculum for so-called minority students grades K through 12 did not adequately reflect the pluralistic American population. The same observation is also true for college students. The instructional practice of advancing a virtually Eurocentric point of view in elementary and secondary school and college actually works to the detriment of all students, particularly those from African-American, Latino-American, Asian-American, and Native American backgrounds. The Task Force called for the development of "positive self-esteem and self-management skills needed in all young people of a pluralistic society" (p. 7). Movement towards intellectual honesty and bias-free education should replace miseducation. The recommendations of the Task Force along with the educational theories of Ira Shor (1987), Thomas Brown (1986), Paulo Freire and Danaldo

Macedo (1987), and Janice Hale-Benson (1986) address the needs of young African-Americans and other so-called minorities. With respect to those theories, this work attempts to address the need for understanding the learning styles and educational content that are relevant to "minority" children, particularly those of African descent.

Finally, with regard to curriculum development, the theoretical approaches, both traditional and contemporary, that support my curricular model will be used. The aim is to merge tradition and innovation. For instance, the concerns of appropriate teaching strategies, the relevance of content to the students' needs, the integration of content and thinking, and multicultural literacy are important to the proposed model curriculum. This curriculum will rest upon the theories of John Dewey (1916), Carter G. Woodson (1933), Paulo Freire (1987), the New York State Board of Education Task Force on Equity and Excellence (1989), Elliot Eisner (1971;1974), and others.

In short, the overall methodology used in this work is interdisciplinary and is similar to the approach of the proposed model curriculum itself.

Educational Aims

The primary aim of this study is to enable educators to adopt a more inclusive approach in their teaching of the major historic exemplars of language, literature, aesthetics, and art. From an artistic standpoint, this study hopes to demonstrate that the so-called "primitive" art of Africa has a substantive and rich historical past, and that art from the ancient African culture known as Egypt has influenced not only the ancient world, but also modern-day African art and even European art in many significant ways. From a literary standpoint, this study also aims at countering the inaccurate belief that the ancient Africans did not document information in writing and that they were illiterate and consequently incapable of abstract thinking and literary mastery. After examining the Egyptian contributions to art, linguistics, literature, history, and aesthetics, it is hoped that the information presented in this work will open new doors to more interesting investigations in the fields of art, literature and aesthetics in general. For instance, in the model curriculum, students will learn that in many African civilizations, such as Egypt, the making of art objects was associated with cosmology, social norms, and rituals. (For example, the pyramids at Gizeh are burial sites of royalty.) Linked to the Egyptians' religious belief of life after death, it was fitting for them to place their nobility in beautifully constructed and adorned resting places. The many examples will include the gigantic temples—which served as the centers of learning and which were found all over ancient Egypt—and the cities. An example of one of these cities is Tell El-Amarna. It was the capital city,

Akhetaten, founded by the pharaoh Akhenaten. In ancient times, this city was famous for its numerous temples, palaces, government offices, suburbs, and sprawling business district. Even though art was an important medium of communicating ideas, literature and many forms of written texts were used to complement art in an effectual synthesis of communication strategies.

When all is said and done, this writer must reiterate that there are other important histories of art, language, literature, and aesthetics besides the conventional Euro-American representation. Also, this study offers its contribution to the larger discourse on multicultural education and towards breaking once rigid boundaries.

Assumptions to be Argued

1. The art and literature of all cultures should be included in the curriculum, so as to foster an understanding and appreciation of the differences and similarities in art and literature from many cultures in our world.

2. Within the context of this work, an education in art and literature will be taken to include art production, aesthetics, art history, linguistic analysis of the written language in Egypt, hieroglyphs, and literary texts. It will also be assumed that these disciplines are the primary areas from which teachers usually select learning experiences and instructions for high school students between the ages of fourteen and eighteen. (Incidentally, instructors at the college level can also make good use of this information.)

3. An understanding of the components of an education in art and language will provide students with a comprehensive body of knowledge. The interlocking nature of these components exposes one to many and varied cultural artistic and literary forms. Such exposure provides an understanding of the past, which is critical to the future advancement of contemporary art and literature. Students will see the differences and similarities among the art of many cultures (e.g., students can compare the columns of Greek buildings with the style of columns of early African architecture, especially in Egypt). Such buildings as the Vatican, The British Museum, and the Capitol building in Washington D.C., which are also designed with columns, can be compared with Kemetic architecture. They will be made aware that before Homer and Shakespeare, the popular literature of ancient Egypt included folk-songs, love-songs, philosophic texts, fables, travel and adventure, tales of ghosts and magic, romance and legend, and rhetoric.

4. Each culture over a period of time develops traditions that reflect its own world-view. Exposing students to the Egyptian view of art and literature would thus allow them to appreciate the art and literary work as an expression of that culture's myths, rituals, belief system, and

technologies. Simply put, this "culture/art" approach shows how culture and art influence each other.

5. Egypt was a black nation. As Herodotus and Anta Diop (1978) clearly show, the first six dynasties constituted a period of undisturbed Black rule during which most of the pyramids and the sphinxes were built.

6. Black art and literature began in Ethiopia, continued in Egypt, and spread its influence across the continent of Africa and abroad, to Europe, Greece, Rome, India, and the Americas (Chancellor Williams,1976, Van Sertima, 1987; Yosef ben-Jochannan, 1989).

7. The developmental period of adolescence and beyond is most appropriate for introducing multicultural education. Some experts, including Lawrence Kohlberg (cited in Goslin, 1969), argue that it is at the transitional period of adolescence that reflective understanding of different world-views becomes possible. Adolescence is a confusing time, dominated by many uncertainties and paradoxes (e.g., the teenager's view of himself as half child and half adult) in a quasi-serious peer culture. Notwithstanding their confusion, adolescents possess some very distinct characteristics that open their minds to new knowledge. Some of these characteristics are identified by many experts in the field of adolescent psychology as the processes of rethinking, reformulating, and reconstructing thoughts and feelings about themselves and their relationship to the world. This is a period of rich intellectual growth in which the student is open to—and most curious about—new knowledge. In the United States educational system, the high school represents the stage when new knowledge is acquired and is the last compulsory formal exposure to an education in art and literature. Many youngsters realize their artistic potential at this stage, during which they attempt to shape and articulate their vision through artistic symbols. Hence the significance of art-making (e.g., sculpture, poetry, short stories) becomes an important outlet for self-expression. Furthermore, it is during this period that teachers can usually influence the student's interest in art and literature.

Justification for Choosing Some of the Cultures of Ancient Africa

Following my research of the artwork and literary texts of Sub-Saharan Africa, I realized that the fact of "art defining culture" was a consistent feature of traditional African societies. Not surprisingly, the ancient epoch of African history also illustrates the African concept that art plays an integral part in everyday life. In other words, art is inextricably linked to the *ethos* of African peoples.

Consequently, an examination of a people's *ethos* and its relation to their artforms and literature becomes important. Clifford Geertz

(1973) explains that the *ethos* of a people is extremely important since it is the tone, character, and the quality of their life, its moral and aesthetic style and mood; it is the underlying attitude towards themselves and their world that life reflects"(p. 127). As a matter of fact, the art and literature of many cultures exemplify the ideals found in Geertz's definition of *ethos*. In the case of ancient African cultures chosen for this work, we find that art and literature provide an insight into their way of life. Through their art and literature, the habits and thoughts of ancient Egyptians are reflected. Some of what we know of these people derives from their arrangement of ethnological objects such as the pyramids, the sphinx, murals depicting secular life, written texts on medicine, science, religion, social and cosmic organization, and the life cycle. If most of what we know about ancient African cultures is found in their art and writing, then an examination of the iconography and culture of ancient Egypt can be most revealing.

Relationship to the Field of Knowledge

My proposed curriculum model would allow students to see how various media such as stone, granite, bronze, clay, and wood paints were used in the production of art objects. Also, that writing—through its chronology from pictogram, to ideogram, to the hieroglyph—has left for posterity a substantial and substantive body of literary works. Students would also learn that the technology and science of ancient Africans significantly influenced their own aesthetics. For example, the builders of the pyramids were highly trained in religion, philosophy, mathematics, and the secret sciences of ancient Egypt. Beyond technology and science, students would also see how the Africans' belief system, rituals, myths, symbolism, communal behavior, and social institutions are reflected in ancient African art and writing. The sculptures of the pharaohs, which represented their belief in the Divine Trinity—Isis, Osiris, and Horus—exemplify Egyptian thought as manifested in art. Accompanying two- and three-dimensional artforms were the written texts. The texts written on the walls of the pyramids are good examples of the constellation of literary works left by the ancient Egyptians. In effect, art and writing were never viewed or presented as separate entities in ancient Egypt. In fact, the same word (𓏞𓏜) was used to signify both writing and art. Overall, students would have an opportunity to examine a chronological history of African art and writing beginning with the ancient to present-day times.

This study would enrich the student's background with new data from another civilization—that of ancient Africa. Hopefully, the courses offered, as envisioned above, will expand the student's knowledge in the visual arts and a wide range of written texts: literature, poetry, hymns, love songs, and master epics. With a broader background, it is hoped, students' awareness of and appreciation for works of art from other cultures will be intensified. Finally, the inclusion of ancient African art and literature might also inspire students to incorporate new artistic knowledge into their work.

Definition of Key Terms

Africa: What we now know as Africa was originally called Alkebu-lan.

African: There ought to be no doubt what this term means: in the words of Kwame Nkrumah, all people of African descent, whether born on the continent of Africa or abroad, are Africans.

Aim: In education, an aim is a general behavioral change expected to be manifested in a learner.

African Ankh: The ankh was the symbol of eternal life among the Egyptians. It is one of the earliest known "crosses" indigenous to Africa.

Art: A definition of art is difficult to pin down, because the phenomenon which we call "art" is characterized by great diversity and nebulosity: thus, attempted definitions are often bewildering. However, as a working definition, this writer affirms that art, whatever else it may also be, is the vehicle with which a culture's institutions transmit and manifest their meanings to life. Given this definition, literary works such as short stories, poems, and hymns are regarded as works of art. There is no real separation in the mind of this writer between art and literature. Art and literature belong to the same complex of human communication: language.

Aesthetics: Beauty is defined in many ways across cultures, thus there is no general consensus on what it is. I have chosen John Dewey's (1958) concept of the aesthetic experience because it is expansive and inclusive. Dewey argued that art itself was widely human and that the experiences manifested in a work of art are the testimonies and celebrations of the life of a civilization (p.326). In other words, the aesthetic objects provided and enjoyed by a people are a direct reflection of the content of their experience and the culture in which they participate. In short, Dewey's definition of aesthetics takes seriously the importance of those facets which contribute to the definition of culture.

Art education, in the context of this work, means an education in art which includes art history, aesthetics, art criticism, and the production of art objects.

Assessment refers to a constrained method of evaluation that examines measurement against a norm of limited value judgements. In addition, it is an evaluative procedure associated with literal or numerical grades, percentages, and rank positions.

Culture: In anthropological circles, the concept of culture has never been concretized in definitive terms. However, to offer some perimeter for the concept of culture, Clifford Geertz's (1973) insights are most valuable. He argues that though culture is an idea, it is not abstract. Although culture is intangible, Geertz contends, it does not go beyond the range of ordinary knowledge. Furthermore, he notes that culture, as transmitter of historical patterns of meanings, "embodied the symbols, a system of inherited conception expressed in symbolic forms by means of which humans communicate, penetrate and develop their knowledge about, and attitudes towards life" (p. 89). If one follows Geertz's conceptualization of culture, then "the transmitters of historical patterns of meanings" would include the various institutions found in all human societies. Thus, these institutions would account for social organization, myth and ritual, religion and philosophy, cosmology, and the world-view of a people. Adopting this perspective, when I use the word culture I refer explicitly to *the institutions which comprise the memory of a society.*

Curriculum: A sequence of formal educational and/or training objectives and goals, the content to be learned, and appropriate teaching strategies are called a curriculum.

Kemet: This was the original name, meaning "Blackland," for what is now known as Egypt. The Africans who lived in this country named it Kemet. The Greeks changed the name of this place to Egyptos, meaning "land of the Africans." The word *Kemet* is also interchangeable with *"kmt"* and *kamit."*

Nubia refers to Nilotic Sudan.

Teaching strategy refers to the overall plan of activities a teacher uses to achieve an instructional goal. It includes the sequence of intermediate objectives, and the learning activities leading to the instructional goal.

Objective is a statement of what the learner is expected to know upon completion of a specific course of instruction.

Secondary school: In the United States such is a school for students between the ages of 14 and 18, or grades 9 through 12.

LITERATURE REVIEW

A review of all the sources used in this text is not possible; thus, the need for this selected review of some of the literature on curricula in the area with which most of my readers are unfamiliar is important. The review that follows also locates the significance of this work by putting it into context.

The information for the model curriculum in this work is drawn from several sources, namely, most recent studies of multi-cultural curricula, *A Curriculum of Inclusion* (1989), proposed by the Board of Education in New York State, and new approaches to curriculum studies, especially as they relate to curriculum for art education. The sources for the Egyptian content included selected archaeological and anthropological studies of ancient Africa, particularly the Nile Valley cultures.

Curriculum Defined

Before discussing the theories that influence curricular studies, a definition of what "curriculum" is conceived to be for the purposes of this study is in order. An agreed definition is still lacking, as the debate between Phenix (1958) and Pratt (1980) bears out. Phenix defines a curriculum as an organized sequence of the school's educational pursuit. He posits that this organized arrangement is characterized by three components: *content or subject matter* to be taught; *method* or how the content is conveyed; and the *order* in which the subject matter is presented. Pratt, however, simply calls the curriculum an organization of a set of formal educational and/or training intentions.

Traditional and Contemporary Definitions for Curriculum Theory

It might be appropriate to begin by considering a traditional philosophical approach to curriculum models. Robert Bullough et al. (1984) aptly summarize the approach to curriculum in the United States by contending that "there is no such thing as individual emancipation separate from the emancipation of others" (p. 18). In other words, one can argue that no group can inform its thinking and gain freedom and emancipation without liberating opportunities for all. Advancing his argument, Bullough suggests that the emphasis on individualism in any culture is destructive. It encourages greed, promising power and the furthering of selfish interest. The danger of this false individualism, Bullough purports, is that it deters people from asking important questions. With the absence of questioning, people blindly follow without a critical view. Bullough observes that the consequence of following the singled-minded path is greater domination, not human freedom. Current curriculum models, Bullough argues, severely limit our knowledge and make it more difficult "to guarantee critical mindedness or high quality critical thinking" (p. 11).

Notably, the traditional curriculum emphasizes our differences rather than recognizing our common needs. Bullough and others contend that the multiple racial groups in America possess the valuable asset of "many levels of interpretation and therefore many possible entry points into uncovering or demystifying that which limits our comprehension and inhibits our control" (p. 12).

If we agree that one of the major purposes of education is to provide us with the freedom to think freely and creatively, then our educational institutions must retreat from what Bullough terms "single mindedness," which constricts the significance of education and of possible approaches to creating meaningful educative experiences (p. 13). Of particular importance, liberal arts must now emphasize aesthetic and cognitive education rather than the technological model concerned with training workers for efficiency and control over the individual's mind.

Lastly, one might conclude that traditional curriculum models no longer serve the rapidly changing society that is the United States. Hence, the new and changing curriculum should serve as the source for openmindedness and help generate ways for new cognitive and aesthetic growth. Other visions and other possibilities must be contemplated if we are going to move forward into the even more ethnically diverse America of the twenty-first century.

With some initial insights for new curricular models in mind, let us look at what some of the experts have said about the contemporary approach to curriculum development.

Principally, an examination of contemporary views on education and curriculum should be prefaced by a brief review of John Dewey's *Democracy and Education* (1916). Dewey's arguments for democratic education exclude no group or groups of people living in a democratic society such as the United States. Dewey holds education to be a necessity of life; as such, it should be used effectively in "teaching and learning, for the continued existence of a society" (p. 4). The school, therefore, is an important agency in the transmission and communication of formal education.

Dewey's insight about the importance of formal education—the school as one agency for the communication of knowledge—was and remains an important consideration as we approach the twenty-first century. He stresses that though people learn a great deal from living together, the educative experience gained in school is not purely incidental. In reality, the educative experience enlarges and improves one's experience. What Dewey seems to imply here is: if adequate and relevant education experiences are not afforded to all, the possibilities for people to benefit from the numerous resources and achievements of a complex society would be lacking. Likewise, the lack of appropriate educative experiences, in Dewey's view, denies young people the opportunity of taking advantage of the wealth of knowledge that is available from numerous sources in schools.

Accordingly, at the center of Dewey's theory is an emphasis on the transmission of knowledge through communication, an emphasis perhaps best stated as follows: "communication [with art and language as examples] is a process of sharing experience till it becomes a common possession" (p. 9). The ultimate significance of communication, he contends, lies in the improvement of the quality of common experience. For in a society in which the institutions and every other aspect of life become increasingly complex, the need and importance of intentional teaching and learning, he argues, become paramount.

Importantly, Dewey's comprehensive treatise on *Democracy and Education* needs greater attention than I can give it here. However, I must refer to his argument for the democratic conception in education. He believes that genuine democratic education should have as its major objective the provision for participation of all groups on equal terms, given the inherent differences in a pluralistic society. In a democratic society, he concludes, education should allow "individuals a personal interest in social relationships and control, and the habits of mind which secure social changes without introducing disorder" (p. 99). The present work's objective of including ancient African art and literature in the school curriculum is thoroughly consistent with Dewey's democratic conception of education.

In the current discourse on curriculum A.V. Kelly's (1979) insights are likewise invaluable. He suggests that a theory of curriculum must be careful not to view each discipline as the ultimate authority. In actuality, Kelly's interdisciplinary approach provides a broad base for information in problem solving. An interdisciplinary approach, according to Kelly, allows us to derive from many disciplines a broad base of knowledge that in turn lends itself to numerous possibilities of teaching and learning. To illustrate this point, he cites questions of value, choice, and commitment that might uncover answers from philosophy, psychology, sociology, and history.

In alliance with the aforementioned thinkers, Richard Hoggart (cited in Kelly, 1979) and the Board of Education of New York State (1989) assert that new curriculum theories should not neglect the effects of what has been called *cultural deprivation*. Hoggart reminds us that we can no longer assert that certain kinds of culture are inferior or superior to others. Elaborating on the concept of cultural deprivation, the New York State Board of Education's *A Curriculum of Inclusion* (1989) affirms that curriculum development cannot focus exclusively on any single culture, but that rather in a pluralistic society such as the United States curriculum planning must include the contributions and histories of all groups.

Geva Blenkin (cited in Kelly, 1979) takes the argument about the cultural deprivation factor in curriculum development even further. He contests that while changes in our views of culture should influence our style of curriculum planning, we must also be aware that the "evolutionary nature of this process creates its own constraints" (p. 48). Of these constraints, Blenkin implies, the curriculum is the product not only of the cultural history it represents but also of its *own* history.

While cultural deprivation plays a critical role in curriculum planning, Meriel Downey (cited in Kelly,1979) and Thomas J. Brown (1986) caution against other dangers and limitations. Downey, drawing upon recent research done in the field of developmental psychology with respect to the way children learn, calls attention to the psychological finding that children have varied learning styles and that some of their learning styles are clearly influenced by the subculture to which they belong. This highlights the issue of cultural axiologies.

Along the same lines, Thomas Brown (1986) is concerned about the learning styles of children from various subcultures in the United States. Brown purports that the classroom pattern of "insist and resist" is prevalent when the culture of the teachers differs significantly from that of the students. His explanation highlights the tension that often exists between some so-called "minority" children and their teachers. Brown elucidates the predicament of these children and their teachers by citing William Ryan's indictment of public education's responsibility for so-called "minority" children's inability to function efficiently in this society. Ryan argues that the problem is not "culturally depriv-*ed*" *children* but rather "culturally depriv-*ing*" *schools*. He insists that the task of the curriculum is not merely to "reverse, amend and repair deficient children" but to "alter and transform the atmosphere and operation of schools to which we commit these children" (p. 2). If the nature of the educational experience—in the form of curriculum—is changed, Ryan insists, we can change its product. He questions the motives of present curriculum planning which defines the problem of curriculum planning as "inherent in the raw materials—the children," which would clearly be a case of blaming the victim. This type of blaming posture is indicative of the current educational inequality in America (Brown, 1986, p. 2).

Ryan and Brown are not the only scholars who are concerned about the problem of the American school curriculum. In several contemporary policy deliberations, for example, the issues of multiculturalism, *A Curriculum of Inclusion,* Education for Liberation, and cultural deprivation have played a crucial role, both from the perspective of basic research and that of curriculum planning. Nonetheless, few have examined the multicultural curricular changes from the particular perspective of literacy and the capacities for it among the various racial groups.

With the critical issue of literacy in mind, I now direct attention to Paulo Freire and Donaldo Macedo's treatise on literacy. Although Dewey's prescription for democratic education is three-quarters of a century old, some educators charge that the crisis of American education he identified has never been more critical than now. In connection with the indictment against American education for marginalizing or debarring whole groups of its citizenry, Freire and Macedo (1987) identify the scope of literacy as the central issue in the debate for significant and effective curricular inclusiveness.

Freire and Macedo see literacy as part of the battleground where people locate their respective histories and become agents in "the struggle to expand the possibilities of human life and freedom" (p. 11).

Literacy, so defined, is in effect political, as it strives to define the means by which the relationship between meaning and power is determined. Being literate, then, is not merely learning to read, but—more importantly—to reclaim "one's voice, history, and future, a precondition for self and social empowerment" (p. 11).

Overall, the theory of literacy espoused by Freire and Macedo does not exclude a definition of *illiteracy,* since they conceive of it as one of the crucial insights about the politics of literacy. The current notion of literacy, they argue, highlights people's ability to identify prescribed experiences of a given society and imply what should be known—"experience of the other," as it were. Viewed from this perspective, *illiteracy* is used as a manipulative tool "over the poor, women and people of color" by those who determine the dimensions of literacy. Therefore, in their attempt to link illiteracy and literacy into the same complex, Freire and Macedo succeed at uncovering "an ideological construct informed by particular political interests" (p. 12).

With literacy redefined, Friere and Macedo position this concept in the critical context of the school and the curriculum. Since the curriculum represents a powerful, multilayered, and contradictory narrative or voice, they insist that *new* curricula ought—by definition—to be *reformed* curricula. In this regard, they urge that the curriculum must be viewed as an integral part of cultural politics. Significantly, however, great care must be exercised to ensure that the curriculum does not serve only as an instrument of "legitimation and domination," but also as a vehicle for transformation and empowerment (p. 20). Put another way, the curriculum should allow the interests, disciplines, and voices of different groups to be heard, so that, in effect, the students' problems, concerns, and needs become fundamental to pedagogy. The corroborating and legitimizing of the students' experiences give meaning to their lives.

Of course, the critical theory of literacy, as advanced by Freire and Macedo, requires educators to understand the politics and ideology that underlie public schooling. They caution us to be aware of the conservative assault on the education system, along with other social and public services directly controlled by conservative agents. Schools and their curricula (especially in a democratic society), argue Macedo and Freire, should not be a training ground for the promulgation of one group's interests. Progressive curriculum planning should respond by ensuring the presence of an indispensable process which upholds the right of expanding human possibilities in a radical democratic society (p. 27).

In review, Macedo and Freire's theory for literacy declares unequivocally that the curriculum, and the pedagogy that accompanies it, are by implication political. As such, educators should not abdicate their responsibility to understand the ideological intentions of learning and teaching.

It would be unwise to attempt a thorough review of what has become a voluminous and rapidly growing literature on multicultural curricula, *A Curriculum of Inclusion,* and the Education for Liberation curriculum. Essentially, this literature can be traced back to Professor Leo Hansberry (1923), Carter G. Woodson (1933), and on through to the 1990s' multitude of contributions. What seems common among most who speak about the "revolutionization" of the curriculum are: the ethical, educational standards, and philosophical implications which Dinesh D'Souza (1991) describes as the "victims' revolution" (p. 52).

Whereas the arguments for a "new brand" of education in our schools have some common ground, the positions taken by many of the proponents are varied and extremely controversial. D'Souza directs our attention to a crucial and important observation. In the wave of sweeping curricular changes, he notes, many universities have diluted their Western- centered core curriculum to accommodate non-Western cultures. Ultimately, textbooks are chosen primarily because of the author's race, gender, or sexual preference. Some universities, D'Souza reports, have opened themselves to closed-minded liberalism, as if everything is appropriate.

Even more destructive, D'Souza remarks, the sharp philosophical differences among teachers have divided them. On the one hand, there are those who pose as champions of minority affairs and interests and as such are "permitted overtly ideological scholarship and immunized from criticism even when they make excessive or outlandish claims with racial connotations" (p. 52). On the other hand, those who object to the newly instituted boundaries are seen as racists and obstructionists along the path of liberal and progressive education. Hence, the battle for these respective positions detracts from the central issue of serious curricular changes.

Amid the struggle for ideological positions and the historical problem of eradicating bias, New York State's Board of Education has conducted an extensive study which focused primarily on education in a pluralistic society. This vanguard research collected data on some very important areas. According to *A Curriculum of Inclusion* (1989), an indigenous Task Force for Equity and Excellence found that the major responsibilities of the education system—to provide positive images and to minimize ignorance—have been replaced by unfortunate modalities of typecasting and misguidance. The Task Force asserts that these disfunctions "have become institutionalized and have become part of the dominant culture enveloping everyone" (p. 6).

Given the arguments against the present curriculum, the findings of the New York State Board of Education research reveal that students from various cultural extractions are miseducated about themselves and others. As a consequence, false characterizations led the researchers to conclude that Americans of every cultural heritage have become the recipients of "intellectual victimization and miseducation" (p. 7). Although all members of the various cultures are innocent victims, the Task Force found that members of African-American, Asian-American, Puerto Rican/Latino-American, and Native American cultures have suffered particularly from the extremely "negative and damaging effects on their psyche"(p. 7).

Attempting to correct the educational deficiencies of all American students, the commission proposed changes in curriculum strategies. The major strategy of the mission is best stated in the following goal:

> Each student will develop the ability to understand, respect, and accept people from different races, sex, cultural heritage, national origin, religion, political, economic and social background. (p. 7)

Since New York is the best example of a multiplicity of various world cultures and histories, the Task Force contends that education of the people must reflect the various cultural contributions toward the Empire State.

A Curriculum of Inclusion stands not only for the importance of the various cultural contributions, but it also emphasizes the importance for the new generations to be provided with information about their parents' cultures. By emphasizing a broader cultural base for instruction, youngsters who learn about their respective cultures and those of others will understand, for example, why some people dress, pray, speak, and look differently. In effect, A Curriculum of Inclusion provides information that is relevant to the learner's history and culture and in the development of self-esteem and understanding of other people.

Structuring an Approach

What is different about the New York State Task Force Report, when compared with the other literature on multicultural education, is that the Task Force identified the problem of culturally depriving education and suggested specific curricular models for teachers to follow in the general areas of social studies, math and science, English and literature, art and music, and second languages. In particular, the criteria used to analyze the new curricular models were sorted into five primary categories: "contextual relevancy and invisibility...consent, stereo-typing and marginality...historical distortion and omission... multicultural form and substance...and Eurocentric conceptualization and modality" (p. 11). The material productions of each major ethnic group were addressed in great detail so as to reveal and document their heritage and culture and thus reflect the diversified nature of American society.

In opposition to the monolithic focus of the present curriculum, the major task of A Curriculum of Inclusion is to seek an approach in the interest of all students to broaden the instructive content, thus showing the pluralism of American society. Therefore, it is important to note that the Task Force does not advocate a total disregard of the old curriculum, for within the old curricular approach there are many valuable lessons to be learned. For example, students from so-called minority cultures must learn about Western culture. By employing the strategy of including all cultures, that ensures against the monocultural error of the earlier curriculum planners.

Recent Views in Psychology and Education Practice on Curriculum Development: The Thinking Curriculum

Lauren Resnick and Leopold Klopfer (1989) offer some insights about the recent developments in cognitive psychology and related fields. They believe not only that the current focus in curriculum planning should highlight the diversity of content, but that educators should also recognize that "all real learning involves thinking"(p. 2). Resnick and Klopfer argue that the thinking ability is not alien to any person or any subject matter. In fact, *thinking*—in mathematics, science, art, history, vocational education, and special education—can be nurtured and cultivated in all students from kindergarten onwards. The integration of knowledge and thinking, in what is called the "Thinking Curriculum," displaces the old notion that education is the acquisition of bodies of facts and/or banks of data.

Modern cognitive theory, Resnick and Klopfer contend, has resolved the conflict between Piagetian and Gestalt psychologists over whether knowledge and thinking are separate, especially as they relate to practiced performance in school. The current view of cognitive theory offers a perspective which advocates that learning is thinking- centered and meaning-centered, yet it focuses on a principal place for knowledge and instruction.

Broadly, the view of cognitive psychologists today is that people are not mere receptacles of information, but builders of knowledge structures, in that to know something means one has collected information which he or she can interpret and relate to what is already known. Similarly, to be skilled means that the individual not only knows *how* to perform a particular skill, but also *wants* to perform it and to adapt the performance to varied circumstances.

Finally, *The Thinking Curriculum* does not ignore traditional instructional theory. Rather it is concerned with all the questions of teaching, such as sequence of information, motivation, feedback, assessment, and evaluation. A transaction of learning and thinking is the ultimate goal of the modern approach.

The Arts and the Interdisciplinary Approach

Since art and literary education is the specific focus of this work, I have elected to review important sources as they relate to my arguments for multiculturalism and the interdisciplinary approach.

John Blacking (cited in Robinson, 1982) provides valuable support for the interdisciplinary approach to the arts in education. He contends that the arts, the artistic process, and aesthetic experience are fundamental to defining the phenomenon we call art. Whereas we find ways of identifying each of these three categories as "a unique form of knowledge," Blacking continues, "there is substantial anthropological evidence which leads us to conclude that there is some form of unity among the arts" (p. 28). (For the author of the present work, language too is an important part of the definition of art. In the African world-view, which will be addressed later, arts, literature, science, and philosophy are not seen as separate bodies of knowledge).

Another supporter of the interdisciplinary approach to art education is Robert Amstrong (cited in Robinson, 1982). He believes that there exists a generalized "artistic process which is frequently manifested in people's ability to switch easily from the enjoyment and understanding of one art to another" (p. 28). Armstrong promotes the multicultural aspect of his argument with the observation of the fact that people of all cultures are involved in the making of art. This fact alone should persuade us to investigate how people in other cultures think and relate to their activities of art making.

Returning momentarily to Blacking, he asserts that the investigation of other cultures' perspectives on art, literature, and aesthetics is most effectively conducted through the medium of modern anthropology. But he thereby amplifies the shortcomings of the traditional Western philosophical arguments about the artistic process and the aesthetic experience. For when placed in the context of other (i.e., non-Western) cultures, these definitions often become meaningless. For broader definitions of art and aesthetics, Blacking uses Edmund Leach's argument to buttress his anthropological approach. Leach purports that anthropological evidence complicates the Western notion of a definition of aesthetic awareness. The varied definitions of aesthetic awareness across cultures are well documented by anthropologists Clifford Geertz (1973), Claude Levi-Strauss (1963), and Leach (cited by Blacking in Robinson, 1982). Their findings clearly indicate that the artistic process and aesthetic awareness need new and flexible canons to describe these concepts.

Lastly, Blacking cautions, aestheticians, art historians, and others in the field of art and literature need not become defensive, since (he claims) the traditions of non-Western and so-called "primitive" civilizations of Asia and Africa have little to teach us about the complexities and problematics of art in modern Western societies. He also cautions against simply adapting techniques from cultures we prefer. That random sampling, Blacking notes, will ruin our aesthetic development. To explicate this point, he cites the example of the distinguished orchestral player who believes he can transform his trombone playing by merely mastering the blowing technique of the Australian aborigine. Furthermore, the musician who fails to investigate why the Australian aborigine blows in a particular way, and what might influence his technique, will certainly miss the factors that will transform his own ability to play the instrument in an innovative way.

Curricular Approaches to Arts Education

Representatives of arts education have been a part of the ongoing debate in education for curricular changes. Laura Chapman (1978) argues that arts education ought to play an important role in a curriculum which includes the arts, sciences, and humanities—from kindergarten through grade school. She asserts that when the arts gain a sense of importance alongside the humanities and sciences, the relevance of an education in the arts become evident. Moreover, Chapman envisions a curriculum with all of these components—humanities, arts, and sciences—providing education of the highest quality. Chapman's curricular framework for art education identifies three major goals: encouragement of personal response and expression in art; the promotion and awareness of artistic heritage (assuming that she is including the various cultural groups in America); and appreciation of the role of the arts in society. Significantly, Chapman connects these three major goals for arts education with the three functions of education in general: facilitating personal fulfillment, transmitting the cultural heritage, and the development of social consciousness.

Elliot Eisner (1971) offers his prescription for advancing the importance of arts education. He urges that "instructional" as well as "expressive" objectives are important considerations in curriculum planning. Eisner contends that instructional objectives should anticipate the expected student behavior or the level of competencies that he or she should display after completing the course of the curriculum. Eisner recognizes, however, that a statement of objectives in behavioral terms may not sufficiently identify the goals and intangibles associated with a student's behavior after a program of study in the arts. Since instructional objectives are insufficient, therefore, Eisner recommends these objectives along with expressive ones. Expressive objectives describe the "experiential" nature of a curriculum. The change in one's view after an educational experience in art is what Eisner terms an expressive objective.

For Eisner, continuity and sequence are crucial in curriculum planning. By continuity he means the selection and organization of learning material in consideration of previous knowledge and acquired skills. Sequence, on the other hand, he defines as the organization of curricular activities which are usually complex.

Finally, Eisner stresses that curriculum planners should consider the learning styles and the complexity of the task in relation to the following factors: the student skill level; the educational significance of the subject matter; and the provision of a variety of learning experiences.

Dwaine Greer (1987) echoes the positions of Eisner, Chapman, the Getty Commission, and others who have recognized art education as an academic discipline. The approach of these art educators is called "Discipline-Based Art Education"—DBAE. Proponents of DBAE argue that aesthetics, art criticism, art history, and art production are the four sources from which the content of an art education curriculum is drawn for the sequential learning and cumulative activities. Greer insists that combining these four components integrates learning from those domains, thereby allowing each component to complement another as the students engage in interrelated learning activities. He concludes that art should be a required and evaluated subject in all schools.

Although June King Mc Fee (1977) was not writing about DBAE *per se*, her suggestions for an integrated curriculum are precursors to Discipline-Based Art Education. She argues that an integrated arts education curriculum, especially from the child's intermediate years, should complement learning activities in other areas of study (e.g., the role of the arts and literature in the student's culture and other cultures). Generally, Mc Fee contends that an education in the arts organizes and relates information from the student's world as a means of communication and invention as the child expresses his or her feelings.

Among others, Martin Rayala (1986) provides a comprehensive guide to curriculum planning in art education. At the base of his philosophy, he espouses that the arts play, as they always have, an essential role in defining "human history, mythology and belief systems" (p. 4). In addition to the notion of art as an integral part of culture, Rayala insists that scientific and philosophical studies confirm that arts education provides a basis for all-around growth and development of the individual. He concludes that art education must be an integral part of both the elementary-and secondary-school curricula. Rayala argues that a carefully planned art-education curriculum can provide support to the holistic and intellectual development of the individual and society. It can and should develop in individuals perceptual awareness, creativity, understanding of their past and present culture, life-coping skills, aesthetic literacy, communication skills, and experience in understanding one's self.

Rayala's prescription for the planning of art-education curricula included goals of conceptual understanding, aesthetic values, creative behavior, craftsmanship and valuing of work, understanding the content of art, and understanding one's self. Besides these goals, the sociopolitical concerns of the classroom activities should respond to "real-life feelings, experiences, beliefs and attitudes" (p. 5). In other words, art education should reflect the contributions of diverse cultures and people, past and present. In addition, he believes that art education can be used as a medium of change to eradicate stereotyping as it relates to race, sex, gender, and physical and mental abilities. When attention is focused on these areas, individual expression is pushed beyond its apparent constrictions.

Finally, the content area of the curriculum in a liberal arts education achieves much wider goals by including aesthetics, art heritage, art criticism, art making, poetry, narrative writing, and short stories.

To recap, the literature discussed above covered some important aspects of curricular development. Among the important aspects discussed, the definitions for curriculum and curriculum theories, both traditional and contemporary were considered. In addition to these definitions, the role of the school and curriculum in a democratic society were also central. With democratic education and the pluralistic composition of America in mind, many educators have argued that the curriculum should reflect the histories and contributions of all the people in the United States of America.

Beyond the inclusion of all the cultures in America, curriculum planners, particularly art educators, have suggested an interdisciplinary approach to an education in the arts. They argue that such an approach will broaden the knowledge base of the student. Art educators have emphasized that an understanding of the theories in educational psychology and as well as defined goals and objectives are essential to excellence in the arts and all other areas of knowledge.

In summary, the appeals for multicultural and interdisciplinary education and for innovative teaching and learning are best exemplified by an education which includes the arts, literature, and language.

CHAPTER TWO

ORIGIN AND DEVELOPMENT OF THE ANCIENT EGYPTIANS

This chapter discusses the origin, development, and interrelationship of the people and the culture of ancient Egypt. When people and their culture are viewed as reciprocal, we can understand more fully the evolution of a culture.

Slowly but surely, American academia is beginning to admit the centrality of Egyptian civilization and its sub-Saharan antecedents to the history of the arts and sciences. It is impossible to reprise this debate in any detail here, but let us at least develop the outlines of the discourse. It is also imperative that ancient Egypt be understood as a Black civilization if it is to be a source of self-esteem for African-Americans.

Consider the following oft-cited remarks from Count C.F. Volney's *Ruins of Empire*:

> There [at Thebes, ancient metropolis of Upper Egypt], a people, now forgotten, discovered, while others were yet barbarians, the elements of the arts and science. A race of men now rejected for their *sable skin and frizzled hair,* founded on the study of the laws of nature, those civil and religious systems which still govern the universe. (Volney 1991: 16-17)

This eighteenth-century scholar was puzzled by characterizations of the "Negro" slaves of the western hemisphere because they looked very similar to the indigenous Africans he met in Egypt. Volney attempted to prove that the indigenous Africans in Egypt were similar to the American "Negro" slaves on the basis of his description of the Sphinx of Gizeh. He described the monument's facial characteristics —a common determinant of racial origin—as identical with all people of the Black races.

Similarly, a contemporary of Volney, Baron Denon (1798), also sought the identity of the ancient Egyptians through an examination of the Sphinx. He described the portraits he examined as having the indigenous African characteristics—broad noses, thick lips, and wooly hair. Denon argues that his drawings document an accurate appearance of the Sphinx's head before Napoleon's troops destroyed some of the evidence of its "Negroid looks" (ben-Jochannan, 1989, p. 14).

The list of historians and artists who affirm Volney's and Dennon's work is long. Among them are the German scholar and explorer Frobenius (1910), and Egyptian art historian Cyril Aldred (1956, 1961;1962). On numerous occasions both scholars have made reference to the racial characteristics of the ancient Egyptians. Hopefully, Reba Ashton-Crawford's faithful rendering of the head of King Aha, or Narmer-Memes (plate 1), together with the photograph of the Boston Museum of Fine Arts bust of Khafre (plate 2), may help convert those who have been misled by the modern falsification that the makers of ancient Egypt were not Negroid and African.

Among other scholars on the long list, Cheikh Anta Diop, who is well known in the disciplines of history, egyptology, and anthropology, has advanced well-researched arguments in support of the position that the ancient Egyptians were Africoid and undoubtedly "black" in racial origin. Supporting Diop is Yosef ben-Jochannan, a renowned scholar of ancient and contemporary history and egyptology. Others supporters are Basil Davidson, Ivan Van Sertima, John Henrik Clarke, Chancellor Williams, Leonard Jefferies, Frank Snowden, and James Brunson.

Foremost, ben-Jochannan (1989) places the controversy in its historical context. Ben-Jochannan and Chancellor Williams (1976) argue that the ancient Egyptians were always referred to by the Greeks and Romans as people whose descendants came from the interior of Africa. He cites many examples from ancient texts which validate the point.

For example, Manetho (early third century B.C.), a high priest of mixed Egyptian and Greek parentage, who wrote the first chronology of the Egyptian dynasties, testifies to the undisputed Negroid origin of the ancient Egyptians. Ben-Jochannan, as if unsatisfied with Manetho's accounts, recalls the many works of Herodotus which referred to the Egyptian as black. Herodotus observed that the probability of encountering men with black skin, woolly hair, without any other ethnic feature common of Negroes, is scientifically nil. To term such individuals as "whites" with black skin because of their fine features is no less absurd than the appellation "blacks" with white skin. If the absurdity of the latter is applied to three-fourths of the Europeans who lack Nordic features, then what can one conclude? Looking at these two appellations and their contradictions, one can conclude that a pseudo-scientific approach has given way to inaccurate generalization (History of Herodotus, p. 115). This decree by Herodotus is but one of many such testimonies by the Greek "father of history," who made many pilgrimages to Egypt in the fifth century B.C.

Over the span of several centuries, from the fall of ancient Egypt to sometime in the 1800s, classical authors of antiquity [cited by Anta Diop (1974) and ben-Jochannan (1989)] had no difficulty classifying the physical characteristics of the ancient Egyptians. Diop commends Aristotle (389—332 B.C.), Lucan the Greek (125—190 A.D.), Aeschylus (525—456 B.C.), Strabo (58—25 A.D.), and Diodorus of Sicily (63—14 B.C.), among many others, for bearing out this evidence about the ancient Egyptians. Each of the ancient historians usually included a graphic description of the ancient Egyptians. For example, Diodorus of Sicily described the Egyptians as follows:

> The Ethiopians say that Egyptians are one of their colonies which was brought into Egypt by Osiris.... It is from them that the Egyptians have learned to honor kings and gods and bury them with such pomp; sculpture and writing were invented by the Ethiopians. (Anta Diop, 1974, pp. 1-2)

Diodorus' account supports Herodotus' statement. Diop employs Diodorus' account to illuminate at least two plausible implications: (1) that Ethiopia is an older civilization than Egypt; (2) that the Egyptians were a different race than the Ethiopians. Diodorus seriously discussed the possibility of considering the ancient Egyptians to be either close neighbors (separated by a physical barrier—a cataract) or actual descendants of Black Africans (Ethiopians). Herodotus, in Histories II (457—450 B.C.), had stated that the Colchians, Ethiopians, and Egyptians bore all of the Negroid racial characteristics of thick lips, broad nose, woolly hair, and dark complexion—a statement that parallels Diodorus' observations, documented many years later.

Despite the testimonies of the ancients, ben-Jochannan and Diop also sought new data to support their position. Ben-Jochannan uses many strategies to advance his claims. Conspicuously, some of the strategies included examining the names and terminologies which the African Egyptians used to describe themselves and their country. He also reviews the works of some of the modern-day scholars who have advanced the claim of an Indo-European/Caucasian genesis for the ancient Egyptians. Furthermore, to counter what he regards as a deliberate attempt to discredit the contributions of a great Black civilization, ben-Jochannan cites the findings from Elliot Smith's examination of mummies from the tombs of Egyptian Royalty (1912).

Ben-Jochannan argues that before the Greeks imposed the name *Egyptos* on the people of *Alke-bu-lan* (modern day Africa), the linguistic and papyrological evidence show that the Egyptians called their land *Kimit, Kham, Ham, Mizrain*, and *Ta-Merry*. It cannot be coincidental, according to ben-Jochannan, that the same words chosen to describe the empire of the ancient "Egyptians" also refer to the land and its people as "children of the sun." The fact remains, these people were of dark pigmentation. And it is no mistake that even the Greek word *Egyptos* means "land of the dark people."

In addition to his linguistic and papyrologic evidence, ben-Jochannan cites that the Nile Valley and (African) Great Lakes High Cultures, peopled by Blacks of Egypt and its close neighbor Nubia, had an organized system of education called the Mysteries System. (This system will be discussed more fully later.) At the height of ancient Egyptian culture, the Grand Lodge of Alexandria was known as the world center of learning. Those foreign to ancient Egypt who did not attend the main educational center received training at the "established subordinate Lodges of the Osirica—which was centered in the Grand Lodge at Luxor, Nubia" (ben-Jochannan, 1989, p. xxv). This puts into a new perspective the well-known fact that the Greek philosophers Socrates, Aristotle, and Pythagoras all testified to the education they received from the Egyptians.

Having established the ancient Egyptian preference for how they wanted to be called and the consistent testimonies of other ancients, ben-Jochannan focuses primarily on several examples of the racist hypotheses which are still used in academic circles as authentic scholarship on Africa, especially as it relates to Egypt.

To expose some of the racist hypotheses, ben-Jochannan examines several attempts to undermine the Negroid origin of the ancient Egyptians. The most striking appeared in the January 9th, 1972 issue of the *New York Times* in a report by Donald Janson of his interview with archaeologist Ray Winfield Smith, of the Museum of the University of Pennsylvania. The article concerned a computer reconstruction of a bas-relief sculpture (see plate 3) in which Queen Nefertiti is shown with the same pear-shaped, elongated torso used to characterize her husband, pharaoh Akhenaten, and all other persons during their reign. Their stylized portrayal represented the aesthetic choice of King Akhenaten and Queen Nefertiti's reign—a shift away from the conventional royal portrayal to a more naturalistic style. In apparent ignorance of the aesthetic shift of the eighteenth dynasty, Smith interpreted Akhenaten's "long, narrow face, hatchet chin, thick lips, thick thighs and spindly legs" (see plate 4) as the manifestation of apparent glandular trouble associated with the syndrome of "a physical monstrosity" (p. 12), namely, "an extreme case of destructive peridontal disease— badly abscessed teeth which results in long narrow face, thick lips, and hatchet chin" (see plate 4). Moreover, he insisted that the outstanding and intelligent achievements of Akhenaten's reign, particularly monotheism, cannot be attributed to him. Instead, Smith credited Nefertiti (who is generally perceived to be of European extraction) with the idea of monotheism, and with the change of aesthetic canons in art. Janson goes on to quote Smith's speculation that the abnormalities of Akhenaten are usually accompanied by sterility, so that Nefertiti's four daughters could not have been his. In his conclusion on Akhenaten, Smith compounded the pharaoh's plight by suggesting that Queen Nefertiti generally stood in her husband's shadow, an indication she had no need to embarrass him about his ineptness.

Winfield Smith's analysis of the Akhenaten bas-relief may not necessarily be racist, but rather one isolated incident plagued with errors. Ben-Jochannan, however, uses this article to illustrate the vicious, deliberate errors and the racism still leveled at people from Africa. He invites his readers to compare the facial characteristics of Akhenaten with those of all people indigenous to Africa and their descendants living in North America, the Caribbean, Brazil, and other parts of South America, and with the descriptions of the Egyptians by ancient Greek and Roman historians. Are we to understand that all those people who seem to fit Smith's description of Akhenaten were/are actually physically deformed?

In his quest to present further convincing evidence about the origin of the ancient Egyptians, ben-Jochannan uses some of the mummies presently on display at the Egyptian Museum in Cario. These mummies represent many of the various facial types present in Egypt before and after the Dynastic periods. Referring to Smith's illustration (see plates 5A-C), ben-Jochannan observes that most "reconstructions" of the ancient Egyptians we generally see are of the "C" type (see plate 5C), which bears the facial characteristics of Europeans. Most people, however, if shown the majority of mummies (plates 5A, 5B) and surviving sculpture in the round, would not have great difficulty deciding the racial origin of the ancient Egyptian. If ben-Jochannan has presented forceful and cogent evidence of the negroid origin of the ancient Egyptians, the findings presented in Anta Diop's great work, *African Origin of Civilization: Myth or Reality* (1974), are utterly convincing.

Like his contemporary ben-Jochannan, Diop presents evidence from the accounts of ancient Greeks and Romans. Beyond the ancients' testimonies, Diop employs several other approaches—linguistic, totemic, physical anthropology, microscopic analysis, osteological measurements, blood-group typing, cultural data, and the papyrus documents which illustrate how the Egyptians saw themselves. From the wealth of data Diop presents, I will focus on his scientific evidence, which has received the greatest attention from people in archaeology, anthropology, egyptology, history, and linguistics.

Diop (cited, Van Sertima, 1989) prefaces his argument by citing the theory of paleontologist Louis Leakey (cited, Diop, 1974), which has received general acceptance. Central to Leakey's theory is mankind's monogenetic and African origin. His evidence shows that man of 150,000 years ago was "morphologically identical with the man of today" and was "living in the regions of the Great Lakes of Africa, at the sources of the Nile and no where else" (p. 9). Justifying the morphological identity claim, Leakey advances two important points. First, it was out of pure necessity that the earliest men were "ethnically homogeneous and negroid" (p. 9). In defense of this assumption, Leakey uses Gloger's law, which posits that living organisms most likely adapt to their environment by developing characteristics peculiar to the given circumstances. In the case of human beings, Leakey insists, "warm blooded animals evolving in a warm humid climate will secrete black pigment (eumelanin)" (p. 9). Leaky implies that if mankind originated in the areas of the tropics, around the latitude of the Great Lakes of Africa, then logic would lead us to conclude that early man of this region had a dark pigmentation. Consequently, those who moved to other climatic regions must have adapted appropriately. Accordingly then, he argues that the "original stock" was split into different races, and this is one possible conclusion. To ensure that his hypothesis is taken seriously, Leakey points to the geographical constraints of early man, identifying the only two routes available to early man for migration to other continents—the Sahara and the Nile Valley.

To support his position about the African origin of the ancient Egyptians, Diop (1974) uses the historical background of the Nile Valley route and the peopling of that Valley by Negroid races. In substance, although the evidence provided by the physical anthropologists can be used to build "reliable and definitive truths, and sound scientific conclusions," the criteria used to supposedly finalize a solution to this problem are arbitrary, thus giving way to "scientific hair-splitting" (p. 129). He cites many studies which exemplify the hair splitting of the varying percentage of negroid presence in the Valley from the distant prehistoric ages to predynastic times. Diop examines one of the conclusions in Emile Massoulard's *Histoire et protohistoire d' Egypt* (1949). Massoulard states that the Negadah skulls are said to belong to a homogeneous group and therefore can provide sufficient data for a general conclusion about the racial origin. He cites that the dimensions of the skulls' total height, length, breadth of face, nasal capacity and so forth, approximate that of the present-day negro. However, he insists that "the nasal breadth, height of orbit, length of palate and nasal index," seem similar to Germanic peoples. Generally, those who argue for the caucasian origin of the early Egyptians bypass the evidence which suggests negroid characteristics of predynastic Negadian people. Instead they focus almost exclusively on the few racial characteristics akin to the white races.

The other studies Diop cites include Thomson and Randall Mac Iver's 1949 study of skulls from El Amrah and Abydos, and Keith Falkenburger's recent study of 1,800 male skulls from the Egyptian populations ranging from predynastic to present day. Falkenburger's conclusions report 36 percent Negroid, 33 percent Mediterranean, 11 percent Cro-Magnoid, and 20 percent are estimated to be either Cro-Magnoid or Negroid. Falkenburger's percentage of Negroid skulls during the predynastic period of Egypt is higher than Thomas and Randall MacIver's findings of 25 percent men and 28 percent women.

Consequentially, Diop's analysis considers the discrepancies among the percentages of Negroid, Mediterranean, Cro-magnoids, and cross-bred individuals. He draws our attention to what is, perhaps, the most salient of all the arguments put forth. Common to all these arguments is that all bodies of evidence converge at a point which shows that the Egyptian population in the predynastic epoch was Negroid. In view of the common and convincing evidence about the Negro origin of predynastic Egypt, those who insist on arguments that the Negro presence came later remain suspect (Diop, 1974, pp. 129-131).

To further reverse the present-day hypothesis of "White African/Egyptians," Diop employs the science of microscopic analysis of skin to accurately define ethnic affiliation. Since melanin (eumelanin), which determines color of pigmentation, is known to be virtually indestructible, and the scientific community widely agrees that the melanin in animal skin and fossils has survived for millions of years, Diop reasons that the skin of the Egyptian mummies (unparalleled specimens of embalming technique) are prime subjects for melanocyte analysis. Although melanin is mainly found in epidermis, it also penetrates the epidermis and lodges in the dermis. For example, the sample of mummies examined from the Marietta excavation in Egypt shows a higher level of melanin than in any "white skinned races" (p. 125). He assures us that if a similar analysis is done on the best preserved mummies in the Cairo Museum, the result will parallel his findings, proving that the ancient Egyptian belongs to the black races.

Osteological measurements were also a part of Diop's scientific analysis. In physical anthropology, the measurement of bones is a more accepted criterion than craniometry for accurately determining the distinctions of race. In other words, by means of osteological measurement one can differentiate the racial characteristics of a white and a black. Citing the study of the distinguished nineteenth-century German scientist Lepsius, Diop reconfirms that the ancient Egyptians belong to the black races, for, even though physical anthropology has progressed in its methodology, Lepsius' findings have not been invalidated by the new approaches. For example, his notation of some specific characteristics unique to the Egyptian skeleton still stands unchallenged. Lepsius contends that the bodily proportions, especially the short arms, are consistent with the negroid or negrito physical type.

Further, in his quest to provide more substantive evidence for the identity of the ancient Egyptians, Diop examines the etymology of the pharaonic language to see what they called themselves. Connected to the idea of self-description, Diop finds only one term that was designated for this purpose. That word was *kmt*, which literally translated means "the negroes." It is, according to Diop, the strongest term existing in pharaonic language to indicate blackness. Likewise, the character used to symbolize the word *kmt* in hieroglyph is "a length of wood charred at both ends" and not "crocodile scale" (as is commonly misinterpreted). Actually, the word *kmt* is etymologically related to the well-known word *Kamit*, which is common in modern anthropological literature. Diop cautions, however, against the manipulation of modern anthropological literature, which seeks to distort the meaning of the word *kmt* to have it imply "white." To guard against misinformation, he redirects our attention to the authenticity of the pharaonic mother tongue where the word *kmt* meant "coal black." (For an extensive discussion of the grammar of the pharaonic language see his *The African Origin of Civilization* [1974], and my chapter 5, below, on language and literary development.)

In divine epithets, according to Diop, "black" or "negro" was invariably used to identify the chief beneficent gods of Egypt. Thus, for example, *kmwr* means the "great Negro" (for Osiris). More importantly, *km* always precedes the names of the revered gods of Egypt: for example, Apis, Min Thot, Isis, Hathor, and Horus.

Many other scholars besides ben-Jochannan and Anta Diop who have succeeded in re-establishing the true origin of the ancient Egyptians also point out the African influence on the development of Greco-Roman civilization. Whereas it is not possible within the scope of this work to review many of those who have argued for the Negroid origin of the ancient Egyptians, I must not neglect to mention the challenging and thought-provoking work of Martin Bernal in *Black Athena* Volumes I and II (1987 and 1991, respectively). *Black Athena Volume I* is particularly important for establishing the racial origin of the ancient Egyptians and their contributions to a great civilization. Convinced by the archaeological findings for at least 7,000 years, he asserts that the Egyptian population comprised African, South-West Asian, and Mediterranean types. Furthermore, historically speaking, the farther south one moves along the Nile Valley, where the upper Egyptian Kingdoms had influence, "the darker and more negroid the population becomes" (p. 242). In fact, the darker and more negroid population is still dominant in these regions today.

Bernal's overall view of the ancient Egyptians is summarized in his introduction. He asserts that the Egyptian population was fundamentally African/Black and that the African dominance was remarkable in the Old and Middle Kingdoms before the approximately 150 years of Hyksos reign, which notably was restricted to Lower Egypt. Supporting the claim of African dominance, Bernal joins Basil Davidson and James Brunson (cited, Van Sertima, 1989) in affirming that the most important and powerful dynasties were I—IV, VI, XI—XIII, XVII—XVIII, and XXV, and that the pharaohs of these dynasties were black (Bernal, 1987, p. 242).

Notwithstanding that Bernal devotes little time to the racial origin of the ancient Egyptians, he echoes the views of Diop, ben-Jochannan, and others with respect to what the ancients thought of the Egyptians. He professes that the ancient Greeks unanimously agreed upon the cultural supremacy of the Pharoanic civilization. Judging from how eloquently and respectfully the ancients wrote about the Egyptians, Bernal believes, if it were possible for the Greeks to review some of the modern arguments that deny the Black African origin of ancient Egypt, they would rebuke the absurdity of early nineteenth-century scholarship. Bernal enforces his position by recalling the fact that the Greeks of the Classical Age went to Egypt to learn philosophy, mathematics, history, and many more arts and sciences. In short, Egypt was the center of learning.

Closely associated with the modern distortion of the ancient Egyptian racial origin, Bernal argues, modern racism and slavery figured prominently in the modern debasement of the negroid presence in early Egyptian civilization. Bernal suggests that those people who imposed the most brutal form of human degradation upon African people through the slave trade employed a strategy which included "proving" that Blacks were biologically incapable of creating a civilization as magnificent as Egypt. By thus establishing the so-called "biological truth," the perpetrators of racism and "continental chauvinism" were able to discount the genius of Black Egyptians and replace it with an Indo-Asiatic, white model of civilization. The mission, then, of many nineteenth- and twentieth-century historians was to maintain this status quo as "truth" despite many contradictions (Bernal, 1987, pp. 240-247).

The arguments presented here are a mere sampling of the voluminous body of findings that addresses the question of the racial origin of the ancient Egyptians. Ben-Jochannan, Anta Diop, Van Sertima, Bernal, and Williams are only a few of the modern scholars who have given credence to the testimonies of the ancients about the racial composition of the ancient Egyptians. The Greeks, in particular, maintained a reverence for the genius of the African civilization, Egypt, which was responsible for so many of their own cultural advancements.

By presenting convincing scientific evidence about the racial characteristics of the ancient Egyptians, Diop in particular helps write an important chapter in human history for the benefit of all people, especially downtrodden African peoples. The findings are overwhelmingly in favor of classifying the ancient Egyptians as belonging to the negro race.

Finally, in my arguments, I have used the work of contemporary observers—Volney, Denon, Aldred, ben-Jochannan, Chandler, Anta Diop, and museums with Egyptian art collections—who have presented written and photographic documentation about the physical characteristics of the ancient Egyptians. In every case that I have cited favoring the African/Negroid origin of the Egyptians, none of the sources sought to discount or discredit the importance of European civilization. In fact, the proponents of the African origin of Egyptian civilization share a common ideological concern, namely that the social and political histories of the Egyptians must be told truthfully. Those who are interested in having this truth told understand the need to recast Egypt into its rightful historical position. Diop and ben-Jochannan warn that the re-establishing of African history should not be used as a tool of divisiveness, but rather as a unifying force on behalf of all mankind.

This chapter has addressed the reconsideration and accurate representation of the origin of the ancient Egyptians. In the discussion I have cited the findings of Yosef ben-Jochannan, Chiekh Anta Diop, and Martin Bernal. Generally speaking, the evidence of ancient Greek and Roman accounts affirms the African influence on ancient Egypt. In addition, scientific data from osteological measurement, eumelanin analysis, and cranium measurements independently support the argument that the ancient Egyptians were Black. As further evidence, the etymology of pharaonic language was examined to find out how the ancient Egyptians referred to themselves. Finally, photographic evidence of ancient Egyptian sculpture supplies mute yet eloquent testimony about the origin of the ancient Egyptians.

CHAPTER THREE

HISTORY AND CULTURE OF ANCIENT EGYPT

The chronicle of ancient Egypt is by no means complete; the records that have survived mainly account for only some of the events of an approximately 3,000-year span. Among the many scholars who have devoted much of their attention to what is, arguably, the world's oldest civilization, David O'Connor (1990) asserts that what we know about the ancient history of Egypt is gleaned from an established writing system, called the hieroglyphs, a centralized kingship, cities, monuments, and other objects excavated by archaeologists. He also suggests that the impact of ancient Egypt can be seen in the religious thought espoused in the Bible. Consistent with earlier arguments for Egypt's impact upon the rest of the world, O'Connor notes that the Greeks, who exercised great influence upon Western civilization, acknowledged that their acquisition of knowledge about art, architecture, literature, philosophy, and science came from the ancient Egyptians. Notably, O'Connor remarks that our alphabet, which evolved from the Phoenician via the Greek, closely resembles the alphabetical systems of the Egyptian hieroglyphs (p.1).

We are told by O'Connor and others that approximately 5,000 years before the dynastic period began (i.e., 8000 B.C.), hunters and gatherers began settlements in which groups of people domesticated animals and grew food. After several thousand years, these scattered communities first became regional powers, then nation states.

Emery (1961) and O'Connor, among others, agree that there were two culturally distinct regions. In the north and in about 5000 B.C., excavated evidence has shown that the sites of Merinda and Maadi, where monochromatic pottery fragments have been unearthed, were organized as a Delta culture. Later, around 4000 B.C., in the southern part of Egypt, there evolved a more flamboyant and varied culture, as is evidenced by the pottery which included bright red, polished wares with black tops, and others with organic and geometric designs. Communities which bore these characteristics of the southern region can be identified as the Tasian and Badarian cultures, and later the Nagada I (Amratian) and II Gerzean.

Generally, the concept of predynastic Egypt can be identified by its two most important aspects: technology and kinship. O'Connor argues that the continuous improvements in technology affected other areas of life, like the building of ships, which in turn encouraged trade and better communication throughout Egypt and beyond. Agriculture also benefitted tremendously from improved technology. Well-made stone and copper tools increased the already high agricultural yields. Not surprisingly, then, from the gradual development of kingship with local regional rulers there arose a fierce rivalry for land. Eventually, the continuous rivalry between north and south was consummated in a great war, after which a single dynasty was formed before or during 3100 B.C. Thus the pharaonic system was established, and would be maintained until 332 B.C.

During the pharaonic era there were thirty-one dynasties that comprised the historical framework of dynastic Egypt. The chronological order divides into three intermediate periods: the Early dynastic Period, 3100—2750 B.C. (dynasties I and II); the Old Kingdom 2750—2250 B.C. (dynasties III—VI); the First Intermediate Period, 2250—2213 B.C. (dynasties VII—XI); the Middle Kingdom, 2025—1627/1606 B.C. (dynasties XI—XII); the Second Intermediate period, 1648—1539 B.C. (dynasties XV—XVII); the New Kingdom, 1539—1070 B.C. (dynasties VIII—XX); the Third Intermediate Period, 1070—653 B.C. (dynasties XII—XXV) and the Late Period, 664—332 B.C. (dynasties XXVI—XXXI) (p. 6). It is important to note that new and significant data about individual dynasties and pharaohs has changed the scope of Egyptian History. More importantly, an examination of the three dynastic periods shows clearly that it was the Old Kingdom that left a formative legacy for the later periods of Egyptian culture.

On the Culture of Ancient Egypt

Looking at Egypt through the window called culture, we must not neglect the education which transmits the culture. In this work, the theoretical framework is similar to the one advanced by Melford Spiro in James Fernandez's *On Symbols in Anthropology* (1982). Spiro argues that for any investigation of religious symbols to be valid, the investigator must first focus on the social characteristics peculiar to the given culture (Fernandez, 1982, pp. 51—52). Likewise, when some understanding of a culture is acquired and used in art and literary criticism, only then are the lines for an adequate interpretation and explanation possible.

In anthropological circles, the concept of culture has never been concretized in definitive terms. However, in an attempt to define the parameters of culture, Clifford Geertz (1973) posits that although culture is an idea it is not simply an abstraction in someone's head: even though intangible, "it is not an occult entity" (p. 12).

Given that culture is usually defined in vague ways, which include references to art, literature, music, and so forth, Geertz contends that culture is neither multi-referential nor unusually ambiguous. Geertz observes that culture is the transmitter of historical patterns of meaning:

> [culture is] embodied in symbols, a system of inherited conception[s] expressed in symbolic forms by means of which humans communicate, penetrate and develop their knowledge about, and attitudes towards life. (p. 89)

If one follows Geertz's concept of culture, then "the transmitters of historical patterns of meanings," include the various institutions found in all human societies. These institutions would therefore account for social organization, myth and ritual, religion, cosmology, philosophy, and the society's geographical conception of itself in the world. Adopting this perspective, in the word "culture" I refer to *the institutions which comprise the memory of a people.*

Establishing a definition of "art" is equally difficult. The phenomenon we call "art" is characterized by great diversity and nebulosity, hence, attempted definitions often miss the mark. The working definition for the present work asserts that *art, whatever else it is, may also be the vehicle which transmits and manifests the meanings of a culture's institutions.* Thus, language, literature, architecture, sculpture, drawing and painting, pottery, jewelry, and other personal decorations are some of the artistic media which can inform us about a culture. These objects can function in a utilitarian, symbolic, or representative mode or in some combination thereof. Finally, with these definitions of culture and art as a base for our thinking, we can now discuss the definition of Egyptian culture through its art and literature.

Geographical Factors

The ancient civilization of Egypt was founded along the banks of the Nile River. In fact, Anta Diop (1974), Frank Snowden (1970),

Chancellor Willliams (1976), and Yosef ben-Jochannan (1989) maintain that prior to 3100 B.C. Egypt was part of what can be loosely called the Ethiopian Empire or Nile Valley civilization. (Some schools of thought go so far as to regard the entire Dynastic Age of 3100 B.C. to 332 B.C. as a fertile offshoot of Ethiopia.)

For a definition of ancient Egyptian culture I will rely on John Wilson's (1956) account, which treats the data about the location, nature of climate, and topography of Egypt as important to our understanding. He notes that the ancient Egyptian Empire was essentially a barren and rainless land. Most of the ancient Egyptian Empire was confined to the western banks of the Nile River, on a north-to-south axis. The Egyptians established their civilization along a narrow strip of fertile soil on the banks of the Nile River in the midst of what was and still is a desert. In Wilson's words, "it is possible to stand with one foot on the lifeless desert sand" and the other on the fertile banks of the Nile. A panoramic view of the ancient Egyptian Empire would have shown the expansive and lifeless sandstone hills in contrast to the fertile valley watered by the muddy river, "which brings life, the life-giving water and soil" (p. 8).

The annual drama of the inundation of the Nile River was eagerly awaited. The surging summer high tides deposited their rich black soil, as they always have, which would rejuvenate even the poorest land. Wilson asserts that the annual gifts of "refreshing water and refertilizing soil in a semi-tropical climate gave an agricultural richness which has been proverbial in all times" (p. 9).

Consequently, ancient Egyptian life was uniquely determined by the influence of its sole source of irrigation and fertility, the River Nile. Ancient Egyptian civilization ensured its survival by harnessing the annual inundation of the rich black soil from up-river that rushed through the valley on its way to the sea. The fertility of the Nile, however, only lasts for a few months. Thus the peasant farmer was constantly actively engaged in his self-preservation by trying to divert the water into areas away from the immediate banks of the river. As we will see later, the ancient Egyptians, out of necessity, became excellent builders of aqueducts and dams that added to the continuity of a lasting economy.

Not that the ancient Egyptians had faced an easy task in efficiently channeling the rising tides of the Nile. As Wilson and ben-Jochannan (1989) both observe, the Nile is not precise in its timing with respect to the inundation. Records over thousands of years show that the river is unpredictable. For instance, a high yield of water between 25 or 26 feet above a zero datum was "normal" and "good" and made for a bountiful crop. A drop of 30 inches below the norm, on the other hand, meant insufficient crops, necessitating conservation and rationing of food. A drop of 60 to 80 inches meant famine until the Nile rose

again to a normal level. Conversely, extremely high tides meant flooding, which was equally perilous. Along with the loss of crops, a very
high Nile would destroy infrastructure such as dams, canals, houses, and
in some cases entire towns. Hence, the ancient Egyptian was constantly on guard against the uncertainty of the Great Nile. In short, the
River was a paradoxical phenomenon of nature for the ancient
Egyptian: a precious gift yet a perilous master.

According to Wilson, the physical contrast of this environment—
desert; jungle marshes near the river; and inundations or lack thereof—
forced the ancient Egyptians to be an organized and ever-vigilant
people. Theirs was a mentality influenced first and foremost by self-
preservation, faced constantly with uncertainties.

Besides the physical conditions mentioned so far, some other
significant environmental factors helped to shape the world-view of the
ancient Egyptians. Wilson notes that the Nile Valley, a narrow strip on
both sides of the river, generally protected the Egyptian from outside
influences. East and west of the valley were scorching deserts which
deterred invading forces. The north was bordered by the vast Sinai
desert which discouraged early Asiatic invaders. Only the Libyan coast
allowed easy access, but people hailing from this direction were peace-
ful—pastoral and non-aggressive—giving the Egyptians little to fear.
Communication was mainly overland, and it took five to eight days for
caravans to cross the desert from east to west. Yet, because of the wide
open desert spaces, the ancient Egyptians saw invading forces
approaching long before they neared the Empire. (The Egyptians'
development of optics made it possible for them to see approaching
forces from miles away). Northern Egypt touches the Mediterranean,
which took the Egyptians at least eight days to cross in ocean-going vessels to contact their nearest neighbor, Crete. Finally, to the south, there
were also the physical barriers of five cataracts. The first cataract did
not present much of a barrier, but as one moved beyond that the wide
inhospitable lands of desert and cliffs presented great difficulties moving north and south.

Psychological Influences

The physical features briefly described above obstructed invading forces
during the earlier days of the ancient Egyptian civilization. Because the
ancient Egyptians were thus spared from constant external attack in the
early dynastic period (i.e., Old Kingdom), Wilson and others believe,
they were able to concentrate more on nation building. Individual citizens, he argues, were imbued with a certain sense of physical and spiritual security and optimism about their world, when compared to their
neighbors, the Babylonians and the Hebrews. In hindsight, the freedom
and confidence of the ancient Egyptians could be traced directly to the

sense of security that the ancient geography guaranteed (Wilson, 1956, pp. 12-13).

While the threat of foreign invasion was thus somewhat muted, the Egyptians still remained cautious of the unpredictable Nile, which held their survival in the balance. Wilson contends that the threat of famine from low water levels and the danger of river flooding forced the Egyptians to conserve and store their resources well in advance of possible disaster. While the Nile might bring harm one year, the Egyptians were confident that, by the following season or the one after, the Nile would be gracious again by rising and fertilizing barren fields. The Egyptians' confidence in the Nile's consistent rejuvenation, Wilson suggests, provided their belief in ultimate triumph over death. In fact, this point is made explicit in the Egyptian *Book of the Dead*. The confidence that the Egyptians possessed in the full prodigality of the Nile's yield was paralleled in their belief in a certain death after which they would continue into the good life. The geographical conditions of ancient Egypt discussed above not only determined the character and world-view of an entire society but shaped and upheld the Eyptians' perception of their own destiny.

Social Organization:
Matriarchy and Mythology

Thus with some knowledge of the geographic features of ancient Egypt, we turn to the physical and geographic conditions that determined the social organization.

Larry Williams, Charles Finch (cited, Van Sertima, 1988), and other scholars of African studies show, with substantive archaeological documents, that the ancient Nile Valley civilization—including the Egyptian, Ethiopian, Nubian, and Sudanese civilizations—exhibited the same matriarchal patterns prominent in later Greek mythology. In support of this argument, Williams and Finch direct our attention to the "most powerful line of black queens—The Candaces (from the Meroitic *Ken take*, which means Queen-Mother)" (p. 12). Matriarchy, they contend, is "probably the oldest form of social organization [and] appears to have evolved first in Africa" (p. 12). Finch and Williams were cautious to add that, although patriarchy supplanted the older social order, matriarchal social organizations are still present in many African nations. Paradoxically, when one thinks about the social stratification of ancient Egypt, the power and importance of the pharaonic theocracy is obvious. In this connection, however, Finch and Williams remark that "inheritance of the Egyptian throne was determined through the female [blood] line" (Van Sertima, 1988, p. 12).

Diop's (1974) observation reinforces Finch and Williams' argument by citing the example of King Seneferu, who sought rulership between the third and fourth dynasties. King Seneferu, Diop notes, married a certain Hetepheres princess who possessed lineage of royal blood. It was only by this union that Seneferu was able to become pharaoh. Other cases are documented where kings married their sisters so as to comply with the laws of matriarchal succession.

In support of the case for a matriarchal social order in ancient Egypt, Eloise McKinney and Johnson (cited in Van Sertima 1988) invoke the Egyptian creation myth. In this myth, the Egyptians attributed many titles to Isis, such as "Egypt quintessential sweet heart, wife and mother," "The lady of a thousand titles," "Great Enchantress," "Lady of Heaven," and " Mistress of Magic." Isis, a mythical queen, was worshiped as the sister and wife of Osiris, the King of the Dead. Johnson relates this primordial myth as follows: Isis and Osiris were the first king and queen of Egypt. While the powerful king was on his crusades conquering foreign lands, his wife Isis continued to rule the great civilization her husband started. Seth, the envious brother of Osiris, slew many of Osiris' followers and later severed Osiris' body into fourteen parts. Isis demonstrated her perseverance by roaming the earth to find all the parts of her slain husband whom she finally resurrected. She later groomed her son Horus to avenge his father's death. Subsequently, young Horus reclaimed his father's reign over the earthly realm while his father, Osiris, ruled the underworld (Van Sertima, 1988, p. 65).

Also defending the matriarchal origin of ancient Egyptian society, Richard Patrick (cited in Van Sertima 1988) informs us that there was an enormous cult following which revered Isis. One branch of this tradition specifically emphasized Isis as the great Enchantress who grew wings to protect the dead Osiris. Another branch, according to Patrick, had a different interpretation for Isis' wings. They believed that she used her wings to transmit to him (Osiris) the breath of life. Patrick identifies Isis as one of the protection goddesses in funerary rites. Isis was frequently shown with her sister Npthys, similarly winged, plumaged arms entwined. Another modus of significance attributed to Isis, McKinney cites Johnson, is the Cobra (Uraeus), a sacred serpent of Egypt which she used to dethrone the god Ra (god of the underworld) so that her husband could take his place.

The literature on the significance of Isis to the social, political, philosophical, and religious life of ancient Egyptians is enormous. However, let us note that in alliance with Mc Kinney, Patrick, and Johnson, Sonia Sanchez (cited, Van Sertima, 1988) argues that the Isis and Osiris myth lays the metaphysical basis for the balance in partnership between the sexes that is consistent throughout ancient Egyptian civilization. Sanchez stresses two salient points in the myth: that women were seen as spiritual beings, and that they were regarded as full partners in civilization-building. This theme of woman's spirituality and partnership was reflected throughout the history of ancient

Egypt. For example, Sanchez contends, the records kept on women show that they were revered foremost as the repository of The Divine, and as essential forces of civilization. In addition, women were the keepers of secrets of society, the mother of the gods, and the manifestations of a universal "feminine" principle which saw the universe, the earth, and the subconscious as a womb for a Divine Will. All of these attributes, in Sanchez's view, solidify the idea that the ancient Africans were committed to women being "allied with, and complementary to man" (p. 49). In fact, women had the same rights as men and were allowed to own material possessions, including real estate. In Sanchez's analysis, she compares Isis and Osiris with the mythic Adam and Eve at the foundation of Christianity. In Adam and Eve's case the woman was "an appendage or after-thought to man" (p. 51). By contrast, in Isis and Osiris' case, woman was a divine equal (Van Sertima 1988: 49—51).

Adding to the claim that ancient Egypt's matriarchal system was directly linked to the Isis/Osiris myth, Sanchez cites the example of Nefertiti, the wife of the brilliant philosopher/poet and pharaoh Amenhotep IV. Beauty and brilliance had elevated her well beyond the norm for royalty of her day. During the time of her co-rulership with Amenhotep (1365 B. C.), Egypt underwent social, religious, material, and political changes. For example, the Nefertiti-and-Amenhotep reign over Egypt was marked by conquest of other lands and access to a great deal of wealth. Gold was plentiful, and Egypt was the center of world trade. However, Nefertiti and Amenhotep were seeking to re-establish some of the religious values that had been lost over the previous centuries. Unfortunately, materialism had overtaken the Egyptians and with it the importance of women declined. Despite the declining female status, Nefertiti was not to be relegated to the position of a subservient queen, incapable of divinity. Sanchez notes that Nefertiti was determined to be an important factor in the reshaping of Egyptian civilization. Of course she was challenged by those in the materialistic world, who dominated religion and all other aspects of life at the time. But Nefertiti and Amenhotep built a new Egypt, marked by a new capital city in Amarna, called Akhetaten. In this new city the arts flourished and men and women lived together in unity, beauty, peace, and happiness.

After the death of her husband in 1353 B.C., Nefertiti ruled Egypt with a strong hand and watchful eye. She also raised and trained the young King Tutankhamen (King Tut). Nefertiti believed as long as the young boy-king was raised by her in Amarna, the great memory and mission she and her husband created would never die. This great queen did everything to maintain the dominance of Ma'at (Truth, Justice, and Righteousness), a concept all pharaohs and queens were supposed to uphold. Unfortunately, however, Nefertiti's dreams were foiled as the young pharaoh "was a disappointment to the politically-minded queen mother" (Virginia Spottswood Simon, cited, Van Sertima 1988: 60).

Diedre Wimby (cited, Van Sertima 1988) also reminds us that Kemit had an illustrious line of queens: Neithotep of the first dynasty, Mer-Neith of the Horus regent first dynasty, Nitocris of the Horus regent sixth dynasty, Ahotep and Ahmose, Nefetere of the seventeenth dynasty, Hatsheput of the Horus regent-eighteenth dynasty, to name a few. Of those just listed, Hatshepsut was the exceptional one. During her reign, she ended the tradition of conquering foreign lands. In fact, Hatshepsut in the time of her reign helped transform Egypt into a noble nation. However, she was criticized and challenged for her philosophy of non-aggression, especially since she followed a line of warrior kings. Unfortunately, her policies grew more unpopular in Egypt, especially when other nations were bent on conquering the land of Egypt. In the end, she was remembered for invoking the conscience of Egypt "by spiritually, physically and intellectually assuming all the ritual apparatus of these male-oriented kingships" (p. 46). She exemplified the spirit of Horus by becoming "darting fire against [her] enemies"(p. 46). Unlike previous queens, Hatshepsut manifested masculine attributes. In truth, she attired herself like a man and often times demanded to be referred to as "he" rather than "she." Hatshepsut was obviously at odds with the paradox inherent in the Egyptian matriarchal system which required a female bloodline to be on the throne.

On reflection, Hatshepsut led the way for her female successors by demonstrating that a woman was capable of being both gentle and harsh when needed. The myth of Osiris, Isis, and Horus influenced the matriarchal system employed in ancient Egypt and in the rest of Africa. There are many renditions of this myth in Egyptian art in the motif of Isis suckling Horus. Many egyptologists argue that from this Isis/Horus representation arose the long held tradition later known in Crete, Greece, Rome, and parts of Europe as "Madonna and Child."

Judging from the precedent set by the Isis/Horus/ Orisis myth, the female in the central role set a distinctive foundation for the social and religious roles of men and women.

With the male/female roles established, we can now look at the social structure of ancient Egypt. First, however, a working definition for matriarchy is crucial, since it is fundamental to the social and ritual proceedings of ancient Egypt. Anta Diop (1978) offers a clear definition of matriarchy and patriarchy in his argument for the existence of a Southern African "cradle of civilization." In social structures which espouse patriarchy, after marriage the woman leaves her own family to join her husband. In a matriarchal system, on the other hand, after the man marries, he leaves his clan to join the clan of his wife. Diop points out that the patriarchal structure is only conceivable in a nomadic life, while the matriarchal flourishes in a sedentary and agrarian way of life. He contends that the matriarchal system is the only one that affords the woman, despite her physical frailty, the opportunity to contribute substantially to economic life. Diop adds that the female "becomes one of the stabilizing elements in her capacity as mistress of the house and keeper of the family" (p. 34).

While supporting the woman's prominence, Diop posits that she owns an important role in "the discovery of agriculture and plant selection while the man devoted himself to the hunt" (p. 34). Since the primary concern in ancient times was the security of the group, Diop surmises that both males and females were responsible for the collective security of the family, thus respect was given to both sexes. Furthermore women, in agrarian societies receive a dowry from their husbands, instead of the reverse which characterizes nomadic life. The sociological implication, Diop maintains, is that the dowry constituted compensation by the males, who were viewed as the less favored sex.

Finally, Diop concludes his discussion of the differences between patriarchy and matriarchy which argue for a dominant female role by identifying the partner that leaves the clan after marriage. Amongst sedentary people, the man must leave his clan, "a stranger," to join his wife's clan. This characteristic, Diop argues, is purely matrilineal; whereas, in nomadic societies, where the wife leaves her genos and becomes the stranger, the woman's movement is very consistent with the patrilineal system (Diop, 1978,pp. 34-35).

Given this working definition of matriarchy and patriarchy, let us now move to the details of the social structure and organization in ancient Egypt. First, the political characteristics of the different types of states must be identified. Diop (1991) identifies at least four types of states: (a) the state known as the "Asian mode of production" (which Marx and Engels claimed to be the model perfected by the pharaonic Egyptian State); (b) the state born out of resistance to the enemy; (c) the ancient Athenian model; and (d) the Spartan and Tutsi type of state. Of these models, Diop believes, the Asian Mode of Production (AMP), which he prefers to call the "Africa"-type state, bears characteristics most akin to the matriarchal ancient Egyptian state (pp. 129–132). One of the outstanding characteristics of this system of government is the extraordinary influence of *civil* power, "as compared to military-dominated systems of government;" furthermore, he explains, in the AMP-type state "military aristocracy is partially absent" (p. 129).

To illustrate this point, in peace time the military is not the focal point of an AMP state. The military takes a defensive posture. Diop notes that AMP states were founded on a collectivistic basis, where all the citizens accepted and depended on the nation for collective survival. Ancient Egypt is the best example of the Asian mode of production. Accompanying Diop's assertion are the geographic conditions and the climate that isolated the people of ancient Egypt. For example, he directs attention to the unpredictability of the Nile River, with its flooding and its low water levels and sediment, both of which lead to devastation. The ancient inhabitants of the Nile Valley survived by rising above an individualistic, clannish, and tribal egoism. They understood that any selfish social behavior brought the inevitable consequence of death. Considering the geographic constraints, Diop posits the emergence of "a supra tribal authority, a national authority, accepted by all, invested with the powers necessary to conduct and coordinate irrigation and water distribution, works essential to the general activity" (p. 130). He goes on to speculate that geography was an essential determinant of this hierarchic system, whose leaders enjoyed great power and privileges over a more or less caste stratification, which was accepted by the people and flourished despite its flaws. The nation survived revolutions and other forms of social disorder simply because a confederation of tribes had to organize and protect themselves against nature. As Toynbee said, to overcome an obstacle to survival, the collective effort of a large group will supersede the isolated interests of any minority group (Diop, ibid., p. 130).

Social Stratification

Together with an understanding of the geographic features and the mythology and religious beliefs to be examined later, we see the shaping of some distinct social and political characteristics in ancient Egypt. Diop (1978) and W.B. Emery (1961) have written extensively on the social distinctions among the ancient Egyptian people. In particular, Diop notes that the royalty and the god-king concept were necessities that evolved from the need for collective agricultural life. The ancient Egyptians, at an early stage, found it necessary to coordinate secular authority and the supernatural or divine character. Even though there were class distinctions, according to Emery, there were no castes. In fact, all men were commoners before the "good god" who was identified as Horus (p. 105).

In the Egyptian belief system, the pharaoh was symbolic of the Falcon god Horus, and was therefore celebrated by the people. Traditionally then, absolute rule was invested upon him by the people, for he was the mediator between themselves and God. In sum, Emery observes that the god Horus was responsible for the fertility and productivity of the land. Given Horus' significance and the fact that the pharaoh was his human manifestation, the pharaoh's life was expected to be lived on behalf of the people whom he served.

Next in the hierarchy was the noble class of the priesthood. Members of this class were referred to as "priest-kings" in the role of "interpreter of the divine will but not a god" (Diop, 1978, p. 151). Since the pharaoh was king and priest simultaneously, he delegated his priestly functions to an official who executed his wishes each day in the temple.

By decree, then, these officials bore great influence and responsibility.

In counting the pharaoh along with his appointed functionaries, the priest-kings, Emery also observes that the officials and artisans who made up their followers and subordinates assisted the King in ruling over the masses of people.

Despite clearly defined social classes, Diop redirects our attention to significant behaviors. In keeping with the fundamental aspiration of survival as a collective, hunting, fishing and farming were activities in which all people, including the king, participated. As a matter of fact, the king was the most dominant farmer. To concretize the paradoxical egalitarianism of ancient Egypt, Diop cites the numerous depictions of the pharaoh digging the soil (a sign of blessing) to open the excavation of a canal (Diop, 1978, p. 155). (Incidentally, in the English-speaking Caribbean, officials of African descent make the first dig to begin a project).

Emery's analysis of the burial practices of the ancient Egyptians is also helpful for a better understanding of the social order. Burial grounds around Menes, the first known pharaoh, differ according to the social stratification of the three ranks in the population. At Saqqara, he points to the evacuation of tombs which appear to be the burial places of the pharaohs, their families, and other great nobles. These tombs were decorated with all the luxurious items that were common for a highly civilized people. Archaeologists have also found another set of tombs across the Nile River at Helwan where the less noble were buried. Significantly in this instance, these tombs are similar in design, but fewer valuables were entombed with the corpses. Notably, the articles found represented a relatively high standard for artisans and masses, who were buried with articles of their everyday activities, such as equipment that was used in their crafts, and farming equipment of domestic life (Emery, 1961, pp. 110-111).

Religion and Philosophy

George G. M. James (1954) is convinced that the geography of Egypt, in relation to its social order, gave rise to very specific religious beliefs, rituals, and cosmology. He cites Mircea Eliade's *History of Religion*, which carefully presents the theory of the cosmic triad. Central to Eliade's theory is the sky (or father god), which provided rain to fertilize the earth (or mother goddess) so that the vegetation (son) blooms. For the meaning to the cosmic triad, James compares these three cosmic divinities to the ancient Egyptian mythological figures of Osiris, Isis, and Horus, who also permeated the religious practices of the Indo-Europeans and peoples of the Mediterranean shores.

To initiate our investigation of ancient Egyptian religion, let us turn to Martin Bernal's *Black Athena*, Vol.I (1987), which elucidates the

Afroasiatic roots of Classical civilization. Bernal argues with great conviction that before the people of the Nile Valley settled in well-organized cities they worshiped many gods. However, with the unification of Lower and Upper Egypt under the reign of a long line of royalty, pharaohs and queens, the idea of monotheism was introduced. Emery, George G. M. James, Bernal, and others indicate that Osiris, Isis, and Horus constituted the divine Trinity which was revered throughout antiquity in the likeness of father, mother, and son. In this relationship, Chandler (cited, Van Sertima, 1989) writes: "Osiris was the greatest God of Egypt, Sun of Saturn, celestial fire and reincarnation" (p. 131). Isis represented the virgin mother and personified nature. Chandler points out that Isis is described as the "woman clothed with the Sun of the land of Khemi" (Egypt); while Horus was referred to as "loved of heaven" and "beloved of the Sun...born from the womb of the world" (p. 131).

Identifying Isis as representative of good that triumphs over evil, Chandler remarks that Horus "is also the substance of his father, that is, being related to death and time, the material manifestations" (p. 131). According to Egyptian belief, the world was judged by Horus, the god of the pharaoh, who was in turn the god-king and the human representation of Horus. His symbol, the serpent, was placed on the crown of all pharaohs.

The ancient Egyptians had continual conflicts over religious worship. During the early history of pharaonic times, around 3100 B.C., many followed Set, the mythological brother and rival of Osiris. As the legend goes, Set killed Osiris. Many of Set's followers regarded him as the supreme ruler of Egypt. However, we know that Horus avenged his father's death later by eliminating Set. But Set, the evil one, still kept a significant following. It was not until the second dynastic period that the Set cult gave way to the dominant worship of the triumph of good.

Principally, Horus, the son of Osiris, held the most important role in Egyptian religion, especially following the unification of the lower and upper monarchies. Emery maintains that all residual god images from tribal and predynastic times were synthesized in the solar god. This synthesis became known as the circle of the sky mythology or sky god, where all previous gods' characteristics were obliterated. Despite the successful eradication of other religious followings, as many authorities have shown, Set proved to be most difficult of the deities to erase. His appeal and presence were never completely extinguished. Throughout the ancient history of Egypt, Set continued to personify evil. Set was represented by "an unidentified animal which had the appearance of a dog, with a vertically split tail and the head of an ant eater with high square-topped ears" (Emery, 1961, p. 121).

Although there was a consistency of religious belief throughout the history of pharaonic Egypt, several major religious denominations survived—e.g., Re at Heliopolis, Ptah at Memphis, Osiris at Busiris, and

Min of Coptos. In every instance, however, Emery states that these religions were recast from the original divine trinity: Osiris, Isis, and Horus.

As one might expect, my introduction to ancient Egyptian religion but scratches the surface of a very complex and controversial issue in the historiography of Egypt. An exhaustive examination of ancient Kemetic religion would take us into an interminable discourse. However, some attention must be focused on one controversy over ancient religion in Egypt: polytheism and monotheism.

Insofar as this controversy is concerned, Chandler (cited, Van Sertima, 1989) notes that some contemporary and traditional authorities on the subject insist that Egyptian religion with its many deities and magic was irreligious. In response to the alleged paganism of ancient Egyptian religion, Chandler invokes a leading and renowned egyptologist and historian, Champollion. Egyptian records, declares Champollion, have supported the evidence of one Supreme God. To make this point, Champollion quotes from the Ebers Papyrus to clarify the notion of monotheism espoused by the ancient Egyptians:

> I came from Heliopolis with great ones from Het-aat, the lords of protection, the masters of eternity and salvation. I came from Sais with mother-goddesses, who extended my protection. THE LORD OF THE UNIVERSE told me how to free the gods (man) from all numerous diseases. (trans., C.P. Bryan 1930: plate 1)

Champollion uses this excerpt from the Ebers Papyrus to make an important point—i.e., that to the ancient Egyptians it was the Lord of the universe who ultimately protects man against danger.

In search of other evidence to support the monotheist concept, Chandler refers to excerpts from Hermetic Philosophy as its major source of reference about the concept of one God as father. Clearly the Pymander makes reference to the concept of one God as father, which is a concept very similar to the Christian belief (Van Sertima 1989: 143).

In a convincing effort, Chandler solicits Heinrich Brugsch's work, *Egypt Under the Pharaohs* (1891), which emphasizes that ancients like "Herodotus, Thales, Parmenides, Empedocles, Orpheus, and Pythagoras, were all known to have made many journeys to Egypt to be instructed in Natural Philosophy and Theology" (Van Sertima 1989: 10). Brugsch posits that, although Moses is credited in the Judaeo-Christian Bible with institutionalizing monotheism, this same Moses had been taught by the ancient Egyptians. Referring to *The Book of the Dead* (1895), which illustrates the forty-two commandments of Egyptian religion, Brugsch contends that Moses modeled his system upon the writings and teachings of the ancient Egyptians (pp. 10-11).

The ancient Egyptians also had a very complex and multilayered philosophical system which grew from their religious practices. George G. M.James refers to the educational system of the Egyptians which the Greeks called *Sophia* ("Wisdom Teachings"). In addition, C.H. Vail's *Ancient Mysteries System*, draws attention to the earliest theory of salvation. Focal in the Egyptian theory was that man's soul, if liberated from its bodily fetters, would attain liberation to become godlike; thus one could see the gods in this life, attained with the immortals (James, 1954, p. 27).

Theophile Obenga, the leading scholar in Egyptian-Nubian philosophy, uses a philosophical text of the pharaonic age to explain Egyptian concepts that were established more than 2500 years before Christ. The Egyptian text was chiefly concerned with speculations in:

> Life and Death, Truth and Justice, social order and chaos, happiness in eternity the Beyond ... the emergence of matter, ...Nun and Maat, created and uncreated beings, existence and existing, being and nothingness, astronomy, sciences, medicine, ethics and cosmogenesis. (Van Sertima, 1989, p. 292)

Obenga notes that from this radical thinking of the pharaohs, the idea of "nothingness" was conceived. Hence, from "nothingness" there came what is "now known or made." Besides, the ancient Egyptian believed that "an abyssal water, absolute" already existed with all the raw materials for a latent consciousness and the manifestation of itself as creation "all of which is, all which exists or will come into being" (Van Sertima 1989: 291-292). Obenga ponders the pharaonic explication for the beginning of all things, as the Universe is composed of everything. The pharaonic theory does not involve God or darkness, which are fundamental to the creation story in the Bible. But at the center of the pharaonic belief system is primal matter emerging from the primeval concept of Water and Nun: the spatial milieu of all existence (p. 295).

Restating James briefly, Obenga concurs that the critical teachings of the pharaonic philosophical concepts above led to enlightenment among the ancient Egyptians. Moreover, these precepts were taught in formal organized institutions known as the Mystery Lodges, with three distinct grades of students:

  (1) The Mortals—probationary students who received instructions but were peripheral with respect to the experience of inner vision;
  (2) The Intelligentsia—those who had attained the inner vision and by implication had received mind or *nous*; and
  (3) The Creators or Sons of Light (the enlightened)—who had become identified with or united with the light, that is, with

true spiritual consciousness.

These three grades are equivalent to Initiation, Illumination, and Perfection respectively. During these stages of intellectual development, students of the Mystery System were put through rigorous disciplinary, intellectual, and physical exercises overseen by high priests who tested them to ensure development of body and mind.

Our present-day university system may echo some of the concepts of the Mystery System of ancient Egypt, as the student's education in the Mystery System not only prepared him for the conditions of eternal happiness, but also demanded knowledge of the ten virtues and seven Liberal arts aimed at liberating his soul. The neophyte was required to manifest the following virtues:

> (1) Control of thought and (2) Control of action,...(3)Steadfastness of surprise,... (4) Identity with spiritual life or the higher ideals,... (5) Evidence of having a mission in life, (6) Evidence of a call to spiritual Orders... (7) Freedom from resentment,... (8) Confidence in the power of the master... (9) Confidence in one's own ability to learn, and (10) Primary ... is readiness ... for initiation. (James 1954: 30)

The final virtue embodies what the ancient Mystery System of Egypt represented in its entirety. In other words, "when the pupil is ready, then the master will appear" (p. 31). James also concedes that the four cardinal virtues taught by Plato are directly derived from the Egyptian philosophical system.

Complementing the ten virtues, the students' curriculum of the ancient Egyptian Mystery System consisted of the seven Liberal Arts: Grammar, Arithmetic, Rhetoric and Dialectic, Geometry, Astronomy, and Music. Beyond this training, successful students, who mastered the disciplines outlined, were admitted to the Holy Orders of the Mysteries priesthood. Their curriculum, according to James, included the specialized secret system of language and mathematical symbolism. In addition to this curriculum, the Egyptian priests' education required a specialization in magic. To explain the phenomenon of magic, James incorporates Herodotus' writing on the philosophical training of the Great Mysteries and magic. Herodotus was convinced that the Egyptian priests were capable of:

> controlling the minds of men (hypnosis), the power of predicting the future (prophecy) and the power over nature... by giving commands in the name of the Divinity and accomplishing great deeds. (James 1954: 27)

Increasingly, students of this inner circle not only learned to exercise control over nature but were also trained from *The Book of Coming Forth By Day*, commonly called *The Egyptian Book of the Dead* in "magical formulae and instructions" aimed at supplying information about the state of the departed souls. This training included post-mortem conditions and their methods of verification.

Summarizing the comprehensive educational curriculum for the priesthood, James identifies as central *The Egyptian Book of the Dead* and the sciences of the 42 Books of Hermes. The 42 Books of Hermes provided the following instructions:

(a) *Odus* and two books dealing with music.
(b) *Horoseopus'* four books for instruction of the priest in astronomy.
(c) *The Hierogrammar* for teachings in cosmography, geography, astronomy, and the topography of Egypt and land surveying.
(d) *The Solistes* books of Hermes addressed the slaughter of animals and embalming.
(e) *The Prophets* are ten books of higher esoteric theology which the high priest of the temple had to know, plus the whole education curriculum of the under-priest.
(f) *The Pastophori*, the six medical books which addressed physiology, the diseases of male and female anatomy, drugs, and instruments.

Given the sketch of the educational system outlined above, one can now begin to appreciate and see the connection of the secret sciences and the social order and its protection as an integral part of the Holy Orders and the Sciences of the Monuments. In the instance of application of the sciences of the Monuments (i.e., Pyramids, Temples, Libraries, Obelisks, Sphinxes), the priest/artist had to master architecture, masonry, carpentry, engineering, sculpture, drawing and painting, and metallurgy in order to build these structures. The secret sciences included numerical symbolism, geometrical symbolism, magic from *The Egyptian Book of the Dead*, myths, and parables. Finally, since ancient Egyptian priests were civil servants, they also received training in economics, law, government, statistics, census-taking, navigation, ship-building, chariot-building and horse breeding, and military sciences. Simply put, the education of the Egyptian priest was multidisciplinary.

In retrospect, the factors of geographical conditions, climate, psychological influences, social order, mythology, religion and philosophy, and education all depended on each other to weave the unique character of ancient Egyptian culture, which included art and literature. The discussion that follows will illuminate the importance of each of these facets of Egyptian culture, and their bearing on art and the development of written language.

Chapter Four

THE ART OF ANCIENT EGYPT— OLD KINGDOM

With the foregoing sketch of Egyptian culture as a frame of reference, let us now look at Egyptian art with all of its social, political, religious, scientific, cosomological, mythological, and philosophical ramifications. Within the scope of this work, the concept of art is taken to include architecture, sculpture, drawing and painting, jewelry, and pottery. One must note, however, that the separation of art and written language which we make here is only done initially to facilitate an understanding of these two facets of the same complex of communicating ideas. In ancient Africa, art and written language were the fruits of a collective experience.

Architecture

What are usually described today as splendid and awesome feats of architectural engineering were accomplished by the ancient Egyptians during the Old Kingdom of the third and fourth dynasties. Rosaline David (1975) cites Herodotus, Flinders Petrie (1923;1885), and Emery (1935), the famous British archaeologist, as authoritative sources for information about ancient Egyptian architecture. Petrie and Emery identify Abydos (of the second dynasty) and Saqqara as the zenith of great funerary architecture. Saqqara, David notes, is the site where the great pyramids still stand (p.14).

Baldwin Smith (1938) cautions us not to take the stone monuments and sculptures at face value. He warns against the tendency to judge them by Western aesthetic rules, further assuming that the history of Egyptian architecture commences with these stone structures at Saqqara. In actuality, Smith argues, the stone architecture has historical beginnings as "primitive prototypes" built of wooden and mud structures in the predynastic epoch of Egyptian history. However, with the introduction of copper tools and other metal implements, the archaic Nile Valley inhabitants eventually decided on stone as the most appropriate material to immortalize their royalty, which was in keeping with their religious belief of life after death (Smith 1938: 14).

The use of limestone and sandstone marked the beginning of an illustrious human civilization. In addition to the actual stone structures built during the predynastic period, the religious issue of the life after death dominated all forms of architecture and other art forms. In short, the architecture and other art forms gave "shape" to the ideas of the Egyptians. Baldwin concludes that Egyptian architecture and art commemorated the institutions of religion. He notes that all Egyptian art "whether sculptural, graphic, or architectonic, was in some sense mortuary" (p. 8).

Paradoxically, however, it must be noted that the Egyptian was not preoccupied with thoughts of death; rather, he was known for his proclivity towards the celebration of life and the implementation of rational habits of mind. With enjoyment, celebration of life, and his obviously great intellect, the ancient Egyptian built a special civic architecture of which we know very little (Smith 1938: 9).

Architecture of the Old Kingdom, Dynasties III—VI (2686-2181 B.C.)

We begin the discussion on architecture of the Old Kingdom by reviewing the overall approach of earlier histories written during the nineteenth and early twentieth centuries.

According to Baldwin Smith, many people focus almost exclusively on the "monumental and elaborate buildings," while very little attention, if any, is directed to the large sector of vernacular architecture (Smith 1938: 11). Much more attention was given to the monumental and elaborate buildings of ancient Egypt for their tectonic attributes, while some historians have neglected the rich aesthetic and artistic valuation that is revealed through a close and thorough examination. The rich underlying aesthetic of style, function, meaning, and technique of Egyptian architecture is also present in the foundations of African thought and architecture.

According to Flinders Petrie (1923), this common aesthetic "thread" of dynastic architecture is rooted in predynastic wattle-and-thatch hutch semicircular-based structures, which were built with a conical or hoop roof. Interwoven reeds, branches and mud were crudely assembled for shelter. Next in chronological order was the mud house.

Predynastic vernacular structures were constructed beginning with sticks placed in semicircular or in circular bases, plaited and thatched. Then the walls were daubed with mud and the dome-shaped or curved roofs were added.

With the advent of what is termed the dynastic or pharaonic reign, Egyptian architecture underwent some significant changes. For example, the circular and semicircular-based structures which were built with curved, conical, or dome-shaped roofs became common. These vernacular architecture structures, according to Smith (1938) and Alexander Badawy (1966), were precursors of later domestic and religious architecture which dominated the ancient Egyptians.

As was mentioned earlier, it was not until the third dynasty that wood and brick construction was replaced by the new stone architecture commonly known today as "Egyptian architecture." Supporting Smith and Badawy, Eberhard Otto (1967) adds that the archaeological findings from excavations at Abydos, the center for the worship of Osiris, provides important information about ancient Egyptian monumental and civic architecture. Otto notes that although Abydos was not the capital of unified Egypt, which meant it had little political focus, it nevertheless was of importance for two separate reasons: Abydos was the site of the continued funerary cult of earlier Egyptian Kings, and the central place of worship for the god Osiris.

Maintaining the importance of Abydos, Petrie notes that the architecture at this site dominated the tombs of royalty of the first dynasty. Unfortunately, however, the original superstructures were damaged and pillaged, thus making it difficult for modern archaeological techniques to recover complete or partial architectural structures. The evidence found, according to Otto, were the original layout of Abydos, remains of mud brick from subterranean buildings, various inscriptions found on funerary equipment, "especially ceilings with royal names and small tablets with records of canals" (p. 15). As evidence of Abydos' outstanding achievements, the tablets of Narmer are among the primary documents supplying information about this place (see plates 6 and 7). Since little is known about the architecture and politics of the second dynasty, it is difficult to do more than speculate through reconstruction of tombs and other buildings.

Based on such speculation, students of ancient Egyptian architecture now believe that significant changes occurred during the first two dynasties. Some are convinced that a radical change in floor plan was introduced. They claim that the radical change is shown in the introduction of the predominantly rectangular base for mastaba, temples, pyramids, domestic dwellings, and courts (Badawy, 1966; Smith, 1938; and Tompkins, 1971).

During the third millennium, Smith and others identify the first gigantic stone architectural complex—the step pyramid. Essentially, this structure, which replaced the mastaba, is described as the world's first stone building—a monumental phenomenon. Architect, mighty builder, and patron of the arts, Imhotep is the Egyptian credited with this legendary structure. In addition to Imhotep's contribution, the reigning pharaoh of Egypt during this time, Zoser, cannot be ignored. For he is also credited as a bold thinker who supported the more permanent sculptural form. Another note on Imhotep helps us to understand some more about the magnificent achievement of his great mind. Imhotep was revered throughout Egypt for his wisdom, which included his positions as "a scribe, sage, astronomer, magician, the father of medicine, and the first user of stone" (Smith 1938: 61).

Step Pyramid and Complex

Imhotep's move to build a permanent burial place for the beloved pharaoh Zoser was a court complex which complemented the great step pyramid. The walled precinct of one square mile had a corridor entrance which was the only entrance to the city of the dead. The diagram (see plate 8) shows that the corridor entrance, at the southeast corner of the complex, was prefaced by a towered gateway. In the gateway there were two large doors leading into the long corridor flanked on both sides by fluted columns. As one passed this impressive line of columns, the Great South Court was next. The rectangular platform was punctuated in the center by two B-shaped masses of stones believed to be altars. On the west side of the court there were three terraces rising in ascending order. The last of the three terraces bridged the great court and the pyramid.

     At the center of the complex there stood the six-step pyramid, which rose higher than any of its complementary structures (see plate 9). This imposing structure, according to Smith, consisted essentially of successive enlargements of the original mastaba. Pointedly, it is important to mention here that there has been much speculation about how Imhotep built this pyramid. Unfortunately, important data about the foundational work has been lost over time. Yet, we know from numerous descriptions of the step pyramid that the customary north entrance to this structure was on the second step and descended to a passage which led to several galleries.

     Smith describes the galleries that were cut into the bed of the rocks, which had elaborately designed vertical walls of alabaster. On these walls are the inscriptions from *The Egyptian Book of the Dead*. A significant inscription honoring Imhotep reads as follows: "First after the King of Upper and Lower Egypt" (p. 81).

     Egyptologists have found an elaborately decorated chamber with the remains of what was once remarkable woodwork. This woodwork was the residue of a coffin which was "marvelously constructed from six inch thick wood, each piece veneered only 4 millimeters while the other surface area was covered with a gold leaf" (p. 79). The wooden coffin, identified as the coffin of the Great Pharaoh Zoser, lay in a room next to other adjoining chambers, which some speculate to have been the resting place of Zoser's queen.

To the north of the Great Pyramid were the serbad, Mortuary Temple, the Court of the Northern palace, and the Great Altar. The serbad was a small rectangular structure built next to the pyramid. This enclosed structure had two holes for seeing into the building which housed the ka—a statue of Zoser. Significantly, the openings allowed the rock-crystal eyes to watch the world of the living.

Next to the serbad was the pyramid temple or the mortuary chapel, which appeared for the first time on the northern side of the pyramid, since the mastaba was the burial place of the pharaoh on the eastern side. This innovation illustrated a development in the funerary burial system advanced by Zoser. The temple had a narrow, maze-like entrance which led one into the building, through two successive courts in front of the temple. The facade of each building had an impressive four-columned portico facing southward from the pyramid. Smith observes that the columns were not freestanding, but rather a facade for heavy stone architecture. The columns, he adds, "are joined together in pairs by a piece of wall" (p. 79). Incidentally, the facade of columns just described is regarded as "classic simplicity" and is quite similar to succeeding examples in Egyptian architecture.

To the southeast of the large north court of Temple T were two palaces which were identified as north and south palaces along with their individual courts. Smith believes that these palaces were two small rectangular buildings, the southernmost one the *"White House,"* symbolizing the pharaoh's dominion over upper Egypt; and the northernmost the *"Red House,"* symbolizing his reign and control over Lower Egypt.

Again, we see on these buildings four tall slender columns attached to the brick walls which bore the weight. The roof was deliberately curved to depart from the overall rectangular look. Each column that actually supported the wall and the roof was topped with a carved capital of "two curved and channeled leaf-like pendants on either sides of the rectangular rafters set between them" (p. 75). Interestingly, the more sophisticated columns and their appendages found in later Egyptian architecture have their roots in the prototype stone columns found at Saqqara.

The building in the southeast corner of the precinct completed the complex of architectural structures at Saqqara. The most significant of the structures in this area of the precinct was Temple T, which was better known as the "The Osiris Temple." This temple was placed in northern and southern locations, each with two entrances. Both entrances led one down halls, the walls of which were supported by columns. In addition to these supporting columns, the walls on either side of the hallways had windows which allowed light to enter the building. However, what students of architecture have found most fascinating about Temple T was its facade. In this regard, one of the outstanding features of the temple's exterior was the imitation of woven matting in stone, quite similar to its precursor that was made out of wood and reed in predynastic time. Smith observes that Imhotep exercised extreme care and also introduced the architectural features of round corner posts that supported the entire building. To conceal these huge posts, the architect curved the smaller torus molding which served as a device to create the illusion of a continuous wall.

Another exemplary feature found only on the Temple of Osiris was the presence of the Egyptian "cavetto cornice," which projected from the walls of the building. The roof of this building was made from flat slabs of stone. Notwithstanding, Smith notes that the flat surface was interrupted at intervals by parallel "corrugation, painted red to represent the round beams of contemporary roof" (p. 71).

Finally, Temple T was served by a court known as Heb-Seb. This court was surrounded by a series of chapels which appeared to function as fences around the religious shrine.

In sum, the above account of the Saqqara precinct attempts to frame the description and discussion of the development of architectonics in ancient Egypt. Regrettably, to appreciate the outstanding quality of Imhotep's work would require a much more elaborate discussion than time and space will permit here.

Development of the True Pyramid

Imhotep's genius in pyramid building was copied extensively in the centuries that followed. His blueprint from the step pyramid at Saqqara was modified throughout the years until reaching its zenith in the fourth dynasty. At the high point of pyramid building, three monumental structures were erected at Gizeh and became known as one of "the wonders" of the ancient world. These monuments still stand as examples of the advanced scientific approach to pyramid building. According to some egyptologists, including Ann Rosaline David (1975), the great pyramids of Gizeh were built approximately 4,500 years ago, where they are still found at the edge of the desert near modern Cairo. However, the transition from the step pyramid to the three great pyramids was bridged by what David and others have determined to be the earliest tomb, which also has been upheld as a "true" pyramid—at Dahshur, which is north of Saqqara, the famous Bent Pyramid, built by Seneferu of the fourth dynasty (see plate 10).

Another student of Egyptian architecture, Desmond Stewart, (1971) notes that although the Bent Pyramid at Dahshur evolved from the step pyramid approach to construction, its final outer surface and general appearance are the manifestation of a unique profile, in which the lower part is steeper than the upper part. Stewart observes that somewhere at the mid-point of the outer surface, the plane inclination decreases sharply to the summit. Rosalie David adds to this observation that the sides incline at an angle of 43 degrees for 36 feet in a broken line, instead of the 52 degrees common to the bent pyramid's successors (David 1975). Thus the unusual tilt of two different angles on the same plane gave the pyramid its bent look.

An important feature of the bent pyramid that cannot be neglected is the appearance of a relatively smooth surface, as opposed to the grid-like surface of the step pyramid. In this instance, the steps were covered by local stone which was finally covered with lime stone, thus making the surface smooth. Undoubtedly, this pyramid (or bent-pyramid) form marked the beginning of the age of pyramid building which peaked at Gizeh (Stewart 1971: 30-35).

Returning to the three pyramids at Gizeh, ancient records tell us that three pharaohs are credited with the construction of this magnificent group of pyramids. The first and the largest of the three great pyramids was built by King Khufu, also known as Cheops. Edward Denison Ross (1931) offers a description of this pyramid, which appeared approximately two hundred years after the prototype at Saqqara. Ross eloquently states that this pyramid was imbued with "mathematical exactness of measurement and line" while its superb design and calculated masses rose to the sky (p. 13).

Not surprisingly, in the view of some, like Peter Tompkins (1971) and Flinders Petrie (1923), there is still great speculation about how stones were cut with such remarkable accuracy and how stones weighing well over a ton were placed next to each other with precision. Petrie notes that each stone was set with joints at ten thousandths of an inch—work as intricate as that of an optician.

Sustaining the magnificence of the great pyramid, E. Baldwin Smith (1938) cites Herodotus' accounts of the great pyramid which ponders over the methods of construction. Herodotus was awed at the fact that tackle and pulleys were not employed to place the huge stones on the summit of the pyramid. Moreover, his research notes that the pyramid took some twenty years to build and it employed approximately 100,000 men whose ration would be estimated at a million and half dollars in today's economy (Smith 1938: 96).

Most convincingly, Peter Tompkins' *Secrets of the Great Pyramid* (1971) offers a copious structural description of the Great Pyramid. He asserts that the pyramid covers a space equivalent to seven blocks of midtown Manhattan with approximately "two-and-half million blocks of limestone and granite" (p. 4). Furthermore, Tompkins calculated the Great Pyramid of Cheops to be equivalent in height to a forty-story skyscraper. He also reports that the enormous structure, with its precisely fitted stones, was covered by a mantle of highly polished limestone, to reflect the rays of the sun.

In support of his observations, Tompkins cites the work of Diodorus Siculus and Strabo. He emphasizes Strabo (24 B.C.), who wrote some forty-seven books addressing the pyramid and its complementary structures. Strabo describes, with great precision, the entrance of this pyramid which differed from its predecessors. Access to the pyramid was gained through a swivel door which opened into a descending passage at an angle of 26-1/2 degrees. Strabo notes that the narrow and low passage descends approximately 150 feet into the live rock below the base of the pyramid. He reiterates that this passage was no new invention. The prototype structure at Saqqara also had this tunnel passage. However, the only technical advancement of the Great Pyramid at Gizeh was the "vertical distribution of chambers, connected by long, sloping passages, which were intended to be concealed permanently in this stone mountain" (p. 4) (see plate 11).

The remarkable architectural feat of suspending chambers, professor Tompkins tells us, was achieved through the deployment of long corridors which led to the queen's and king's chambers. Each suspended corridor and its chamber were supported by a corbeled vault, which served as a buffer against the pressure of gravity. In addition, as part of the new evolution in interior design, Tompkins records that a Grand Gallery connected the king's and queen's chambers. This gallery was supported by the corbel vault with its "stone masonry as a roofing construction, similar to [that] used in the case of the chambers" (p. 246).

Interestingly, the pyramids of Chephren and Mycerinus, which were constructed later, are very similar in design to the Great Pyramid of Cheops. The only remarkable difference is their size. Chephren appears larger than the Cheops because it stands on a higher plateau. But in actuality, it is smaller, while the Mycerinus is definitely the smallest of the three.

Similar to the Zoser step pyramid of the third dynasty, the three Gizeh pyramids were not isolated monoliths as they appear now. Each pyramid, though it was the focal point of the burial site, belonged to a vast complex of buildings. In fact, the pyramids could not function without their complementary constituents.

Finally, all pyramid precincts which followed the Zoser prototype are similar, hence there is no need to repeat their description. In addition, one should not be left with the impression that pyramids and temples were the only architectural structures in a precinct.

Sphinx

A discussion of the great pyramid complex at Gizeh would be incomplete without mention of the colossal monument of the Sphinx. The Great Sphinx, according to Tompkins (1981), lies about "twelve hundred feet southeast of the Pyramid of Cheops near the valley building of Chephren" (p. 33). The impressive monolith is carved from a single sandstone knoll towering 66 feet high, extending 240 feet in length, and spanning 13 feet 8 inches at its widest part (see plate 12). The anthropomorphic image is part man, part lion. Notably, some egyptologists argue that the human portrait is identical with that of the pharaoh, Chephren. However, even if the reports are inaccurate one can be quite certain that the headdress with the cobra and the falcon on the forehead belongs to the long tradition of royal symbols used by the pharaohs.

Tompkins and others believe that at one time the Sphinx may have been coated with limestone plaster which was painted in the various colors of a pharaoh's regalia, as well as his natural skin tones. More importantly though, the great Sphinx of Gizeh was not a mere aggrandizement to the pharaoh; rather it served many symbolic functions, many of which unfortunately remain an enigma to modern man. Hence, the monument has aroused much awe and speculation. For example, Sir Norman Lockyer, a British astronomer, suggested that the sphinx's crouching half-lion with human face "symbolizes the junction of the constellations Leo and Virgo which occurred at a summer solstice in the fourth millennium B.C" (p. 33).

In another instance, Tompkins reviews Cassini's incomplete theory of the adoption of a geodetic which was to have represented 1/6000th of a terrestrial minute of an arc. Tompkins surmised that Cassini was unaware that such a foot had been in existence for thousands of years, and that "the sphinx, which could be used as a geodetic marker to indicate the equinox, also once had an obelisk between its paws" (p. 33). The shadow of the obelisk, Tompkins contends, could be used to calculate the correct circumference of the earth as well as the variance in the degree of latitude (Tompkins, 1971, p. 33).

The speculations do not stop with the positing of scientific theories. In fact, some students of Egyptian history believe that the Sphinx was built upon a labyrinth of secret passages which connect subterranean structures including the three pyramids. This particular belief remains a speculation to this day.

It is important to point out that there were many sphinxes, although they may not be as famous as the one at the Gizeh Pyramid complex. It was also common for many pharaohs to immortalize themselves by having sphinxes carved in their likeness. For instance, Rosalie David (1975) shows us an example of the sphinx of Ramesses at Memphis (19th Dynasty, New Kingdom). She argues that the Sphinx at Gizeh was the likely precursor to the Ramesses II model. Amenophis II at Karnak of the 18th Dynasty is another example of a Sphinx in the likeness of a pharaoh.

Significantly as well, sphinxes were represented not only in the lion/man anthropomorphism but also in the lion/ram-head mold. Examples of such sphinxes were placed along the avenue leading to the temple of Karnak, middle to later period (see plate 13).

Finally, our most secure knowledge of a function of the Sphinx, according to David, is that "Shesep Ankh represents royal power, protecting good and repelling evil" (David, 1975, p. 28). Remarkably, the data provided by David supplies insight about the most significant functions of the sphinx.

Obelisk

Affiliated with the great sphinx at Gizeh is the obelisk. Tompkins (1971) describes an obelisk as a "tapered four-sided pillar [with a pyramid at its apex] used for measuring shadow length [and it is] usually inscribed with hieroglyph[s] proclaiming the achievements of the pharaoh" (p. 390) (see plate 14). In addition, Tompkins (1981) contends there is a significant difference between an obelisk and its imitator. The United States' Washington Monument is a perfect example of the difference: the Washington Monument, the tallest in the world at 555 feet high, was assembled from "36,000 separate blocks of granite faced with marble" (p. 3), whereas a true obelisk is quarried from a single piece of granite.

Some egyptologists argue that although there are no complete examples of obelisks, records from the old kingdom, the first five dynasties, show that the obelisk's forerunner first appeared with the pyramids of Gizeh. Tompkins also verifies that the pharaohs from the fifth dynasty "added to their pyramid complexes of vast solar temples built around a huge 'ben-ben' (the Egyptian word for obelisk)" (p. 3). Notwithstanding, these huge needles were not true monoliths, but rather, obeliscoid structures, comprised of separated blocks which rose from a truncated pyramid base (Tompkins 1981: 4).

Albeit, the earliest example of a true obelisk is traced to King Senusret of the twelfth dynasty, at Heliopolis. This was the major one of the huge needles where the temple of Amon-Re at Karnak was also located. Outside of the temple two great obelisks were erected, one on each side of the immediate entrance. Baldwin Smith (1938) notes the religious importance of the obelisk by citing Amenhotep III's statement, "When my father rises between them, I am among his following." This verse, he believes, helps to cast light on the importance of sacred "pyramidions" (p. 155). Along with the religious significance, which is the worship of the sun god, the obelisks also served in the scientific realm of Egyptian life. Again one recalls Tompkins' observation: "by measuring the shadow [of the two obelisks of Amon-Re] at the solstice, it was possible to extrapolate the meridian circumference of the planet" (p. 210). Further, Tompkins adds, with the employment of a series of obelisks, "the ancient Egyptians could have physically measured minutes and seconds of a meridian arc, along a meridian" (p. 211).

Unfortunately, of the hundreds of obelisks which stood in Egypt, only nine still remain erect. Many were taken away by invaders, while the remaining needles are either buried or lay broken as a result of the "religious fanaticism of competing cults" (Tompkins 1971: 4).

Temples

Henceforth I want to focus specifically on the next most popular Egyptian architectural structure—the temple. Besides the three famous pyramids of ancient Egypt, the temples that served the pyramid complex are known for their large rectangular edifices, impressive columns, colored granite walls, and fine masonry (see plates 15 and 16). Whereas only fragments and ruins remain, the pyramid temple of Khafra, with its basalt foundation, provides the best evidence of the outstanding architectural features in the Old Kingdom and throughout Egyptian history. Since the T-shaped temple at Khafra was the only surviving example of early Egyptian temple architecture, it might be important for us to examine this temple of the Fourth Dynasty, whose architectonics were merely modified in the succeeding centuries.

To the casual visitor, the site of the Khafra temple is a mere ruin. But Smith's (1938) reconstruction of this temple, using an intact rectangular edifice 110 meters long, is most important. This colossal structure was situated on the east side of the Khufu Pyramid. Smith suggests that there was apparently one enclosed entrance and corridor leading downward into the valley. To the right of the entrance was the chamber for the guardian, while to the left there were the vestibule and its auxiliary structures. The floor plan, writes Smith, demonstrates that from the vestibule there was a columnar passage that led into the T-shaped hall with its square monolithic piers of Aswan granite. At the end, the reception hall opened into a court whose perimeters were fortified by large granite piers, in front of which there stood a statue of the pharaoh.

Nominally, the actual temple was a low rectangular mass of masonry, crowned with a flat roof which was supported by solid walls made of limestone blocks faced with heavy granite ashlar. On the inside, the rose-colored granite walls were punctuated by pillars that serve as part of the support system for the massive stone work. Smith's speculation leads him to believe that in keeping with the religious austerity of early Egypt, relief work in stone, together with the hieroglyphs, must have given the walls an impressive appearance.

The twelve-meter-high walls had their upper edges rounded in the style of earlier brick-and-mud construction. (The brick laying method used was quite similar to modern methods of laying rectangular bricks). In addition to the fine masonry, Smith believes that the symbolic significance behind the choice of only two doorways into this temple might be linked to the North and South Kingdoms that existed during the early dynastic period. Each doorway was flanked by two lion sphinxes, symbolic of the pharaoh and his power. It was believed that the magical and divine power which were associated with the lion sphinx would serve as a protecting force for the temple.

Quite predictably, as Smith continues, although temples were built in succeeding years with modifications, they maintained the basic features of massive proportions and freestanding stone support. For example, a temple with some modifications, Smith notes, was the temple at Abusir of King Sahure of the Fifth Dynasty. In this temple, the simplicity of the massive walls was replaced with painted stucco and carved reliefs. The columns were carefully sculpted to resemble the common plant forms in the Valley. The palm-leaf capital dominated the columns at Abusir. The structure of these massive granite monolithic columns "imitated bundles of papyrus plants bound together, the flowering heads standing erect instead of spreading into a campaniform," which would have been common to the Khafra T-shaped temple of the fourth Dynasty (Smith 1938: 120-127).

In sum, the basic plan and architecture of the Egyptian temple varied little throughout its history. Generally, each temple represented the dwelling place of the god. The entrance was flanked with a massive pylon or gateway leading into a series of open courts and pillared hypostyle halls, then to the sanctuary of the god, where the most scared rituals were performed. Literally, temples functioned either as the place for worship of the deity who dwelled within them, or as a mortuary reserved for the worship of the dead and deified pharaoh. The temple of Horus at Edfu is an example of a deity worship site, whereas the Ramasseum at Thebes is a mortuary temple dedicated to the warrior king Ramesses II.

Regardless of how massive and elaborate the Egyptian temple was, with its pylons, courts, and halls, in the final accounting all structures were built around one small room, which was the sanctuary where the god lived. Even with the New Kingdom's noteworthy artistic achievement of overblown and grandiose colonnades and halls in the temples of Amun at Luxor and (particularly) at Karnak, we see that these temples were still built around the axis of the sacred sanctuary (David 1975: 92-98).

Architectural Achievements
Outside the Pyramid Complex

If the impression given so far has been that the pyramid complex was the only high point in Egyptian architecture, then I must hasten to mention the science of urban planning, manifested in the highly organized ancient cities and towns.

Despite the ruins, some rebuilt and others buried, Baldwin Smith believes that the archaeological evidence from ancient Egyptian cities provides important information about the history of urban planning. He argues that ancient Egyptian urban architecture illustrates, "many of the natural stages in early development of communities." Accordingly, Smith contends that the architectural plans of ancient Egyptian cities clearly show the first systematic and geometric town plans. For example, the use of geometrically arranged streets, though some may argue that it was a "natural and inevitable stage in the development of early urban life," attests to the Egyptians' consciousness and foresight with regard to the final layout of a city (Smith 1938: 210).

It should be clear by now that Egyptian life was dominated by the Nile river, making it necessary for the ancient Egyptians to gather into communities. We have already reviewed Badawy's (1966) account of the predynastic-to-dynastic evolution of houses, from the one-cell dwelling and circular plan to the rectangular model. In the discussion to follow, I will attempt to show how the development of houses went hand-in-hand with the evolution of towns and cities.

Before ancient Egyptian cities can be examined, it might be instructive for us to look at the fundamental features of an embryonic Egyptian town. Smith describes a prototype of a town in the making as comprised of "a casual grouping of clan, tribal, or frequently communal huts around the totem house of the high priest and chieftain" (Smith 1938: 210). As the need arose for defense against invading forces, the houses were protected within a roughly constructed circular fortification which looks quite similar to those seen in some African societies today, namely, the Zulu and the Maasai.

Now let us consider one of ancient Egypt's most famous cities. While the ancient city of Akhetaten, now known as Tell el- Amarna, is today perhaps the most famous Egyptian city, we must not neglect to look at the first known city of Egypt, Memphis.

Memphis was chosen by the first pharaoh, Menes, as the capital of the newly unified Egypt. It was the focal site for an agglomeration of villages, precincts, and defensive towns which gradually merged together, not unlike the city of London. Smith descibes the city of Memphis from the findings of Flinders Petrie. Memphis was about eight miles long and four miles wide. Within the metropolis, Petrie reports, Memphis was not congested with streets lined by houses; instead, careful allotment gave large gardens and fields to the various outlying villages and precincts. He makes the important observation that a total of nineteen temples might be evidence of a combination of villages, towns and precincts which finally coalesced into the city of Memphis.

Smith also relies on Herodotus' accounts, which admirably set forth the plan of Memphis. He reports that the city was geometrically planned with streets running from north to south and crossing at right angles. Apparently, these were rectangular blocks of uniform houses on parallel streets. Closely following Herodotus' observations, Smith concludes that the planning imposed on a city like Memphis could hardly grow from the natural evolution of the primitive village. He is confident that there was deliberate intellectual activity at work in the approach of the city builders of ancient Egypt. Smith suggests that the preconditions for such urban planning were present at the beginning of dynastic history.

Principally, the pharaohs of this epoch in Egyptian history—Old Kingdom—are known for the elaborately constructed cities of the dead, built in the deserts. For example, the pharaohs of the Thinite Period, first Dynasty at Abydos, were the first to construct many rectangular graves around their eternal abodes. The graves that surrounded the pharaohs' tombs served as a defensive wall, similar to the fortifications seen in many traditional African societies. By the fourth Dynasty, the intellectual concept of planned towns and cities was not restricted to the pharaoh's city of the dead, but also encompassed the domestic lives of the living Egyptians. Despite modifications in city and town plans, the basic features of later defensible cities—clusters of dwellings around the palace-temple of the king—mirrored those of the embryonic town.

Given the knowledge of basic town and city planning, we can look at the domestic architecture. Badawy (1966) identifies five models of domestic houses. He calls the first one "Terrace with two ventilators." In this instance, the entrance to the house was controlled by a singular gateway which opened into a central courtyard. In the courtyard there were a sheltered water tank and granaries. The house was situated at the back of the court, which was enclosed on three sides by a low parapet wall. Badawy notes that a porch ran in front of the house and was supported by four columns with bases. The entry door opened from the portico into the rooms of the house. Usually, there were a few flights of stairs that took one to the terrace. On each end of the terrace there was a vaulted opening. The space between these vaults was occasionally enclosed by a balustrade which interrupted easy movement on the terrace.

The second model of domestic dwelling Badawy calls "Terrace with columned shelter." The space between the two ventilators, in this instance, was used to erect an awning supported by three or four columns. This superimposed structure functioned as shelter from the sun and from the dampness of cool desert nights.

The third model of house was identified as "Terrace with various levels." A small stairway from the roof of the portico allowed access to the terrace. Badawy remarks that the innovation of multi-terracing was the forerunner of the multi-storied house. "Terrace with columned portico" seemed like the next logical step. The two ventilators were replaced by an upper portico which now occupied the entire upper floor, the full width of the house. This floor rested on two side walls and on the same number of columns as the lower portico. A window on each wall was opened and allowed air to enter.

Finally, with the two-storied house the most elaborate modification, the entire ground level including the portico was surmounted by an entirely new floor for dwelling. In this instance, the second floor portico became the facade of the upper story. The columns of this story were usually shorter, but generally more in number than on the ground floor. A stairway on the lateral took one to the highest point of the house where there were two ventilators. For better security the walls around the courtyard were built as high as the lower story.

Concluding, Badawy directs our attention to architectural elements of domestic houses that are noteworthy for their specific features. The walls, for example, were generally built of brick, plastered and painted with horizontal white and red strips. Roofs were either vaulted or dome-shaped. He believes that the rationale for the employment of vaulted and dome shaped roofs was an understanding of the physics of resulting stresses. Badawy argues that a flat curve could be tolerated for the vault over the ground floor, while a higher one had to be used in the upper story. Stairways were generally external, and they ran along the left side wall of the court. Winding stairs led one to the various stories.

In addition to the structure at large, door panels were usually decorated while the doorways were trimmed with a hood molding. Windows were barred with either vertical mullions or horizontal elements. In the case of the rectangular or horizontal windows, they had hood molding over them and a projecting sill. Columns were simple cylindrical shafts supported by a base (Alexander Badawy 1966: 10-17).

In retrospect, it is important to re-emphasize that the domestic architectural development faithfully transmitted the fundamental lessons of the Old Kingdom throughout the history of ancient Egypt.

Sculpture

Like the architecture, the plastic art forms of sculpture, painting, pottery, and jewelry reflect the many statements of belief, hopes, and world-view of the ancient Egyptians. Lionel Casson (1965), E. Denison Ross (1931), Eberhard Ott (1967), Cyril Aldred (1962), G. Maspero (1960), and others contend that Egyptian art was highly influenced by religion. They observed that the art form which dominated Egyptian life was sculpture. Moreover, many students of Egyptian art seem to agree, it was the divinity attributed to the pharaoh, the god-king, the human incarnation of god that drove the production of an aesthetic canon called "pharaonic art."

In principle, maintains Denison Ross, Egypt, the cradle of the arts, has left us with the legacy of some of the first examples of representative art, especially human portraiture, which is clearly deliberate and self-conscious. Aldred (1962) and Denison Ross have no doubt, as their claims are supported by excavated artifacts, that the development of sculpture goes back to predynastic times. Meticulously, Denison Ross builds the argument that predynastic sculptural objects were made not purely for a decorative purpose, but rather for some magical motive. He emphasizes that the important principle of magic must remain foremost in our minds if we are going to understand the art of ancient Egypt.

Aldred supplies us with some more fundamental insights about Egyptian art. He contends that the portrait statues that the world admires today as magnificent creations of art were not made to move the emotions of the spectators; rather, they were to ensure through magical means the immortality of the person represented. We will see later in the discussion a stoic and introspective reverence which is synonymous with royal Egyptian portraiture (see plate 17).

To commence the discussion on the early development of human portraiture, Ross points to the evidence we now have from Badarian and predynastic tombs. Evidently, mud from the Nile river was modeled into human and animal figures. While the appearance of these figures may suggest that they were ornaments, the fact that these objects were found at burial sites compels us to conclude that their creators' intention must be connected with the later common practice of furnishing the dead with objects that he or she might require in his/her second life (p. 16). To say, then, that Egyptian art, from the earliest stage of predynastic times, and even into its later development, is for decorative purposes would constitute a major misconception of this art.

Given this underlying aspect of philosophy in ancient Egyptian art, we can now take a brief look at predynastic sculpture. Ross persuades us that predynastic art can be classified into two broad categories: representational and non- representational. Bearing these two broad classifications in mind, for instance, he defines representational art as "that which attempts to reproduce or imitate [an object] that already exists in nature or manufacture" (p. 17). On the other hand, Ross decrees, non-representational art (e.g., architecture, pottery, and jewelry) is the creation of objects that are not necessarily copies of anything that exists. Regardless, he cites the case of the artist who adds statues or reliefs to a building, or paints on the ceiling of a temple, or makes a fish-like vase. Such an artist, he proclaims, has crossed the boundary

back into the domain of representational art. Judging from his definitions, Ross implies that non-representational and representational art
can cross each other's boundaries. He argues that the intermingling of
these two forms of art does not diminish the practical separation
between representational and non-representational art.

Based on the definition of representational art outlined above, it
would not be difficult to classify the majority of ancient Egyptian sculpture as in the realm of representational art. We see in early sculpture
of humans and animals, seemingly crudely rendered, efforts made to
indicate, for example, the characteristics of an ox. In the case of the
human figure, Ross draws attention to the two ivory figures from the
votive deposit at Hierakonpolis. These two figures do not accurately
render of the entire human anatomy, but care was taken with respect
to the salient features of the face. Ross speculates that the reason for
the stiff and somewhat awkward appearance might have been lack of
control over tools and material. He notes that ivory in particular is very
difficult to work with if one does not have the appropriate tools.

Subsequently, with the improvement of and mastery over tools,
plus the use of other materials such as basalt, Ross asserts, the foundation of clever portrayal of racial characteristics in the face became
the hallmark of the Egyptian artist.

By the advent of the First Dynasty, sculpture in the round was
accompanied by simultaneous development in bas-reliefs. The famous
palettes of Narmer testify to bas-relief sculptural technique. These palettes
are perhaps the best known early monuments which document the reign
of King Narmer. The relief work, executed on slate, demonstrates high
technical skills of composition. To illustrate some of these skills, Aldred
(1962) shows us two of the palettes. One palette from Hierakonpolis (predynastic period) is 17 inches long. On both sides is carved a jackal which
conforms to the outline of the palette. The surface area of the palette is
crowded with portraits of real and imaginary beasts. Aldred observes that
these animals are anatomically accurate, thus setting the standard for the
rendering of animals in the future (see plates 6 and 7).

The second palette, "Parading in Triumph," demonstrates a different kind of compositional sensitivity. In fact, this palette has three
compartments, each apparently portraying one phase of a narrative.
For this palette I will refer to Gaston Maspero's (1960) very clear
description. He describes the central compartment by pointing to the
two leopards confronting each other. Their extravagantly elongated
necks curve and interlace around the central depression. The grimac-
ing faces of the opposing animals form a crown, as it were, above the
circular configuration. Behind each of the animals is a man (apparently
each animal's keeper), both dressed in short skirts and wigs and each
restraining his beast from biting the other.

Above, in the central compartment, there is an imposing figure, presumably the pharaoh. (We can assume the imposing figure is the pharaoh because he wears the diadem crown—crown of a warrior king—and short skirt from which hangs the fox tail). He is bare-footed and armed with a scourge and club. The warrior king is followed by his wife with vase and sandals in hand, while a procession of four standard bearers carry what are believed to be the flags of the four quarters of the world. Beyond the standard bearers, two rows of decapitated enemy corpses lie flat on the ground, loosely bound by their wrists, their heads neatly placed between their legs. Below the central compartment, a sturdy bull, a symbol of the pharaoh, demolishes an enemy's brick fortress and tramples the fleeing party.

On the reverse side, instead of three compartments we see two. The pharaoh's figure dominates the larger compartment, which occupies about two-thirds of the palette. On this occasion, he wears the tall white miter crown of a sovereign with one escort, his groom. He strikes down on the head of a kneeling subject with a club. Above the head of the kneeling chief is a group composed of:

> the hieroglyph of a papyrus marsh from which the head of a man emerges, and a falcon poised with one foot on three of the stems; with the other, which terminates in the arm and hand of a man, the bird holds a cord passed through the most of the head.

In the second compartment, Maspero notes, the two naked figures fleeing for their lives represent the rest of the defeated tribes in the struggle to unify Egypt. Noticeably, the other palettes of Narmer also illustrate episodes of war and the depiction of domestic life after unification of lower and upper Egypt (Maspero 1960: 23).

In his analysis of bas-relief sculpture, Maspero identifies some important characteristics that were to remain central to Egyptian relief sculpture for centuries. Chiefly, the craftsmen focused on bringing out the "principal lines of their models to fix their contours, to simplify their reliefs, to coordinate their movements and their postures" (p. 4).

Regardless of the story told, whether it was a battle, a hunt, or a religious procession, the craftsmen exercised great care to render the figures in soft gestures. The harsh emotions associated with a battle, for example, were not implied by the angles and quality of line used in the reliefs. Lines were generally used in a manner that minimized harsh abruptness.

Finally, a careful examination of the bas-relief sculpture of pre-dynastic Egypt clearly shows that this art form, and perhaps others, were well regulated. Detail pre-planning and the acquisition of a high degree of technical skills were demanded of the practitioners. One can perceive the roots of later conventions and, ultimately, of the whole tradition of relief sculpture, already in place during predynastic Egypt.

In support of the thesis that predynastic roots have influenced bas-relief sculpture of dynastic times, Maspero draws our attention to some recurring conventions. He contends that some of the conventions of the great age of Egyptian sculpture can be discerned in the predynastic epoch. For example, "the dry and angular rendering of the shoulder and the arm, the stiff, almost benumbed bearing of many of the persons," are characteristic in bas-relief from the predynastic era and throughout the history of Egyptian art (p. 23). He also points to the artist's use of gravity and purity of line which are accompanied by the touch and spirit of movement.

To complete his description of bas-relief, Maspero highlights the Egyptian artist's technique of firmness in modeling and the learned simplicity that complements it. Above all, the techniques of keeping the reliefs low and indicating planes by light touches are exclusive to Egyptian bas-relief.

Now that we have some background on predynastic art forms, particularly bas-relief sculpture, it is possible to proceed to a discussion of the sculpture of dynastic Egypt. The sculpture of Egypt, especially during the first six dynasties, reached its peak of artistic development under the descendants of the predynastic artists. Chandler (cited, Van Sertima 1989) and Maspero agree that the early dynastic craftsmen had at their disposal the ruling ideas, conventions, techniques, and skills necessary to perpetuate the unique Egyptian features of originality and character.

For instance, many examples from the Old Kingdom illustrate the unmistakable development of the Egyptian genius through the making of bas-relief and sculpture in the round. We have already reviewed some of the achievements of Egyptian architecture and some of the sculptural forms which accompanied it, so there is no need to recapitulate them here (see above, pp. 53–60).

Generally speaking, the sculpture of the Old Kingdom is referred to as either pharaonic art or, on account of the numerous depictions of pharaohs, queens, and other royal dignitaries, as simply royal (see plates 18 and 19). We will see, however, that the ordinary Egyptians were also represented and that their portraits were handled somewhat differently from those of the ruling class.

Fundamental to our discussion of the artistic achievements of the Egyptian artist, some explanation must be offered about his role and functions so as to minimize our difficulties understanding his work. As an important part of our understanding, we should acknowledge that the builder, painter, and sculptor belonged to a community which followed prescribed conventions. In other words, the artist was not a self-conscious individual, like the artist of modern societies. In addition to the collective approach, the work of the ancient Egyptian artist usually manifested the religious, philosophical, and general world-view of his culture. For example, many of his pieces were repositories of the super-natural force of life after death, a concept which dominated Egyptian life. Perhaps Aldred (1949) best describes the function of Egyptian art when he claims that the art, particularly the statues, were objects that the ancient Egyptian saw as having the capacity to be animated "with divine power; or that after death, the spiritual essence of a man could reside in the statue for all eternity" (p. 1). Once this function is under-stood, we may begin to appreciate the tightness and controlled man-ner with which the work of ancient Egypt was executed. To Aldred's description I would add that even though the religious aspect of life per-meated most of the art forms, other areas of Egyptian thought—e.g., science—were also present in the making of art.

During the first two dynasties of the Old Kingdom, according to Ross, Aldred, and Maspero, the artistic ideas and forms became clearer as they were influenced by the political and cultural unification of lower and upper Egypt. Primarily, the arts played a very important role in the consolidation of the newly formed Egyptian civilization. In his attempt to explain the role of art at the beginning of the dynastic period, Ross notes that the plastic arts were used to instruct other artists and future generations on how the gods, kings, and great ones of the earth should be represented. In actuality, the plastic arts became the teaching medium through which the "proper way of representing [the pharaohs'] figures, their clothes, their crowns and their emblems was first arranged in a regular convention" (p. 12). However, it was not until sometime between the third and fourth dynasties that conventions were cemented. By that time, most students of ancient Egyptian art history agree, the lagging development of the plastic arts was finally approaching the lev-els of the architectural feats seen at Gizeh.

To illustrate some of the outstanding achievements in the plastic arts, Maspero cites the Memphite school of the arts as testimony to rapid development. He believes that the art of Memphis, an important cultural center of the Old Kingdom, was the most influential and gifted of all Egyptian art schools of that time and even of later periods.

As with the architecture of the third and fourth dynasties, stone was the favorite material for sculpture. Pink or black granite, diorite green, breccia, schist, red sandstone alabaster, green and dark slate, red quartzite, and limestone were commonly used in statuary. Incidentally, although not many pieces have survived, sculptures in wood were also produced during the Old Kingdom.

Indeed, the achievement of sculptors working in these hard mate-rials cannot be overstated, especially since there is no traceable evidence of steel tools. From archaeological findings, the tools used during this period (Old Kingdom) were made of flint, bronze, and untempered iron. Maspero advises us not to blame the absence of steel tools for the apparent lack of "manual dexterity which caused them not to disengage certain statues and groups entirely" from the slab of stone (p. 75). It was common to see a seated sculpted figure's back remain attached to a solid rectangular support that looked like the back of a chair. As part of the Old Kingdom convention, he adds, when the figure was standing we see that it had a rectangular wall acting as an obvious support. Maspero observes that the wall against which the standing figure leans "is reduced to the semblance of a pillar terminating squarely at the level of the shoulders or the neck or in a point which is lost in the hair" (see plate 20 for an illustration of this point).

To resolve the conflict in our minds about the figure's attachment to a buttress, Maspero and Cyril Aldred assure us that the sculptor's use of a back support was not exclusive. He (the sculptor) retained the buttress in keeping with the tradition of longevity of the piece. As evidence, there are several examples where we see the back support absent. Some of these are the alabaster Chephren, the limestone statue of Prince Hem-On from Gizeh, an alabaster statuette of a fourth-dynasty princess, and a painted limestone statue of a seated scribe (see plate 21).

Sculptors of the third and fourth dynasties also learned to maintain control over the forces of balance and gravity by placing the arms close to the upper torso. Several arm positions were used. For example, there were figures with arms down at the sides, and some with arms placed on the knees. We can speculate about the obvious structural value of the arm placement, but there are some definite symbolic functions for each of the hand placements.

As the sculptor gained more confidence and experience we see that the figure was allowed interaction with space. In truth, what we are seeing is the birth of kinesics in sculpture. Apparently though, the new liberty kinesics afforded to Old Kingdom sculpture was not generally practiced in stone. Aldred (1956), Maspero (1960), and Ross (1931) agree that since wood, ivory, and metal were not difficult materials to work with—but also because not highly valued—the sculptor could stand to experiment with kinesics in these media. Because of the lack of importance attributed to these materials, however, the pharaoh, deities, and most members of the royal class were not generally represented in common materials of wood, ivory, and metal.

Thus, the first "breakthrough" in the emergence of sculpture in the round occurred when sculptors in wood transcended the "insecurity" of representing feet and hands, which were still either blocked out or paid little attention in stone. The Sheikh-el-Beled—a work in wood—is a good example of the liberty furnished by kinesics, which expedited the development of Old Kingdom sculpture (see plate 22). In this instance, the sculptor placed and extended the left arm away from the figure with what Maspero calls a "ceremonial wand" that is attached to the base of the sculpture. The legs are also astraddle and quite resemble the stance seen in contemporary stone pieces. Most significantly, the modeling of the anatomy equals that of contemporary stone sculpture.

Besides "introducing" the science of kinesics to sculpture, the Sheikh-el-Beled epitomizes the degree of realistic form attained in Egypt and other contemporary cultures at this time. Recognizing that the Sheikh-el-Beled is a pivotal piece, Aldred describes the 44-inch wood sculpture as "remarkably naturalistic in conception," with evidence of great technical ability, control over the material, and acute attention to details—e.g., "the convolutions of the ears and their ridges of close cropped hair" (p. 34). Maspero (1960) adds that the sculptors of the Sheikh-el-Beled also captured the male's social status and some of the attitudes associated with it, such as the figure's rustic appearance, smooth-shaven features, and stocky build, with short thick legs. Maspero suggests that such characteristics were common to people of the plebeian class. He concludes that this and other similar pieces of this period were rendered back and front with "truth and brutal honesty" (p. 85). On one hand, we can understand Maspero and Aldred's high appraisal of the Skeikh-el-Beled, since the form is innovatively naturalistic by comparison with its precursors. On the other hand, in the sculpture of the royal class, the sculptors are bound by their religious conventions. Maspero contends that they took the liberty of stylizing the features of their models "as far as this was compatible with the exigencies of likeness" (p. 81). In other words, the basic likeness of the pharaoh was always maintained but enhanced by canons of idealization. If some physical abnormalities of the subject's actual face would have detracted from the pharaoh's nobility, the artist was careful to correct them. In fact, all pharaohs, from the middle of the Fourth Dynasty throughout the Old Kingdom, were always portrayed with prominent eyes, muscular cheeks, and a muscular physique with wide shoulders, high pectorals, and a muscular midsection that tapered into a small waist. The legs were usually exposed to show muscular thighs and calves. In effect, pharaonic sculpture revealed an idealized form of the male figure carved according to Old Kingdom stylistic canons.

The female figures of the royal classes were likewise sculpted according to the canons of proportion. Their bodies were proportioned and displayed the grace of soft femininity. The example of Mykerinus and his Queen exemplified the idealism of male and female court art of the Old Kingdom (see plate 18). Aldred observed that while the restrained feeling of simplified masses were a common style in the Old Kingdom, there is also frank depiction of the intimacy that existed between a husband and wife of equal status. The element of emotion evoked from this piece adds a secular feeling to the monumental tradition that underlies pharaonic art.

The *Triad of King Mykerinus and Goddesses* also address the question of idealism and monumentalism with respect to human emotions (see plate 19). The king is placed in the center, flanked by the goddess Hathor and the goddess of the Jackal district. The goddess on his right affectionately holds the king's hand while the goddess to his left tenderly touches his shoulders (Ross 1931: 102; Aldred 1962: plates 25, 26).

Though it is possible to identify some stoic and aloof examples of pharaonic sculpture, there are an overwhelming number of couples which transmit feelings of affection and equality between a king and a queen. To say, then, that the genre of Old Kingdom sculpture is purely formalist, idealist, and religious would be inaccurate. The sculptural genre of the Old Kingdom is best described as a combination of religious and stylistic canons common to this period of Egyptian art.

In my analysis of sculpture in the round in the Old Kingdom, I do not mean to leave the impression that naturalistic renditions of figures were never carved in stone. Ross, Aldred, and Maspero draw our attention to the significant *Painted Limestone Statue of a Seated Scribe*. (See plate 23). Aldred comments on the remarkable attention given to technique in the carving of the "bony structure of the face, shoulder, and hands, and the adiposity of the trunk and thighs" (p. 34). He believes that the realism of this piece distinguishes it from all other examples in Egyptian art. In sum, the poise of the *Seated Scribe* can be characterized as a confident, well-educated, and pensive individual. From the scribe's distinctly non-athletic physique, one surmises that he spent a great deal of time away from outdoor physical activity.

Bas-Relief Sculpture of the Old Kingdom Dynastic Era

Bas-relief sculpture developed along very different lines from sculpture in the round, and was a typical part of tombs, temples, and pyramids. Like sculpture in the round, bas-relief sculpture has its genesis in the predynastic epoch or earlier. We return to the previously examined Narmer palettes, which also were significant in the development of bas-relief sculpture. The technique and composition used on the Narmer palettes reveal much about the development of bas-relief. Again, we see the preference for materials such as wood, limestone, sandstone, as well as alabaster, schist, granite, serpentine, and diorite.

Artistically speaking, bas-relief was usually the composition of one or several narratives. Maspero stresses that each figure was drawn with one continuous line, which shows the assurance and freedom of an artist who has mastered fluent linear technique. Skillfully, the transition between the soft outline and the background is subtle, hence one must carefully discern the planes that separate figures from ground. As a result of the combination of soft contour line and low relief, the composition is placed in an atmosphere of serenity even if the subject matter of the particular scene depicts something brutal.

In like manner, the handling of the mass within the contour is very subtle. The inner details are characterized by a combination of soft but definite lines, which create "almost imperceptive modeling" (p. 67). For example, the individual volumes of the face, nose, eyes, and mouth are made prominent through the vigorous use of point and sharp edges.

As if a deliberate contrast were intended, the hard-edged line in the eye, mouth, nose, and facial area strikes a balance with the treatment of the rest of the anatomy, which is rendered in more amorphous edges (see plate 24).

Bas-relief sculpture epitomizes another one of the Old Kingdom's unmatchable contributions to the fine arts: the mastery and control of line with chisel and brush. Maspero (1960) encourages us to observe linear techniques to manipulate plastic space and volume according to the movements of those figures. The bas-relief sculptors were aware of bone and muscular-skeletal anatomy of the pectoral region. He achieved such understructure with delicate projections, depressions, and quality of line and edge. Maspero and Aldred have noted that, given the limited tools at the sculptor's disposal and considering how difficult limestone is to carve, the renderings of bas-relief during the Old Kingdom are quite a remarkable feat (Aldred 1961: 24).

Aside from the definition of projections and depressions with line and edge, it is particularly revealing to examine the bas-relief sculptor's approach to composition. Several surviving pieces from the Old Kingdom offer some insight. Both human and animal figures were arranged consecutively on the same horizontal plane in profile (see plate 25). In many instances, the artist preferred to position all figures looking in the same direction. There are, however, a minority of instances where figures look away as if distracted. Although two-point perspective was not followed precisely in many of these pieces, there are clear indications that the artist possessed understanding of receding planes. On the stage setting, as many term the bas-relief scenes, there are obvious attempts to overlap figures, to show front, middle, and back (see plates 6 and 7).

A frequently preferred compositional device is the "staging" of a narrative in pictorial compartments. A lower compartment represented the foreground action, while the level above showed middle ground and finally the background, sequencing several events as if to occur in space and time. Based on the examples under observation, there are no grounds for concluding that the ancient Egyptian artist did not understand the technique of perspective.

Of course, bas-relief sculpture was portrayed in the hieroglyphs on temples, pyramids colonnades, facades, and walls, even on the base of monumental or freestanding sculptures, and the inscriptions of the formal names and titles of individuals. The fine work was usually painted to enchance details, especially where lighting was insufficient (see plate 26).

Drawing and Painting

Flinders Petrie (1923) identified the high degree of skill attained in drawing and painting of early dynastic times. The exemplary depiction of a pair of geese at Medum not only captures a convincing naturalistic rendering of the geese, but also has executed a convincing treatment of stalking along a meadow amid tufts of herbage through the facility of paint and line (p. 56).

However, it is Ross (1931) who best describes the drawing and painting of the Old Kingdom. He stresses the keen observation and trained mimetic power with which the early dynastic artist executed his work. In particular, Ross points to the freedom demonstrated in scenes that were from daily life. Without the constraints of religious obligations and conventions, Ross argues, animals and plants are rendered with a meticulous accuracy, comparable to present-day illustrations of zoological and botanical manuals. In short, from the evidence of their drawing and painting (see plate 27), the Egyptian artists were "supreme mimetic art-workers" (p. 18).

Pottery

The Old Kingdom artists were not restricted to representational imagery and forms. They also excelled in non-representational art. We know from earlier discussions that the Egyptians were highly advanced builders of architectural forms which, for purposes of argument, can be considered as non-representational art. Thus, the abundance of surviving stoneware made by the ancient Egyptian potters demands recognition. In this respect, Petrie and others are convinced by their archaeological findings that predynastic Egyptians were already very skillful potters. In fact, Ross notes that the pottery from the Tasian and Badarian periods demonstrate the early techniques in pottery. One technique mastered in predynastic times was firing.

By dynastic times, potters had developed preferred styles that varied in form and color. These innovations were possible because of the advances in glaze firing. Ross reports that early in the Old Kingdom, hematite was excavated and made into slip for glazing. When pots were fired with a coat of this slip, the result was a rich, warm, red color. Furthermore, complicated methods for decoration of vessels were developed. For example, applications of grease, we are told, were painted as a resist on certain areas of the pot before firing to retain the color achieved in the first firing. In this way, it was possible to achieve polychrome designs on the pottery. Artistically speaking, many of today's ceramic techniques, such as painting designs, incising patterns, and polychroming, were first used by early dynastic potters for decoration. The most noteworthy feature of the pottery from early Egyptian potters is the great attention given to color and form (Ross 1931).

Significantly, the most striking of early dynastic pots were made of stone. Petrie notes that the hardest stones (diorite, basalt, syenite, and porphyry) as well as the softer stones (alabaster, slate, colored limestone, and serpentine) were all used to make the magnificent examples which have survived five thousand years. Observers of these pieces are constantly amazed by the symmetry and fine finish obtained without tubular drill and circular grinding equipment, for example. Petrie calls a vase from Heirakonpolis in black and white syenite the greatest triumph of Egyptian stone-work (see plate 28). All the vases from early dynastic times were hand cut, and the artistic achievements have not been surpassed even in modern times (Petrie 1923).

Jewelry

Besides pottery, there are many other examples of non-representational arts. Of these so-called minor arts, jewelry is outstanding. Many of the pieces found date back to the Old Kingdom and bear witness to a preference for personal adornment. Gold, electrum, agate, jasper, carnelian, garnet, amethyst, and turquoise were abundant and precious to the Egyptians. As evidence of their appreciation of precious stones, exemplary necklaces, bracelets, chains, pectoral pieces, and crowns were skillfully crafted. With an acute sense of design foremost, several techniques were employed in the making of jewelry during the first dynasty. One method for bracelets required the craftsman's precise execution of separate pieces which were later assembled as one complete overall design. Another method employed the mold technique, whereby the necklace was cast; afterwards, the surface of the cast metal, such as gold, was hammered and chiseled to create the patina (Casson 1965; Ross 1931; Petrie 1923) (see plate 29).

By the fourth dynasty, a "loop-in-loop" technique was employed to make gold chains. Individual gold rings were fashioned into double loops which were then connected to each other. Petrie has stated that by far the most impressive Egyptian jewelry found dates back to the twelfth dynasty at Dahshur; this work, he states, "is graceful and sincere in design and pure in color" (p. 87). Petrie was also impressed by the exemplary rendition of careful harmony and perfect finish. Colorful stones of carnelian, turquoise, and lazuli were outlined in gold, a technique widely used by the Egyptians to prevent tarnishing (Petrie 1923).

Much more could be told about the jewelry of the twelfth dynasty and the eighteenth dynasty, particularly during the reign of King Tut-Ankh-Amen. "King Tut's" tomb is known for its abundance of jewelry, especially pectoral ornaments. These pectoral pieces were made from open-work gold plates, which were engraved on one side with precious stones inlaid on the other. Despite the many segments of each piece, some with clear open spaces and others with detail and intricate engraving, the balance between the segment and negative space is unified in an appearance of strength and symmetry.

Summary

Throughout this discussion of ancient Egyptian art, I have focused primarily on the achievements of the Old Kingdom in the areas of architecture, sculpture, drawing and painting, pottery, and jewelry, as these influences were carried over into later periods. The examples were chosen for their innovations and remarkable artistic and technological excellence established during the Old Kingdom.

As also discussed, the mastabas, the geometrically designed tombs, were transformed, over an approximately four-hundred-year period of developing building technology, into the great pyramids and the temple complexes at Gizeh. During the Old Kingdom these structures were built in honor of the supreme god-king, the pharaoh.

By the period of the Middle Kingdom, the king had become "secularized", in as much as he was revered as a man and not as the incarnation of the god Horus. The pharaoh was still, in effect, equal to the gods. With this change of metaphysical philosophy, however, the original burial site—the pyramids—was abandoned for a new funerary complex. The most prominent example of a funerary complex survives at Deix-el-Bahri, near Thebes, the tomb of the pharaoh Nebhepetre Mentuhotep. Built against the wall of a rock cliff, it ascended three levels. On the upper level stood the pyramid, but it was not the pharaoh's burial place as has been common earlier. The tomb was re-established within the bed of living rock at the back of the complex, with a brilliantly decorated interior.

The altering and rebuilding of funerary architecture in the New Kingdom were undertaken by the pharaohs. The world-view of the ancient Egyptians was somewhat modified—extended to influence all the arts. New Kingdom architecture, according to Aldred (1961), was the repository for the "wide variety within the conventions of Egyptian style" (p. 1). Attention was shifted from pyramids and was redirected to the temple, which became one of the most significant architectural contributions of ancient Egypt.

Egyptian sculpture, paintings, and drawings complemented architecture. For example, in the tombs and temples, many stone statues of the pharaohs were erected as part of the ordained ritual of the dead. In this connection, we see that the pharaoh was the most exalted subject of Egyptian art. In support of his exaltation, artist communities worked as agents who executed the principles of the established tradition of Ma'at—Justice, Truth, and Order. Hence, for all practical purposes, there seems to be stylistic and structural consistency in Egyptian art, although variations in details are evident from the Old through the

Middle and into the New Kingdom.

The Old Kingdom, however, must be credited with providing the aesthetic canons of Egyptian sculpture that endured throughout its long history. Hitherto, sculptures of the pharaoh rarely depicted outbursts of emotion, with exceptions in the Middle Kingdom. The pharaoh's portraiture was consequently motionless, introspective, devoid of passion, and above all, it was serene. The figure was generally posed as seated with his hands on his knees. When in a standing pose, one foot was astride and his arms were close to his sides or clasped across his breast. In those instances in which a pharaoh and his queen were represented, she extended her arm around his waist as an indication of partnership with her husband. Usually, the pharaoh was portrayed as confident, with a youthful muscular athletic physique and a face that exuded majesty.

During the Middle Kingdom with its political changes, the pharaoh's power became limited by the priests and provincial leaders. He was portrayed as a heroic man, with more of a human personality than the detached godly majesty of the Old Kingdom. The portraiture of Thutmosis III exemplified the arrogance of a mighty conqueror. Sculpture during this time displayed a mastery of technique, plus the introduction of the subject's psychology.

Finally, New Kingdom sculpture wrought major changes. With Egypt regaining its great wealth, the once again exalted pharaoh was portrayed in sculpture with a delicate and refined look quite unlike the simple and stoic forms of the Old Kingdom. The sculpture and architecture of this period were massive and monumental. Along with sculpture in the round, bas-reliefs were used in tombs and temples as teaching aids with the narrative of the re-creation of the dead. We see the artists adhering to the canons of the established aesthetics. For example, a pharaoh is always the central figure and much larger than his dwarfed subjects. His head and legs are shown in profile while the shoulders, chest, and one eye are frontal.

Figures of people and animals were usually arranged in a straight line and care was taken to ensure accuracy. On such points, the artist was concerned with conveying a message through the conventions of his "grammar" and was not absorbed with the devices of perspective, foreshortening, and complicated overlapping. Unlike the wooden sculpture of the Old Kingdom with its attempts at naturalism, Middle Kingdom bas-relief focused on archetypal "definitive statements" from daily life, work, games, and public ceremonies.

The Middle Kingdom had accommodated certain changes, some of which allowed for greater "animation" of forms, more freedom of design, and greater self-assertiveness. With the regulation of the pharaoh's dominance, and the assurance that all people, regardless of social status, had a right to an afterlife, there was a greater demand for art, thus opening the way for varied interpretations among craftsmen.

Finally, the New Kingdom brought sobering changes not seen in the Middle Kingdom. The bas-relief reflected the gloom and doubt that pervaded this period. In a way the final decline of ancient Egyptian civilization was best articulated in bas-relief sculpture.

When we turn to painting and drawing, some changes like those in sculpture are observable across the span of the three Kingdoms. Like all other art forms discussed earlier, drawing and painting were rooted in predynastic times. Initially, during the Old Kingdom, paint was used to enhance sculpture in the round and bas-relief carving. Actually, during the Old Kingdom, painting and drawing were used—sparingly—as separate media on plastered surfaces instead of expensive wall carvings. Nevertheless, early painters were just as skilled with the brush as their counterparts in sculpture were with the chisel. Generally, the artist made a preliminary grided sketch before the final execution in paint. Sketches conformed to the artistic tradition of the Old Kingdom.

By the Middle Kingdom, drawing and painting reached their fruition, each becoming a major medium, inspired, and executed with great vigor. The pieces done on tombs continued to be conservative, bounded by the constraints of the Egyptian world-view. However, the work depicting secular life took on new dimensions. With newly found freedom, artists could opt for careful attention to the naturalistic treatment of their subjects. The most significant changes occurred in painting and drawing. During the eighteenth dynasty, under the rule of Akhenaten, there was a deliberate attempt to change the religious tenets and artistic canons. Larger spaces were devoted to painting, which may have opened the door for mural painting. These depictions included new subjects, such as landscapes, architecture, and figures interacting in a natural way. As the key figure in this new movement, the pharaoh Akhenaten allowed himself to be represented in his natural, pear-shaped torso, contrary to the muscular athletic look of his predecessors. But, as expected, after Akhenaten's death, drawing and painting and other artforms returned to the tradition of the ancient Egyptian past.

Though most students of the history of Egyptian art tend to categorize jewelry, pottery, leather, and wood work as minor arts, the craftsmanship displayed—particularly by potters and jewelers—matches that of the painters, builders, and sculptors. The stone vessels of the Old Kingdom are remarkable for their symmetry achieved without the aid of a potter's wheel, and the fine finish without either glazes or polished surface. After all, the skills and techniques of the Old Kingdom were never equalled or surpassed in the Middle and New Kingdoms. Finally, some observers of Egyptian art, including Aldred, Maspero, and Casson, go so far as to speculate that the expertise gained by making stoneware laid the foundation for work in the sculpture and blocks of monumental stone work.

Last, but by no means least, jewelry-making was also important among the so-called minor arts. Gold and precious stones (such as agate, turquoise, jasper, carnelian, and garnet) were highly valued by the Egyptians. These media were crafted into necklaces, crowns, chains, pectoral pieces, and bracelets. The high point of jewelry-making was the twelfth dynasty, which produced some of the finest pectoral ornaments of inlaid colorful stones on engravened cast gold frames, never surpassed either in ancient Egyptian history or even today.

Analysis

The prevailing view of Egyptian art is that it is generally religious, very conservative, and traditional. While this impression is true to a certain extent, after a careful examination across each Kingdom, the data give rise to questions about long-held generalizations about Egyptian art. Some attempts have been made in the above discussion to show the versatility of the Egyptian arts despite steadfast religious traditions. The question as to whether Egyptian art is religious or not needs a full length discussion to present substantial facets of this issue. Such a discussion constitutes my examination of aesthetics in chapter 5. In any case, what is clear beyond the shadow of a doubt is that the achievements of Old Kingdom art laid the foundation for the periods that followed in ancient Egypt, as well as in other civilizations.

Finally, a keen student of ancient Egyptian art will discover that, although the art from the Old Kingdom appears to be formalistic and static, it does not lack inventiveness and innovation. In other words, the craftsman adhered to a religious tradition; but within the boundaries of that tradition, liberties were taken. We see that wooden figures were shown interacting with their kinesphere. In addition, the demonstration of naturalism on non-pharaonic figures was not uncommon. Furthermore, although the pharaoh's figural portraiture was stylized according to canons of idealism with a youthful muscular torso, the sculptor retained the facial appearance of the individual.

In hindsight, Old Kingdom art in particular and Egyptian art in general possess some admirable qualities no student of art can ignore. Some of the noteworthy qualities are: The attention to symmetry, regardless of scale of object; the skilled handling of bas-relief and sculpture in stone; and the plasticity and nuance displayed in the use of line and color of wall paintings.

CHAPTER FIVE

TOWARD AN UNDERSTANDING OF ANCIENT EGYPTIAN ART

Now that we have established our approach to ancient Egyptian art, let us investigate a workable position in aesthetics which is manifested in the art, culture, history, and origin of the ancient Egyptians.

The Problem

Much has been written about the pervasive influence that religion had on Egyptian art, especially in the Old Kingdom. However, I wish to depart from the conventional approach and focus on other facets of the Egyptian culture which have equally contributed to the prevailing theory of aesthetics in ancient Egyptian art. The central point I hope to illuminate in this discussion is one that appears to be a commonly debated issue among art critics and laymen alike. For example, some art historians, including Aldred (1949) and Maspero (1960), have examined ancient Egyptian art as having been influenced largely by religion, and to a lesser extent by the political persuasion of each Kingdom. It is my intention, however, to add other insights and provide a broader understanding for judgements about ancient Egyptian art.

In offering further insights about the missing dimensions of ancient Egyptian art criticism, most of my examples will be from the Old Kingdom; additional examples from the Middle and New Kingdoms will be introduced as appropriate. My emphasis on the Old Kingdom is cogent because in this period the foundations were laid for the development of the arts and other areas of Egyptian life. For those who recast Egyptian art history in the domain of ancient African art history, the story of the Old Kingdom is important, since recent evidence suggests that the first six dynasties were unmistakably Black.

Mode of Analysis

Referring to the cultural history and art theory of ancient Egypt outlined so far, a discussion of the aesthetics of ancient Egyptian art is in order. Following John Lofland (1971), the first precept one must consider is that the cultures or subjects under examination have their own ways of representing their own view of life. In the view of many anthropologists, such as Claude Levi-Strauss (1963), Clifford Geertz (1973), Daniel Crowley (1977), and Victor Turner (1982), people have a well-defined structure to their thoughts about culture and art. The culture and art of ancient Egypt reveal a remarkable amount of order and structure around which Egyptian culture was organized.

If culture does influence the making of art, then, when we analyze the art of any society, we cannot analyze art apart from the order of that society's world-view and their explicable and coherent view of reality. So, armed with the "culture/art" theory, I will examine ancient Egyptian art in comparison with the texts of religion, geography, philosophy, education, symbolism, science, and myth to define the meanings of aesthetic forms. The comparative analysis of culture and art lends itself to the qualitative mode of analysis. John Lofland contends that the foremost principle of qualitative analysis provides an explicit rendering of cultural structure, order, and pattern found among the people under observation (pp. 6-7).

It is also appropriate at this point to mention that the concept of beauty is defined in many ways across cultures, thus there is no general consensus on what it is. I will use John Dewey's (1958) concept of the aesthetic experience because it is expansive and inclusive. He discusses the aesthetic as a "body of matters and meanings, not in themselves aesthetic, but becoming aesthetic as they enter into an ordered rhythmic movement toward consummation"(p. 326). Dewey argues that art itself is widely human and that the experiences manifested in a work of art are testimonies to and celebrations of the life of a civilization—a means of displaying the development and the ultimate quality of that civilization. Moreover, Dewey contends, the aesthetic objects provided and enjoyed by a people are a direct reflection of the content of their experiences and the culture in which they participate. Dewey's definition of what is aesthetic takes seriously the importance of those facets which contribute to the definition of culture. I must also draw a parallel between Dewey's definition of aesthetics and Geertz's attempt at defining culture. Central to both definitions is the fact that a people's experiences and institutions are reflected in both art and culture.

Factors that Influence Art Making in Ancient Egypt —Religion, Philosophy, and Science: A Synopsis

On the religious influence on Egyptian art, Paul Wingert (1965) offers some important insights. He contends that in any culture, regardless of the historical epoch, the motivation for the creation of art stems from a people's need to develop systems which satisfy the needs to depict man's implementation of traditional beliefs and meaning given to life. Wingert argues that although these needs are common to mankind, yet there is a major point of separation, and that point of separation influences the different methods used by each culture (p. 27).

More specifically, the ancient Egyptian's elaborate belief focused on a life-after-death scenario to give an understanding of the causes and effects of certain natural phenomena. Accompanying their belief system, there were a finite number of rituals and rites for some security against misfortunes that could befall them in this present life and also in the after-death experience. In this regard, Aldred (1962) notes that sculpture was frequently used as the most powerful medium to procure the mana or divine power—the spiritual essence of man—which is necessary for the continuity of life through all eternity. Aldred asserts that each statue of the pharaoh, upon completion, was treated with great respect and reverence as if the person were still alive. To ensure the statue's proper treatment, a special chamber or *serdab* was reserved.

Besides the care and respect for the revered funerary statue, it is clear that the statues of the "sitter" are given a perceptual and an idealistic treatment. Except during the Akhenaten reign, the pharaonic figures were generally depicted as young, alert, muscular, and confident. For it was the belief that a healthy body was the best place for the spirit to dwell throughout eternity. Pointedly, because the Egyptians believed that the head was the part of the body where the spirit actually resided, great attention and care was exercised in rendering portraits. African sculpture of the sub-Sahara, similarly emphasizes the head form—or it's replacement, the mask—presumably for the same reason as the Egyptians.

While I acknowledge that religious beliefs influenced many areas of Egyptian life, and that art is no exception, there are problems with the commonly held view that Egyptian art was developed mainly as a vehicle for religious ideas. So as not to under-rate the sophistication of African science, mathematics, and astronomy, and the precision of their calculation, the approach employed in this work will carefully consider these areas of Egyptian life. In all of Africa, including Egypt, art serves several functions. The most popular one concerns art as it is used to concretize the spiritual world. Inescapably, the concept of portraying the spiritual world in a physical context is inherently contradictory, but such is the nature of the aesthetic idea in the African world-view.

Furthermore, since historians and aestheticians of Egyptian art tend to use religion as the sole determinant of ancient Egyptian art while neglecting the context of religion, the general tendency is to view the art work as mere icons in the quest for immortality. Even if religion were the determinant of ancient Egyptian art, an in-depth examination would reveal the complex interface of Egyptian religion with every aspect of Egyptian life. Therefore, it becomes fundamental to clarify some of the important dimensions of ancient African religion in relation to art.

Chukwunyere Kamalu (1990) contends that African religious beliefs, both ancient and traditional, are not a haphazard collection of "myths or superstitions without consistency or significance"(p. 42). Rather, those beliefs derive from a fundamental system of coherent and intricately consistent ordering of thought. (See Mbiti [1969] and G. M. James [1954], for explanations of the philosophic and educational system.) Kamalu and others argue that such a system has led the way for the philosophical approach that influenced the development of art, science, and ethics. For the most ancient Egyptians, then, religion interfaced with science, art, and philosophy.

The recognition, then, that religion in ancient Egypt was more than the quest for immortality, but also included reasoning through art, science, and philosophy, bears several implications. One maintains that those components of ancient Africa are interrelated, which is nothing new. Many others, including Kamalu, Schwaller de Lubicz, and Beatrice Lumpkin (cited, Van Sertima 1989) have studied the Egyptian temples and pyramids and have arrived at a similar conclusion. In fact, nowhere can one find a better synthesis of science and art, or reason and emotions, than within Egyptian art.

Further clarification on the place of science in Africa is required because it differs sharply from Western materialism. Kamalu explains that for Africans science does not merely concern itself with naturalism or materialism but also "recognizes the existence of psychic forces or phenomena" (p. 75).

Unlike the African concept of science, Western science since the "Enlightenment" focuses only upon the material or physical world, and as a consequence does not recognize the psychic forces of nature beyond the physical world. (The time in Western civilization when theology was viewed as the "queen of sciences" is now but a dim memory.) Kamalu (1990) argues that when the definition of Western science is imposed on other cultures, like Africa's, then the nature of African science is misrepresented in the West as "magic." The process of projecting the system of one culture upon another has led to an inaccurate conclusion: that African science is "magic" and is therefore irrational and inexplicable.

An explanation of the African concept of science will be helpful in our discussion of the nature of art and of African arts and their relation to the sciences. In particular, according to G.M. James (1954), the Egyptians identified the arts as spiritual sciences. The term "spiritual science," Kamalu notes, refers to the resolution of conflicts and contradictions of human subjectivity in relation to the physical world. In an effort to support the interrelatedness of the arts and sciences, Kamalu invokes George Thompson's description of the scientist and artist. To paraphrase his thesis, the artist and scientist are both concerned with changing the world: the scientist concentrates on the "external world of man's objective relationships with nature," and the artist is concerned with the "internal world of his subjective relation with his fellow men" (Kamalu 1990: 75). Put another way, the *scientist* explicates the contradictions of his consciousness of the *external* world and seeks to resolve these conflicts through scientific hypotheses. Conversely, the *artist* seeks to resolve contradictions in his consciousness of the *internal* world, which he attempts to solve through the making of artworks.

In either case, the creative act is involved in both art and science. Thompson concludes that the scientist extends our knowledge about the external world and the artist enlarges our social awareness. Additionally, he states, "the artist succeeds at heightening our knowledge of human nature through self knowledge together with social interaction" (Kamalu 1990: 76). Thus, one glaring implication about art and science is: they are not completely incompatible methods of inquiry nor does the difference in their subjects necessitate that they be. They are held in conversation by a common thread: that, in fact, neither artist nor scientist can ignore the subject or object of the other's work.

Finally, if one recalls the earlier discussion of the Egyptian mysteries system, at once it would be clear that these ancient Africans did not establish a division between reason and emotion—a dilemma vehemently debated in modern Western discourse. The common view of today's technological Western cultures places reason and science above emotion and art. Science is seen as purely rational and art as emotional.

The problem with this line of thinking, where reason and emotion are placed in a hierarchy, is that those who espouse this notion ignore that "reason and emotions are both inseparable and essential elements of human nature" (Kamalu 1990: 76). With respect to the recognition and respective importance of reason and emotion as found in science and art, the ancient Egyptian philosophical and educational system ensured that its students were trained in the seven liberal arts and sciences. Hence, the artist-priest, for example, was schooled in astronomy, mathematics, physics, drawing, and so forth. It is apparent that the ancient Egyptians recognized the value of man's rational faculties in order to derive meaning beyond gut reaction. Those who argue that the Egyptians depended solely upon either empiricism or intuition are inaccurate; rather, a combination of the two was used.

Throughout the above discussion, I have stated that African societies, particularly in ancient Egypt, made no distinct separation among the tenets of their world-view. Religion was in constant conversation with science, and the synthesis of the two was concretized in ancient Egyptian art.

Supporting the position argued above, Hunter Adams (cited, Van Sertima 1990) contends that the combinations of religion and science, philosophy and psychology, history and mythology were all considered realities which run through the fabric of daily life in ancient Egypt.

Since the African conceptualization of science does not match the Western definition of science (i.e., "material phenomena—based mainly on observation, experiment, and induction;...deductions from self-evident truths"—Oxford English Dictionary), I must offer the following working definition. Henry Adams and Wade Noble (cited, Van Sertima 1990) aptly describe the meaning of science by placing it in the critical context of cultural domain. Adams posits:

> Science—all science, be it the physical sciences, the social sciences, or the spiritual (and by this, I mean music, art, philosophy/religion)—is the search for unity or wholeness within or without all human experience. (p. 31)

With his insight of the conglomerate approach to science, Wade Noble, a theoretical psychologist (cited, Van Sertima 1990) contends:

> science is the formal reconstruction or representation of a [people's] shared set of systematic and cumulative ideas, beliefs, and knowledge (i.e., common sense) stemming from their culture. (p. 32)

Science, as viewed from the standpoint of a given culture then, according to Noble, is consistent with a people's common sense.

One of the implications of the definition of science offered by Noble and Adams is that science is not culturally universal and that no one culture has the monopoly of superiority on the ways of knowing values and ideas. The construction of reality is as varied as the numerous cultures in our world. Hence, in a culture we do not understand, it is unwise to dismiss unknown ways of knowing as unscientific or magical.

Given, then, that religion, art, and science are interrelated, let us chart an understanding of ancient Egyptian art. First, the geography and climate of the Nile Valley, discussed earlier under my description of culture, greatly influenced the Egyptian's adaptation to his environment.

Because of the fluctuating water supply from the Nile river, the ancient Egyptians developed drainage and irrigation systems to grow food in an arid desert. Naturally, it was the employment of science in the form of agricultural technology that aided the building of dams and the cultivating and harvesting of such crops as barley and einkorn wheat. Van Sertima (1990) reveals that the large agricultural complexes in the Sudanic and Nile Valley areas domesticated over twenty-five food and fiber plants, and that animal husbandry was also a serious concern.

By and large, the archaeological data which supplies the evidence about the Egyptian's botanical knowledge, crop cultivation, and irrigation technologies, also gives crucial insight about the way the Egyptians organized their thinking in the face of a hostile climate. To organize farming—particularly, knowing when to plant to ensure a bountiful harvest—requires

> a knowledge of astronomy ...in response to [a need for] more accurate predictions of events affecting agriculture such as the seasons and the annual overflow of the Nile. (Pappademos, cited, Van Sertima 1990: 181)

Van Sertima reminds us that the observations associated with astronomical science involve "precise record keeping, a capacity to measure complex distances and times, to calculate orbits and azimuths and convergences" (p. 14). The underlying foundation of astronomy is science, because it depends on complex mathematical formulae to solve problems.

Scientific Influence on Egyptian Art

With the importance of science explicated, one can make connections about the scientific modes of thinking employed in Egyptian life, especially as they relate to art. The connection of the arts and the sciences in Egyptian art is exemplified in the construction of pyramids, temples, and obelisks.

As far as the relationship between science and art goes, Beatrice Lumpkin (cited, Van Sertima 1990), Peter Tompkins (1971), Flinders Petrie (1885), and others agree that without the use of an exacting science and a command of technology it would have been impossible to build the monuments of Egypt. Lumpkin reveals that the stone structures hold the secret about the "level of science, technology, and administration required for their construction" (p. 67). She argues that advanced engineering and mechanical skill, along with experience and discipline were required to complete the pyramids, temples, and obelisks.

Central in the claim for the employment of science in art is mathematics. Lumpkin argues that more advanced mathematical concepts than those of the Euclidian era were employed in the building of such monuments as temples. She cites George Sarton's (1971) thesis in *The Life of Science,* which reveals that the Moscow mathematics papyrus copied by the scribe Ahmes substantiates the claim for the use of advanced mathematics in Egyptian architecture. For this reason the respected historian of science writes:

> Here we have a mathematical treatise which was written more than thirteen centuries before the time of Euclid....it contains already such elaborate results that we must consider it, not as a beginning, but rather as a climax, the climax of a very long evolution. (Van Sertima 1990: 68)

Sarton's findings leave little doubt that the Egyptians employed the science of mathematics to ensure that accuracy was an important part of their approach to architecture. (Because mathematical calculations are very involved and elaborate, coupled with fact that the present work does not allow for an in-depth discussion of this nature, I must direct the reader to the works of George Sarton [1971] and Peter Tompkins [1971;1981] for a detailed description.)

Along with the use of mathematics, Lumpkin debates that Imhotep's construction of the first stone pyramid at Saqqara could not have been successful without the stonecutters' skills, which were developed over centuries through the delicate carving or sculpting of stone pots.

Perhaps more central to careful planning were the use of the *pi,* the square, and the triangle, which were found in some surviving scale drawings of front and side elevations of temples, pyramids, and other buildings. Of great importance, however, to historians of mathematical science is the employment of rectangular coordinates to draw a curve —the precursor of coordinate geometry. In this instance, equally spaced vertical lines (much like our common graph paper) appeared. Lumpkin observes that the "height of the vertical lines gives the desired height at the horizontal location indicated by their spacing between vertical lines" (p. 77). Equally important was the employment of rectangular coordinate grids restricted to sketches for construction and for drawing and painting (see plate 27).

In a brief overview, scholars Schwaller de Lubicz (cited, Peter Tompkins 1971), Diop (cited, Kamalu 1990), and Lumpkin (cited, Van Sertima 1990) have substantiated the employment of pure mathematics in ancient Egypt—the number *pi,* the Golden Number, and transcendental numbers in the building of temples, pyramids, and obelisks. Lumpkin clarifies that the Egyptian's knowledge of the *pi* ratio, for example, was achieved with remarkable accuracy, compared with the Greeks. She observes that the perimeter of the base of the Great Pyramid at Gizeh when divided by its height, yields the value of *pi* and that this attests to one of the advanced elements in mathematics known by the Egyptians.

Along with the above mentioned mathematical knowledge of the *pi* ratio, the knowledge of the Golden Number is an important factor for building construction. Schwaller cites the Temple at Luxor to illustrate the point about this mathematical precision that is fundamental to building and design. For example, through his study of the dimensions of the doorways, he observes that the Egyptians were familiar with the Golden Number, which also has a direct relationship to the transcendental number *pi*.

Finally, after reading the existing literature attesting to the highly developed mathematics found in the everyday life of the ancient Egyptians, Diop notes, among other things, "a diagrammatic representation of a transcendental number" (Kamalu, p. 78). A transcendental number is a non-algebraic number which cannot be written down in a finite series of digits. It can, however, be represented, but only in geometric diagrammation. Simply put, the transcendental number is the squaring of a circle. For example, according to Tompkins (1981), "the Pyramid base is a square whose perimeter is equal to the circumference of a circle whose radius is the Pyramid's height"(p. 197). Consequently, for the ancient Egyptians, the superimposition of the square on the circle reveals not only the perimeter of a pyramid's base, but it also signifies the circumference of the circle it represents. (For further information see George Cantor's 19th theorem on the transcendental number.)

A careful look at ancient Egyptian sculpture will illuminate the use of other sciences as well. Although Aldred's (1962) account of ancient Egyptian art does not explicitly discuss the role of science, particularly mathematics, he does inadvertently allude to it. Aldred claims that the Egyptian was claustrophobic and that this fear was expressed in the Egyptian's concept of space, "which is as geometrically finite as the cubic block of his stone sarcophagus" (p. 10). This rationale for the Egyptian's use of geometry seems somewhat misleading, because he blames claustrophobia for the conceptualization of space. Despite his hypothesis, however, Aldred goes on to discuss that the Egyptian artist carefully "delimits the boundaries of his universe with an Elymas-like touch as though to emphasize that he is aware not only of its extent, but of its essential rectilinearity" (p. 10). This rectilinearity is demonstrated in the floor plans of temples, city layouts, pyramid complexes, and the block pattern of friezes and borders; and even in the "square word-groups" of Egyptian hieroglyphic inscriptions, as well as in each scene which makes up the composition of bas-reliefs and paintings. At this point, it is significant to note that sculpture *in the round* emerged from an implied *cuboid*. Evidence of the cuboid foundation can be gleaned from the rectangular back support, rectangular base, and the initial block-like appearance given by Egyptian sculpture in stone.

To find the answer to what might seem like a mystery behind the repetition of the square, we must revisit George James'(1954) description of education in ancient Egypt. James notes that the ancient Egyptians believed that the world was founded upon contradictions, which are not necessarily logical. Nevertheless, they tried to give meaning to the contradictions through the Principle or Doctrine of Opposites (which, incidentally, is wrongly attributed to the Greek Heraclitus by the European world). In fact, James cites the origin of the doctrine by showing diagrammatically *The Four Qualities and The Four Elements* which form the foundation of the education system in Egypt commonly known as the Mysteries System. *The Four Qualities and The Four Elements*, are *Hot, Dry, Wet, Cold; Air, Fire, Water, and Earth.* Hence, the schematic square in which Air is diagonally opposite Earth (or vice versa), Fire diagonally opposite Water, Hot opposite Cold, and Wet opposite Dry. Also implicit in the configuration of these qualities and elements is the concept of *duality*, which plays an important role in Egyptian art.

Besides the obvious use of mathematics in the skill of sculpture, Egyptian artists also studied other sciences such as anatomy and physiology for skillful and accurate representation of proportions. The athletic physique of the pharaoh is exemplary in its depiction of muscularity and proportion. Additionally, portraiture, for which the Egyptian artist is most famous, requires knowledge of cranial structure and the muscular disposition of the skull.

From what we know about the architects of the pyramids, temples, sphinxes, and obelisks, it seems that they relied on the following sciences: geography, physics, acoustics, geology, mechanics, astronomy, and mathematics. Although not all these sciences were necessary for the making of bas-relief and painting, the artist obviously studied mathematics to facilitate the composition and execution of his work.

Pharaonic Philosophy and Its Influence on Art Making in Egypt

According to Obenga (cited, Van Sertima 1990), to affirm the "ordered" and "beautiful" in pharaonic art is insufficient. For it is the Ma'at philosophy of Order, Truth, and Justice that permeates Egyptian art. Obenga contends that each work of art "is a tension of numerous essential qualities, moral... philosophical...and aesthetic." He notes that along with the sciences used, the ancient Egyptians "had to respect the divine laws of the national canon which was itself from Ma'at" (p. 319).

To stress the importance and precise relationship of pharaonic philosophy to Egyptian art, Obenga points out that the Egyptian temple and all places of worship (which included lakes, pyramids, obelisks, and palaces) belonged to the cosmic order of Ma'at. The link between man and the cosmos in Egyptian thought and art, argues Obenga, is signified in the symbolic decision to align the axis of sacred edifices in line with the "energizing lines of the Universe"(p. 318).

Other examples of the integration of man and universe as a cosmic whole are revealed in the paintings on the walls and ceilings of the temples. Usually, the subject matter illustrated celebrates the "starry Universe in a state of constant and perpetual creation" (p. 318). Hence we see the sun-God Ammon-Ra as supreme in religion; more specific to our concerns, the disc representing the sun is common in the art of Egypt. In addition, there were a number of ceremonies in which the performance dramatized the relationship between human and cosmic forces in Black Pharaonic Egypt.

In their research on Egyptian art's representation of the celestial bodies and the cosmos, Scwhaller de Lubicz and Norman Lockyer (cited, Tompkins 1971) ascertained that the orientation of the sun temples of Egypt was intentionally designed to disclose specific information about the heavens. Lockyer cited the two temples of Dendera—one dedicated to the goddess Hathor and the other to goddess Isis—both are mythological personifications of heavenly bodies. He contends that the dual function of these temples was: (1) worshipping places for the goddesses, and (2) "horizontal telescopes with the same number of pylons gradually getting narrower toward the holy of holies." The brilliance in this arrangement of pylons, Lockyer describes, was that it allowed "a beam of horizontal light coming through the central door [to] pass uninterruptedly into the sanctuary to mark the rising of the celestial body" (p. 168). Lockyer observes, in his conclusion, that the columns served to shield the eyes from the rays of the rising sunlight, so that the rising of the sun could be accurately calibrated.

Schwaller de Lubicz's findings support Lockyer's theory. The ancient Egyptians clearly understood "the procession of the equinoxes... and...[that] an equinox brought with it a new constellation into position behind the rising sun at a vernal equinox every 2,000 years." The acquisition of this knowledge, Schwaller de Lubicz concludes, can best be attributed to the astronomical function of the temples, and the obelisks.

The vivid demonstration of opulence and majesty displayed in the art of Egypt can be accounted for by the concept of *Ma'at*, the primodial matrix of Order, Truth, and Justice. For Obenga, the argument for the presence of *Ma'at* is clearly demonstrated in every aspect of Egyptian life and is explicated in the Egyptian decree that "all men living in society must conform to Justice and Truth, to *Ma'at*, the supreme Virtue, guide and measure of all human activity" (Van Sertima 1990: 317).

In the spirit of dualism, a feature integral to pharaonic philosophy, Obenga reveals that one can observe the presence of *Nun*—the
complement of *Ma'at*. This theory claims that "it [is] possible for life
to pre-exist in matter but only reveal itself as a creative force in intelli-
gence." Thus, the idea of God is conceptualized by the ancient
Egyptians, the spiritual world as an abstract ideogram with no beginning or ending. Such a world is where "matter and spirit move together
towards their own identity" (Van Sertima 1990: 317). In line with such
abstract thinking, Egyptian art illustrates a symbolic and self-perpetu-
ating and mysterious geometry.

Since the principles of Nun and Ma'at are fundamental tenets in
pharaonic philosophy, and since the task of the scribe, architect,
painter, and sculptor was to bring the metaphysical into the understanding of the physical, the art of Egypt, then, communicated the
paradoxical nature of Black Pharaonic thought. Therefore the artists
worked in a symbolic and surreal style that evoked such enigmas. In
short, Egyptian art should not be taken too literally, for these artists
maintained the "mirror" of dualism that is remeniscent of the fundamental principles of Nun and Ma'at.

Symbolism in Egyptian Art

From the outset of this discussion of symbolism in Egyptian art, we must
in the context of this work restrict examples to a few. The pharaoh,
the god-king, is the living example of paradox and symbolism, for he
represents the ideas of absolute truth, justice, and order, and yet is
human with all the inherent fragilities thereof. Although great reverence
was bestowed upon the pharaoh, it was the *ideas* that he represented
that were so highly valued over and above his or her mortality.
Therefore, the artist with absolutes in mind had but one option: the perfect execution of the pharaoh's portraiture.

In the social context, the pharaoh's statue faithfully reflected the
traditional symbolism. As such, Lionel Casson (1965) tells us that the
crowns of the pharaoh can be distinguished, based upon which disposition of the king was to be conveyed. The white crown, or White
Miter, is a familiar icon among the kings of Upper Egypt. On this and
others to be mentioned later, we see the royal emblem of the serpent,
which protects the region between the physical and the underworld of
the after life. The red crown signifies Lower Egypt. But after the reuni-
fication of Egypt, the forms of red and white crowns were merged in
a single double crown. It was only in battle or at military functions, however, that the blue war helmet was worn (p. 58). Interestingly, the colors that symbolized Egyptian royalty—red, white, and blue—are also
used by some European royalty e.g., France, England, and even the
United Sates of America.

In addition to the different crowns worn, Chandler (cited, Van Sertima 1989) tells us that the common affect of the serene pharaonic statue signifies the majesty associated with divinity, and also captures the temperament of "a relatively gentle and charitable nature," typical of the Egyptians of the Old Kingdom. Although there were periods in Egyptian history when these characteristics were modified, they generally evoked a feeling of peace, not war (p. 141).

Moving to another important genre of Egyptian art, the numerous examples of mother-and-child images, we observe again the symbolic and dualistic nature of the art. The madonna-and-child image illustrates the Isis, Horus, Osiris myth—the original creation myth of Egypt, which was discussed fully earlier.

There are many interpretations of the Isis/Horus representation. Among them, Isis, wife and mother of Osiris, gave birth to their son, Horus. The importance and reverence attributed to Isis, Chandler argues, echoes a "strong matrilineal foundation," which characterizes African social order. She was, to the ancient Egyptians, the giver of life, "Virgin Mother...womb of the world...and the woman clothed with the Sun of the land of Khemi [i.e., Egypt]." Hence the numerous examples of Isis suckling her son, Horus. Upon her head is a crown, a crested disc, obviously symbolic of the sun, the central celestial body of worship. As mentioned earlier, Isis and Horus also symbolized part of the divine trinity—father, mother, and son (Osiris, Isis, and Horus) (Van Sertima 1989: 131-141).

Sculpture, ornaments, and objects of daily use were buried with the pharaoh. The pharaoh was given the figural portraiture, known as the *ka*, which depicted him in his various roles. Along with his figural representations, his large group of servants, also represented in sculpture, were supposed to attend to him when he reawakened from his sleep/death. Most importantly, however, was the presence of a boat which was to transport him into the after-life—through death, which was believed to be a mere sleep. Food and all the articles to which the pharaoh was accustomed adorned his tomb (Casson 1965: 172).

Color as Symbol in Egyptian Art

Most noteworthy was the symbolic meaning of color in pharaonic art. As a matter of fact, the use of color, especially red ochre and black, have been at the center of the controversy of the ancient Egyptians' racial origin—the so-called "dark-red race theory" (Van Sertima 1989).

James Brunson (cited, Van Sertima 1989) studies the meaning of color on statues and paintings. He posits that "red ochre, an oxide of iron, was combined with a vegetable gum binder by the ancient Egyptian painter to create the now famous dark-red color" (p. 53). Brunson cites Mircea Eliade (1978) to verify the presence and use of red ochre in Africa, tracing it back to between 27,000 B.C. and 41,000 B.C. Of paramount importance is the magico-religious symbolism attached to red ochre and that its meaning is similar across Africa. For several centuries before and during the dynastic period of Egypt, the corpse of the deceased was elaborately painted with red ochre. Eliade is persuaded that the application of red ochre symbolizes reincarnation or rebirth of the soul.

He points out that Africans, especially those from central Africa (who predate the Egyptians), depicted man in red ochre and woman in yellow ochre. The meaning behind the use of these colors, Eliade posits, is that man painted in the color red symbolizes the "blood of life" and woman painted in yellow is goddess of agriculture. The yellow also represents fertility. In retrospect, since Africans of earlier times used the red ochre color, in particular, it should come as no surprise that the Egyptians opted to use it as a sacred symbol (Van Sertima 1989: 56).

Besides the well-known but controversial issue generally associated with the use of red ochre and what it may indicate about the racial origins of the ancient Egyptians, Brunson contends the importance associated with specific colors throughout Africa there remains a perceived sensibility associated with the color black. "Blackness," he notes, is "inextricably bound to the conceptual cycle of life, death, and rebirth." The impact of blackness, Brunson insists, still influences Judeo-Christian symbolism from ancient to modern times. For the Egyptians, blackness was a concept that represented the "Lord of the Hidden Treasure, guardian and divine consciousness which raises the human spirit from obscurity to light" (p. 56).

To sum up the symbolism of the color black, James Brunson (see Van Sertima 1989: 56–57) offers seven possibilities:

1. Black symbolized the black land and soil of Egypt.
2. Black symbolized divinity and reverence toward the ancestors—deification.
3. Black had a spiritual or religious connotation, symbolizing rebirth, or regeneration; this entailed a rhythmic cycle suspended in eternity, which included plant and animal life.
4. Black symbolized death and the underworld or netherworld, known as Amenta.
5. A connection was made between black soil which flowed into Egypt from Nubia, and which occurred during the inundation; a further association was attached to Nubians themselves, who were literally black-skinned.
6. Ancient memories and traditions connected the original transmission of the "gods and goddesses" from ancient Egypt's black-skinned ancestors.
7. Only the king, queen, and neters were allowed the symbolic use of black in funerary rituals; this, prior to the advent of

the Middle Kingdom, would bar or restrict anyone else
black in skin tone from being depicted as such (pp. 56-57).
As one reflects on Brunson's reference to black as a color reserved for
the elite, it seems appropriate to add that all of the Egyptian gods,
deities, and royalty—Osiris, Isis, Horus, Hathor, Min/Amen,
Thutmosis, Tutankhamen, and Queen Tiye, to name a few—were usually painted or rendered in coal black, ink black, jet black, or blue black.
(See Richard King's *African Origin of Biological Psychiatry* [1994] for
an equally insightful discussion of the spiritual, psychological, and phys-
iological significance of the "color" black.)

Finally, no discussion about symbolism in ancient Egyptian art
would be complete without mention of the most symbolic modality in
ancient Egypt, that is, the ubiquitous hieroglyphics, which were especially inscribed upon sculpture and architecture. The hieroglyphics are
best described as picture writing. For instance, symbols of man, animals,
flora, and everyday objects were assembled in such an order as to
express words and complete ideas.

Although the Egyptians had no alphabet as we know it, their system of symbols represented every consonant sound of their speech.
Amazingly, the hieroglyphics were such a consistent and uniform system that they were listed in a pictorial glossary which differentiated
homonyms, so that from near homonyms the reader could grasp fully
the intended meaning. For example, to refer to more than one man or
woman, the determinatives of two parallel strokes made below these
figures would indicate such. The hieroglyphics did not remain a vernacular for ordinary people; they took on a sacred character, and
meanings were deliberately obscured by scribes and priests to the point
that the signs became incomprehensible to outsiders.

Dualism

While continuing the discussion of the manifestation of African thought
in ancient Egyptian art, one must account for the dualistic nature of this
art. In the discussion of symbolism so far, references were made to the
dual functions of the pharaoh and his statue as secular ruler and spiritual representative of god, creating the tradition of god-king. Since
numerous examples of dualism exist in Egyptian art, only a few are
needed to illustrate this concept.

Pointedly, the famous architectural structure, the pyramid, epitomizes the meaning of dualism. The pyramid, we know through Peter
Tompkins, Octavio Paz, Beatrice Lumpkin, and others, is a projection
of the quadrangle, which derives from the Principle of Opposites—the
four cardinal points. Pyramids were sanctuaries and burial places for
royalty, reveals Paz (1990). The upper part from the platform, usually
composed of thirteen layers, was the sanctuary; while the nine subter-

ranean chambers functioned as the tomb. In Egypt, India, Mesopotamia, and Mesoamerica, the pyramidal form symbolized a mountain. Paz states that in these ancient systems of thought, the *world is* a mountain, the archetypal mountain which is represented by the pyramid (Paz 1990: 15). More specific to the ancient Egyptians, notes Cyril Aldred (1980), the Creator-god Ptah was also represented by the "primordial mound of earth that arose from the waters of elemental Chaos and on which all life began, just as the annual inundation of the Nile" (p. 11).

The pervasiveness of duality was apparent, both explicitly and implicitly, in ancient Egyptian thought and aesthetics. An example of explicit dualism is the numerous anthropomorphic images, for instance, the sphinx—part man, part lion—or any of the Egyptian gods and deities. The ram-headed God Khnum, for instance, was, in the ancient Egyptians' creation mythology, a potter who molded the first human out of clay. Similarly, the god Thoth, the inventor of the arts and sciences, has a bird's head with a man's physique. Noteworthy, as is the case with all gods of Egypt, Thoth has a female counterpart, another expression of the passion for balance in Egyptian life.

Space and Time in Egyptian Art

In the view of ancient and traditional Africans, argues J. Mbiti (1969), space and time are not separate within the world of human experience. Essentially, space, time, objects, and events belong to a common matrix of human experience. To illustrate the integration of time and events in African thought, Mbiti contends that Africans seemingly avoided the numerical calendars that organized the Western linear concept of time. Instead, Africans employ the use of, "phenomenon calendars which are dictated by events"(p. 19).

In the West, we recognize that time is punctuated by events. But for Black Egyptians, each pharaoh's phenomenon calendar was signified by temples, pyramids, statues, sphinxes and other art work. The marking of events in this way certainly helped ancients and moderns to locate events within specific time frames. With particular reference to space, as with time, "it is the content of space (i.e., objects) which define it" (p. 27). As further proof of the integral relationship between time and space, Mbiti states, the same word is often used for both.

Environmental Influence on Egyptian Art

The development of a genre for ancient Egyptian art is influenced by its geographic disposition. Egyptians of a unified land quickly became exploiters of the available natural resources to create stable living conditions. It should come as no surprise, then, that the quest for stability permeated every aspect of their life, especially since art was one of the teaching mediums of ancient Egypt. Besides, in a dry climate such as the desert, careful consideration must have been given to the choice of material to be used in the construction of architecture and the making of other art objects. Dry and arid conditions are hostile to material such as wood, often resulting in cracking and decaying. The choice of more durable material such as stone became an attractive option. Fortunately, the Egyptians had easy access to the stone quarries of Aswan. To provide the greatest assurance of permanence, stone was well suited for a people who believed in immortality.

Besides the ready availibility of appropriate material for art making, Aldred notes, the surrouding flora and fauna of the Nile River obviously provided ample inspiration for the creation of objects out of clay, stone, metal, and minerals. For example, the crowns of the colossal stone columns in much of Egyptian architecture were carved respresentations of the lotus flower and the papyrus plant, both of which are found near the Nile River. The wooded areas of the Nile Valley harbored many birds such as the crane and the geese, which became motifs in the paintings and bas-reliefs. Other motifs—cow, deer, lion, dog, crocodile—were also included in Egyptian art, as they were common animals in Egyptian daily life.

On reflection, the influence of the expansive desert with the heavens as its canopy upon the massive architectural structures cannot be ignored. Man's awareness of his natural and cosmic environment is supremely illustrated in Egyptian art.

Summary and Analysis

To put all aspects of my argument in the critical context of aesthetics, I must return to the Dewian framework discussed earlier. Dewey maintained that the art produced by a people are the testimonies and celebrations of the development and quality of a civilization. In the light of these testimonies and celebrations, we have seen in this study that ancient Egyptian art was generally influenced by its religion and philosophy, myth, sciences, prevailing environmental influences, and technologies, all acting together as an integrated world-view. As a consequence of these cultural arrangements, peculiar to Egyptian life, we find a unique approach to life and, ultimately, to aesthetics.

In association with the Egyptian world-view discussed above, one can conclude that the art of this civilization is largely symbolic and, as such, acts as a sort of window frame to a world of complex human experiences. To support the claim that Egyptian art and icons are symbolic representations of human experiences, I evoke Ortega's thesis (cited, Charlotte Otten, 1971) on the meaning of art and icons: Central to his argument, he asserts that the work of art is but a mere entrance to the matrix of meanings and experiences common to a culture (Otten

1971). If this contention is true, then Egyptian art with its multiple meanings (i.e., the pharaoh's statute as the expression of god-king, falcon-god, and male appearance undergirded by the concept of matriarchy) is definitely reflective of the cultural beliefs characterized by many cultural symbols.

Keeping the idea of symbolism in mind, the art of ancient Egypt was primarily utilitarian in function as it sought to teach and convey meaning first rather than simply gratify the senses. For example, the paintings give vivid pictures of everyday life in all its bustle. Put another way, art for the ancient Egyptians was not a mere accoutrement to everyday life, but rather it was a celebration of and an integral part of everyday life.

In the final analysis, this discussion merely opens the door and offers a few insights which assist on the journey through the voluminous works that have survived the three millennia of pharaonic rule. One could argue that without some background knowledge of Egyptian culture and world-view, as discussed above, an informed and intelligent discussion would be impossible. Only after acquiring some understanding of the ancient Egyptian culture may one begin to appreciate why some specific choices were made in their art-making process. Aldred (1980) reminds us that the spectator cannot but be conscious of the Egyptian culture which permeated sculpture, painting, and architecture. In actuality, the main subject of Egyptian art is man and his many activities in an Egyptian milieu. Among the life-size, larger-than-life, and diminutive pieces of sculpture, one sees the magnification of "heroic and beneficent qualities of divinities and kings," rather than "the horrific power of tyrants or demons" (p. 12).

Finally, if one must offer a concise definition of Egyptian art (as if it were possible), then a nearly accurate response would include that it reflects admirably the quality of restraint and a good sense of balance, of order over chaos, all of which constitute the hallmark of a sophisticated society that followed the counselling of a philosophy of moderation. Egyptian art, like all art, can be best understood in the context of its own culture.

CHAPTER SIX

WRITTEN LANGUAGE IN ANCIENT EGYPT

One facet of the ancient Egyptian communication system (viz., the visual arts) has been treated fairly extensively in the foregoing chapters. Now we are compelled to examine the other facet of this system by looking at art's complement, written language.

In some academic circles today, and in most popular belief, the inaccuracy persists that Africans, particularly those of ancient times and/or from so-called "primitive" societies, were and are non-literate and that the continent of Africa did not develop a formal writing system of its own. The implication is that written language was not a contribution of African peoples. To dispel this misinformation, following a line of investigation and examination that looks at the cultures and civilizations at the source of the Nile valley arguably about 40,000 years ago, I will present updated evidence that Africans indeed had formal and informal written scripts and complete languages. For instance, the ancient Ethiopian Empire's Ge'ez and Amharic scripts, Sudan or Nubia's Meroe script, and the great civilization of Egypt with its hieroglyphics are examples of both formal and informal writing, that is, systematic as well as sign communication systems. However, since the information of written language covers such an extensive historical period, the decision has been made by the researcher to focus particularly on Egypt, because the Egyptians have the most complete history of written language available to modern scholars. Consequently, the following broad areas become central to this research: a working definition of language; the historical context that precedes written language in Egypt; features of informal and formal writing (grammar and function); and the legacy the ancient Egyptian language has left for the

Greeks and Romans and—by extension—all European cultures which in modern times have expropriated large parts of the extracultural space of Nile valley cultures for expansion and civil organization.

Definition of Language.

It is commonly accepted today that language is a complex phenomenon accounting for numerous forms of communicative behaviors. For example, writing, speech, all forms of non-verbal communication, signs, symbols, pictograms, and ideograms contribute to the linguistic complex. With these images in mind, the modern "speech-act" theory espoused by scholars in poetics and semiotics offers a corrective to the abstract individualized concept of language. Thus, students of linguistics, philosophy, aesthetics, criticism, anthropology, and the arts now have a way of moving beyond the realm of language as an autonomous, self-contained, and grammatical system into the arena of language as a sociocultural practice. Language then, can be defined as: all communicative behaviors that help the participant to construct and convey information that is meaningful, shared, organized, and dynamic.

Adding to the foregoing definition of language, Umberto Eco (1976) offers a most succinct definition of language through the use of semiotics. He conceives of language as a variety of systems of signification and communication (from verbal language to gesture, from visual images to body positions, from music to fashion). In this modern view of language, Eco's semiotic theory argues that there are a wide range of "languages" influenced by different conventions and laws that can be investigated at the elementary level, such as words, colors, physical formants of sounds, geometrical or topological shapes, and—at the more complex level of text and discourse—narrative structure and figures of speech. Most important to note is that the composition of any text requires productive labor to display features such as articulation of pseudo-combinational units, vectorializations, programmed stimulations, and stylizations (Eco 1976 :260).

Arguably, the written language of the Egyptian hieroglyphics is one of the best examples of what Eco and other deconstructivists conceive language to be. In the hieroglyph the semiotician is presented with fertile ground for the examination of sign/function communication.

A Short History Of Writing in Africa

In literature and popular text books it is the exception rather than the rule to find the African as contributor to the history of the written text. African cultures are generally considered exclusively oral. However, many African scholars have successfully challenged this narrow view of ancient Africa's literacy. For example, Gerald Massey (1881) and Theophile Obenga (in Van Sertima 1989), among others, argue that to rediscover the African past, in the widest sense, ancient African cultures can speak for themselves when language, religion, myths, art, and symbols are the sources of information.

As a precursor to formal written language, archaeological evidence bears out that Nilolithic man—and in fact man from all over Africa—reserved public and sacred spaces which were clearly designated to communicate messages, both social and religious. These messages, one conjectures, were for teaching and possibly for the benefit of posterity. Many examples of visual communication in the form of ideograms, pictograms, scripts, and writing can be cited from the walls of rock art of the Atlas Mountains, the desert east of the Nile river just below the Delta, the central Sahara, East Africa, Ethiopia, Sudan, Tanzania, West Africa, Southern Africa, and Central Africa, particularly in Zimbabwe. In these "early ideograms," according to Rosalind Jefferies, although men were more frequently depicted,the images of women were unmistakably outstanding in postures of great significance. An instructive example is the many illustrations of women's roles: they are depicted in leadership roles, as heads of communities, as leaders in ritual ceremonies, as healers, hunters, warriors, as primordial Mother Creator with power of fertilizing and nurturing, as Giver of Life, and as mediators between the Spiritual and the concrete physical worlds. In essence, woman was the symbol associated with the protection and survival of the race (Rosalind Jefferies, in Van Sertima 1988).

As Africans sought more permanent communities around defined cultural practices, the need to succinctly perform written communication arose. Hence, definitive language systems were devised to capture their mythologies, religious beliefs, code of ethics for society, laws, and everyday life experiences. To gain a critical understanding of the written ancient African text, one must bear with the following discussion.

Chronology of the Informal Script

The situation of the informal written script in Africa can be traced to pictograms and ideograms. Pictograms were drawings used to convey messages, while ideograms were ideas conveyed in drawings. These early evidences of informal modes of writing mark the starting point for the evolution and change of record-keeping in ancient Africa.

As was alluded to earlier, archaeologist Mary Leakey (1971) recorded that in Tanzania, dating back to approximately 40,000 B.C. and earlier, pictograms and ideograms were employed to communicate messages. In addition to these finds in Tanzania, explorer Henri L'Hote found in the Sahara Desert, in Algeria, in Lybia, in Mali, and in the Sudan other examples of cave painting dating back to about 8000 B.C. The Zimbabwean and South African examples were much more recent, with a date of approximately 4000 B.C. Picture writing continued its steady evolution into what some historians call "historic" times.

Notably, in "historic" times (or predynastic Egypt), the most sophisticated development of pictograms and ideograms can be seen on the Nubian incense burners from ca. 3300 B.C. discovered in old Sudan at a place called Ta Seti. Although numerous pictorial records can be cited throughout the period from 40,000 B.C. to 4000 B.C., it was not until the discovery of the picture writing of Ta Seti that the attention of archaeologists, historians, and linguists was captured.

Among the many painted vessels excavated at Ta Seti, the Qustul collection studied by William Flinders Petrie (1923), Bruce Williams (in Van Sertima 1989: 90-104), and others, holds the greatest significance. According to Williams, the incense burners from this collection encapsulate information about records of victory in battle, the rise of rulers to the throne, castles, temples, and, above all, the presence of the development of an official religion. He points out that the falcon-Horus symbol of the pharaoh—which would be the definitive symbol of royalty—was already developed. To illustrate the precursors of dynastic Egypt, Williams selects the popular *Archaic Horus Incense Burner* (see plate 30). Williams describes the three-ship galleon depicted thereon as follows: The first ship is the vessel with a captive held in submission. In the middle ship (even though the image is unfortunately almost destroyed) Williams detects the outstanding white crown of Upper Egypt and the falcon's tail in front of it, the falcon being another symbol of kingship. The third ship carries a rosette, which is yet another symbol of royalty before the first dynasty (Van Sertima 1989: 96-97).

In my research, this burner is critically important in the context of the documentation of ideas. Significantly, this incense burner was etched "in the sunken silhouette style related to rock drawing" (Van Sertima 1989: 96). The decision to remove the message from its stationary position (a rock wall) to a mobile object (an incense burner) could lead one to conjecture that the ancient Africans, Old Sudanese, Nubians, and ultimately the Egyptians were most conscious of the dispersal of the message, regardless of what it was. Hence the employment of the incense burner as a vehicle to convey a message, as opposed to the walls of a rock cave (which limited the broadcasting of the message), was a conscious and deliberate movement by the ancient Africans. Equally significant are the three clearly demarcated segments on the Horus Incense Burner, which can be read as three chronological sequences, as it were, from left to right. I would also suggest that the seeds of more elaborate media such as books and manuscripts were already planted in this artifact from the predynastic epoch of Egyptian history. (A more detailed discussion about the function of the text is forthcoming in this chapter.)

The question to be pursued is whether the unfolding evolution of documentation has any effect on what some scholars, including Gerald

Massey (1881), claim as the beginning of formal writing, the hiero-glyphics (or *medu neter*) in northeast Africa about 3100 B.C.E. in Khemet. Massey posits that formal writing—in Egypt—precedes cuneiform (the script of the Sumerians in Mesopotamia), Sanskrit (the early writing in India), and the Chinese calligraphy found on bones.

In an effort to advance the argument for the ancient Africans' con-tribution to writing, other predynastic examples further chronicle this evolution. Aside from the very explicit pictograms, such as the one men-tioned above of the Nubian Incense Burner, decorated pottery and pot marks provide the rudimentary beginnings of the hieroglyph. Following in the tradition of egyptologists such as Petrie and W.B.Emery (1961), William Arnett's (1982) work attempts to illustrate how such motifs were the "early means of expressing ideas or words" which were later used in the hieroglyphic lexicography (p.5).

Arnett believes that the incised markings on Predynastic and Protodynastic pottery are not mere decoration for adornment, but probably represent the idea of ownership (the property of someone) and authorship. Adding to the corpus of ideas about the significance of pot markings or pictures, John Wilson (in Hoffman, 1991) argues that the inscriptions served to indicate "that a standardized picture may be used as a symbol to convey words and that words which cannot easily be pic-tured may be conveyed phonetically by the rebus principle" (p. 293). It is significant that generally the markings occupied only a small selected area on the pottery and they did not compete with already dec-orated painted spaces. The speculation here locates pot marks as rep-resenting the need for people of the Nile Valley region to develop a parallel system of communication to complement the brilliant artistic narratives they are known for. Indeed, the late Predynastic Egyptians and Nubians were on the verge of developing a system of writing.

Against this background of the need to document ideas and words, it is important to examine these expressions without the use of the more elaborate pictorial narratives that characterized the modus operandi of communication. For example, in Predynastic Egypt, there were many symbols used to represent land, territory, region, country, and district. Arnett identifies several examples of the symbolic repre-sentation that indicated land of some sort. The symbol is "represented as a grid pattern with six parallel vertical lines [which are] intersected by three horizontal lines" (p.8) (see plate 31). He attempts to convince the reader that these motifs found at Tarkhan, Naqada, and Ka-Ap's at Abydos are related to the hieroglyph *sp>t*. Another example given by Arnett which conveys a geographical meaning, common in histor-ical times and certainly still widely used today, is the *niwt*, an encircled Ⓧ. This symbol represented crossroads and was also used to indicate village or town. The *sp>t*. and the *niwt* belonged to the rubric of geo-graphical expressions.

Added to the sp)t. and *niwt*, the semicircle represented one of the most basic ideogrammatic concepts of the predynastic and later Dynastic epochs. Henry Scott (1968) shows us through his illustrations that the semicircle symbolized a loaf of bread, a staple of the Predynastic peoples and their successors. Given the importance of bread, the semicircular symbol held a very important place in their repertoire of symbols. There are many examples of ideograms and pictograms, too many to chronicle in this work, but one cannot neglect to identify the overwhelming geometric characteristic of the symbols, such as straight lines, semicircles, circles, angles, and variants. In either instance, whether it was geographical or geophysical, the use of a geometrical shape was very common. Thus we find that hill slope (◿) according to Scott and others, was rendered as a triangle. Further, a joined series of triangles without bases (i.e., ∿∿∿) represents water as well as the phonetic symbol for the consonant *n* which is pronounced as "n"(as in *noon*). Similarly, the oval shape (◯) used to represent mouth is the phonetic symbol for the consonant r, which is pronounced as "r" (as in *right*).

In the final analysis, the so-called "primitive" hieroglyph on pots and palettes, which some have identified as approximately 3,000 motifs, allow egyptologists to identify the beginnings of political identity and geography through the symbol of the crown (both white for lower and red for upper Egypt). According to Arnett, the hawk motifs found on Badarian pottery and palettes of predynastic times are remarkably similar to the hieroglyphic hawks which evolved into falcons (see plate 32), and were used on standards to identify the "Followers of Horus," the king, in late predynastic times and throughout pharaonic rule for almost three thousand years. Other significant motifs which are clearly from predynastic Badari and Naqada were continued on standards and in the hieroglyph corpus of dynastic Egypt. These include the jackal, the hawk, the cow, the bull, and the serpent. In addition to these motifs (hawk, serpent, and jackal) functioning in politico-royal capacities, they also served to represent deities and spirits sought by the people for daily protection. One can speculate on two major steps toward organized and civilized societies: (1) that there was an attempt to recognize people along lines of distinct groups (society); and (2) that there was a corpus of ideas that contributed to their belief system (the cow for instance, symbolized the Sky goddess, Hathor, who was worshiped in dynastic times).

The argument that the pictograms and ideograms of predynastic Egyptians indeed subscribed to the Egyptian writing system is very controversial and it is difficult to find any consensus, for the very definition of writing is constantly challenged by those embroiled in this controversy. However, regardless of the function of pot marks, palette reliefs, and paintings, Petrie and other egyptologists have shown us that the connection between the forerunner (Predynastic motifs) and the full-fledged Egyptian hieroglyphics cannot be totally denied. More careful investigation is still needed to put this issue to rest.

Even more tenuous is the argument over the racial identity of those who peopled the region of the Nile Valley, before and during dynastic Egypt. The claim of my research, *The Ancient African Tradition of Writing*, by implication, places me at the center of this controversy. Since this argument is well documented earlier in this text, I shall direct the reader to those sources that address the issue of racial origin most persuasively. For example, the controversial "Dynastic Race" theory advanced by those who would trace the origins of the pre-dynastic and dynastic Egyptians to either Aryan, Asiatic, Hamitic (white), or mixed races (see Hoffman 1991: 293), has been constantly challenged and debated by many African historians such as George G. M. James (1954), Chancellor Williams (1976), Yosef ben-Jochannan (1989), Cheikh Anta Diop (1976, 1989, 1991), and a long list of researchers of the African historical contributions to human civilization.

One must be aware that there are still some people who will continue to argue that Predynastic and Dynastic Egyptians were not Africoid despite overwhelming evidence from Egyptian mythology, linguistic links, physical human characteristics, many examples of cultural unity of ancient Black Africa (e.g., matriarchy, royalty, symbolism, art, and religion) and scholars invoking the writings of ancient Greek eye-witnesses such as Herodutus, Strabo, and Diodorus Siculus. Those who argue that the ancient Egyptians were Africans, especially in the Predynastic and Old to Middle Kingdoms, and those who oppose this position, simply reflect how sharp disagreements are an integral part of history and academia at large. Regardless of the stance, what cannot change is that ancient Egypt was by definition an African civilization, and that even today Egypt remains part of Africa.

Beginnings Of Formal Writing in Africa

Now that the backdrop for the hieroglyph has been set, we can proceed to examine the formal writing system of the Egyptians.

Students of the hieroglyph and egyptologists have identified The Narmer Palette of 3100 B.C. as one the oldest surviving historical records of early Egypt (see plate 33 A and 33B). According to Lenore and Henry Scott (1968), among others, The Narmer Palette is a commemorative piece which affords some insight into the period just before the First Dynasty in Egypt. Bruce Williams (in Van Sertima 1989) tells us that the palette depicts the king's victory (*recto*) and the political unification (*verso*) of Lower and Upper Egypt into what marked the beginning of 3,000 years of continuous civilization, which is the longest known period for any culture (p.90). The palette displays a number of fully developed hieroglyphs. For example, in the main scene (*recto*), the king (believed to be Narmer-Menes) is wearing a White Crown, which represents Upper Egypt. He is shown defeating his enemy. Just above him to the right, there is a vignette which depicts a falcon holding a rope leading from a man's head. Significantly, the head is combined with the "land" sign (see plate 33 B) and with the papyrus plants (which represented the inhabitants of the northern, papyrus-growing delta land). On the opposite (*verso*) side of the palette, the king is wearing the Red Crown of Lower Egypt. Narmer is accompanied by standards and servants while reviewing the slain enemy. What we find on this palette is not a mere story of political unification of the two lands but also readable characters from the hieroglyphic repertoire such as the *crown* (a common hieroglyhic determinative) which signified royalty, the *falcon* or symbolic representation of the god-king (a bilateral), and the symbol for *land*.

Among the phenomena of ancient Egypt, writing developed much faster than any other area of the culture. The hieroglyphs were recorded everywhere, from monuments to everyday objects and personal letters. The abundance of written material indicates that there was already an appreciable level of literacy in early Egypt. What gives this speculation some support is the fact that the profession of scribe and its designated deity, Thoth, the patron god of writing and wisdom, were already highly revered. The scribe was kept busy, according to David Silverman (1991), copying religious treatises, legal documents, love poetry, and cures for veterinary problems (pp.1-2). In addition to these records that have survived, George James (1954) refers us to the several papyri of mathematics (namely, the famous Moscow papyrus); medical papyri with diagnosis, treatment, and prognosis; and the Pyramid Text, commonly called *The Egyptian Book Of the Dead* (which was translated by Wallis Budge in 1920). These texts are among the numerous writings left behind by the writing culture of ancient Egypt. Even though modern findings of ancient Egyptian hieroglyphics are voluminous, the body of extant texts represents only a fraction of this highly literate culture. At the center of this culture were the highly regarded scribes. In fact, Silverman points out that the word *sesh*, "scribe," was among the most frequently used titles in ancient Egypt. Scribes constituted a very sizable bureaucracy of the ancient civilization of Egypt (p.33).

Concerning the deity of writing, according to Budge, the ancient Egyptians believed, from as early as predynastic times, that Thoth (also referred to as Tehuti) was a "self-begotten and self-produced" god who was responsible for the calculations and stability of the heavens, stars, and the earth; that he had mastered the laws of both "physical and moral conceptions" and that he had knowledge of "divine speech." Tehuti was also credited as the inventor of the sciences and arts, "lord of books," "scribe of the gods," and "mighty in speech." He was viewed as the author of many of the funerary works which enabled the deceased to gain everlasting life. Tehuti's ability to write set him apart from even the highly revered Osiris, the god of the underworld, and Ra, the Sun god of whom he was the heart, i.e., mind, reason, and understanding (Budge 1969: 400-403). The textual evidence shows that Tehuti, the god of words, occupied quiet a prominent place in Egyptian culture, a telling indication of the importance attached to the spoken and written word.

The documentation of writing in ancient Egypt after 3100 B.C is copious. According to Lionel Casson (1965), in the earliest times, Dynastic Egypt possessed the all-important prerequisite tool for the advancement of successful centralized rule. The vehicle used to propel the transition of the political machinery from two separate lands into a unified nation of Egypt was writing. It was most important in the new epoch of Egyptian history to keep records, issue instructions, record poems, stories, essays, and narratives which, formerly, would have been committed to memory. *Literature was born in Egypt.* In addition to the aforementioned records, Casson reports that methods of calculating, say, time and space paralleled the development of writing. In this regard, the Egyptians were able to compute taxes accurately, survey the land with precision, measure weights and distances, create the calendar, and calculate time. Writing allowed for the genesis and advancement of medical sciences for which the Egyptians have received worldwide renown and recognition, even among skeptical classicists. Also, through the use of the pen, the early pharaohs were able to direct monumental projects, such as harnessing the Nile river by way of a system of tributary canals that reclaimed once flooded land (p. 14).

The fact that the ancient Egyptians have documented so many areas of their culture is ample reason for the researcher to investigate, though briefly, the features of the Egyptian hieroglyphics. In the earliest times, located by Silverman and Casson, the hieroglyphs were used to represent an idea, a word, a person, or a thing in a concrete and recognizable form. As the writing developed, Casson observes, most of the signs adopted phonetic values. Signs were used to stand for sounds and when combined with other hieroglyphs, the combinations were able to "spell out words that had nothing to do with what the pictures portrayed" (p. 141). An instructive example would be if one combined the picture of a *bee* with that of an *eagle*, resulting in the phoneme "beagle," or the combination of a *bee* and a *leaf* to be read "belief." In effect, the hieroglyph became much more than pictograms, which merely represent what was depicted, but rather, the combination of signs lent itself to the equivalent of what the linguist regards as phonetics.

Interestingly, Egyptian writing did not proceed at random. In fact, there are some clear lines of development which the written text followed. Generally speaking, egyptologists have identified five generic stages of written language development in ancient Egypt. W.V. Davies (1987) cites the first stage, called Old Egyptian (2650—2135 B.C.), as the period when the first continuous texts appeared. At the second stage, Middle Egyptian (2135—1785 B.C.), the idiom appeared. (Also during this stage, the written text of the First Intermediate Period of the Middle Kingdom is regarded as "classical," as it was used in literary, religious, and monumental inscriptions until the time of Graeco-Roman domination over Egypt. However, the structure of the language remained close to that of Old Egyptian.) The third stage, Late Egyptian (1550—700 B.C.), saw the documentation of everyday language, particularly in secular documents. Late Egyptian was different from the former stages, notably in its verbal structure. As a continuation in the development of Late Egyptian, its successor, the Demotic written script, lasted from 700 B.C. to 5 A.D. The final evolution of the hieroglyph was called the Coptic script, and it is the only stage of the language where "vocalic structure is known and from which distinguishable dialects are recognized" (p.9). Despite the several styles of writing and other structural features throughout the course of almost three thousand years, all the script styles have had some noticeable relationship to the hieroglyph (see plate 34).

Development of the Hieroglyph

Now that some chronology of the evolution of the hieroglyph has been established, a close look at some of the features and functions of the written language in the early stages is appropriate. The early Egyptian "alphabet," unlike that of Europe, was not borrowed from another culture; the Egyptians simply selected 24 of their own heiroglyphs to represent 24 different consonantal sounds (see plate 35).

Most historical linguists are clear that there were no written vowels, but some caution must be exercised about such an extreme formulation, since a few letters seem to function in Egyptian like vowels do in English. These "semi-vowels" (a description Joseph and Lenore Scott [1968] give to the anomalies) are still technically considered consonants. Nonetheless, although the true vowels were omitted in writing in the early stages, the Egyptians inserted vowels in their correct places in spoken language, just as in today's Arabic, and other Semitic languages such as Hebrew (p.13).

Not unlike other areas of Egyptian life, there were some definite principles that governed the writing system. According to W.V. Davies (1987), the hieroglyphs are known to have three major types of signs, each of which functions differently. The first type of sign is identified as the *"logogram,"* which represents a complete word; second is the *"phonogram,"* which defines a sound—the phoneme of the language, as it were; the third type of sign, the *"determinative,"* was used to make sure that a word's precise meaning was grasped. A point to be noted here is that logograms and determinatives are concerned with "sense" or "meaning" rather than sound and, as such, they are generically classified as *"semograms."* However, Davies cautions us that there are many instances of overlapping between categories where it is not always easy to distinguish semogrammatic and phonogrammatic usage. Even more complex is the fact that within each category, "sense-signs" and the "sound-signs," there are further variations. The superficially drawn lines of three categories of demarcation, then, are mere boundaries to give a sense of a working definition (p.32).

Examples which illustrate the three categories of the early hieroglyph might aid our understanding of the major principles that governed this writing system. Davies' example shows the simplest form of the logogram would be a word that is "directly represented by a picture of the object it actually denotes" (p.32). A disc with a small circle as its center signifies "sun" (⊙) and a rectangle with one of its long sides broken (▭) depicting the floor plan of a house, signifies "house" (pr). It is clear that a writing system that simply relied on logograms would be impractical, since thousands of signs would have been required to accommodate a very extensive vocabulary. Even more difficult, it would be very troublesome avoiding unclear and ambiguous definition for words that are not easily represented by pictures. In order to eliminate any ambiguity, it seems logical that the Egyptians had to devise another sign-vehicle to avoid possible confusion. That sign-vehicle was the phonogram.

Phonograms were derived, according to Davies, from "a process of phonetic borrowing, whereby logograms were used to write other words, or parts of words, to which they were unrelated in meaning but with which they happen to share the same consonantal structure" (p.31). By combining phonograms, or sound pictures, scribes were able to form a rudimentary version of a word. For example, "to express the three consonants for their word for crocodile, which may have been pronounced as "meseh, miseh or emseh" after vowels were added, the Egyptians combined three single consonant signs" (Lionel Casson1965: 152) (see plate 36). It is highly possible that a purely visual symbol of a crocodile may have been added for emphasis.

The purely visual symbol added to a word for emphasis is the third major category in the Egyptian writing system. Like phonograms, determinatives were also derived from logograms. These symbols were placed at the end of many words to ensure that the exact meaning was extrapolated. For example, a word indicating a person is walking, running, or advancing toward an object is followed by the determinative (∧) which represents legs (Scott 1968: 22). Besides the function of the determinative just mentioned, the determinative served at least two other important functions. First, if an intangible thought were to be expressed, a sign was needed to show that the idea was abstract. For instance, when the Egyptians wrote a word associated with hearing, the ear of an ox was often used. Second, since the written Egyptian text consisted of signs in a continuous sequence without a break for spacing, the determinative which usually followed the ends of the words served as breaks between recognizable words and sentences. A rubric, written in red, while the rest of the text was in black, sometimes served as the indicator for the beginning or ending of a sentence (Scott 1968: 23).

Direction of Writing

Generally speaking,the writing of texts in the hieroglyph was not done in a haphazard manner. Jaroslav Cerny (1952) has identified four different directions in which the text could be (and was) written: (1) from right to left, horizontally; (2) left to right, horizontally; (3) from right to left, vertically; and (4) left to right, vertically. To eliminate any confusion as to how a given text should be read, some rules were established. The reading direction was determined by the direction in which the "animals" and "people" were "facing" in the hieroglyphs. For example, if the faces were turned toward the left, that meant the text proceeded from left to right (see plate 37). Significantly, the right-to-left orientation was the most usual. Many experts have suggested that the preference for right-to-left orientation might have been influenced by the fact that most people are right-handed. In addition to the direction, one had to take into consideration that when one sign was placed above another, the top sign must be read first. Overall, a very deliberate sense of design and layout characterized the hieroglyph whereby the signs were not merely written in a linear sequence, but were displayed in an arrangement of "imaginary" squares. It is clear that the ancient Egyptians viewed the hieroglyph as more than writing but also as art. In fact, in Egyptian the symbol for "writing" was the same as that used to denote "art."

Having enunciated some of the features of writing orientation, it seems appropriate to examine briefly some typical sentence structure and grammatical features. It must be noted, however, that the discourse on Egyptian grammar is voluminous and complicated. To find rules and formulae to explain the grammatical structure of ancient Egyptian relegates its study to distortion. To avoid such distortion as well as long explanations of grammar and the many issues of Egyptian grammar, this research will address only a few important issues.

What follows is merely an abbreviated introduction to the grammatical structure of early Egyptian. According to Wallis Budge (1966), W.Davies (1987), and other scholars of Egyptian linguistics, sentences in Egyptian are loosely grouped into verbal and nonverbal. (Students

familiar with ancient Egyptian will know that the verb form is most prob-
lematic and controversial.) Davies declares that context is the most
important factor in defining distinctions such as "tense and mood and
the difference between main and subordinate clauses," which are not
always clearly expressed in writing. His examples seek to illuminate the
relationship between subject and predicate in nonverbal sentences
which generally are not expressed in writing. In a literal English translation, an Egyptian text reads: "the sun in the sky." The verb *is* or *was*
is omitted. But within the stated context, the verb *is* or *was* may seem
appropriate to insert here. "The master in the house" is another example which illustrates the importance of how verbs are understood within
a given context (p. 43). The 'absence' of the verb should not be a surprise; rather it is consistent with the implied vowel in early Egyptian.

In the instance of the verbal sentence, Davies also posits that
"the predicate is the verb, most typically one belonging to the so-called
suffix-conjugation," of which the basic pattern is verb stem + suffix pro-
noun (p.43). Joseph Scott (1968) adds that most of these sentences
begin with a verb such as "ran, love, or wish" followed by the "subject,"
or person performing the action, for example, *I, you, boat,* or *it.* Next
comes the received action of the person or object. Hence the normal
verbal sentence sequence reads as follows: verb, subject, object (p. 58).

Morphology: Gender and Number

John B. Callender (1975) points out that in Egyptian nouns are identified by either of two genders, male or female. Male nouns have no
special ending, but female nouns are identified by the half disc, which
is equivalent to the *t* sound. For example, the male noun *sinw* means
"doctor, physician" and *rri* means "boar, pig." In the case of the female
gender, the noun *hijmt* means woman and *sndwt* means "kilt, skirt."
With respect to number, Egyptian grammar distinguishes three: singular, plural, and dual. The plural ending for masculine is *w:* for example, *snw* means brothers; singular for brother would naturally be *sn.* For
feminine case the plural ending is *wt,* thus, "sisters" would be *snwt;* singular case of sister *snt*). The dual form is used for pairs of things. The
masculine dual ending is *wy,* thus, "two brothers" is *snwy.* In the actual
hieroglyph, two male figures would be preceded by two parallel lines.
In the feminine case the dual ending is *ty,* thus sisters would be *snty.*
In the hieroglyph, one would see the half disc and two parallel lines
before the representation of two kneeling women (p. 14).

According to Davies (1987), adjectives adapt their "gender and
number from the noun they describe and are placed after the noun."
For example, "good man" is *s nfr* and "good woman" *st nfrt;* "excellent brothers" is *snw ikrw,* "excellent sister" *snwt ikrwt* (pp.41-42).

Grammar

The corpus of Egyptian grammar is expansive, as is English grammar. Items of grammar include the articles, demonstrative pronouns, personal pronouns, possessive pronouns, dependent pronouns, prepositions, verbs, features of syntactic categories, and so forth. Since the present work cannot do justice to the full range of the grammatical features of the hieroglyph, the reader is referred to the voluminous works of Wallis Budge as well as Alan Gardiner's *Egyptian Grammar*, which lay out in detail the grammatical features of ancient Egyptian.

What did the Egyptians Write?

We know by now that the Egyptians spent enormous effort and time concretizing their ideas in writing. From the collection of books, manuscripts, papyri fragments, the pyramid texts, funerary texts, and inscriptions found on monuments all over Egypt, we have a wealth of testimony as to what this great civilization taught about itself. The following discussion will survey the functions of symbolism, mythology, religion, philosophy, the sciences, literature, and self-description in ancient Egypt.

The complex of philosophy, mythology, religion, and symbolism is viewed as the foundation of Egypto-Nubian civilization by many modern scholars of African history. Some of these scholars include George G. M. James (1954), Cheikh Anta Diop (1974; 1981), Theophile Obenga (1989), Yosef ben-Jochannan (1989), and Ivan Van Sertima (1989).

Obenga (in Van Sertima 1989) cites the translation of the "Ancient Egyptian Pyramid Texts" of the fourth, fifth, and sixth dynasties, as exemplary of what the Egyptians thought about the "universe before the present universe." The translation reads: "When I was born in Nun before the sky existed, before the earth existed, before that which was to be made firm existed, before turmoil existed, before that fear which arose on account of the Eye of Horus existed" (p. 291). This statement, Obenga declares, is a description of the beginnings even before the creation of the world. It is in fact the myth the Egyptians used to explain the concept of nothingness and being, which became the foundation of their philosophy and religion. Pharaonic Egyptians had long been contemplating the "radical question of questions" about the origins of this world, the cosmos, and the events that led to man's appearance. According to *The Egyptian Book of the Dead* (the oldest illustrated book in the world: 1700—1200 B.C.), before there was the universe, Creator-God, Nothingness, and Chaos, there was Nun. Nun was represented by "an abyssal water" which contained all the raw material, the preconditions as it were, for the emergence of life. The primordial water bore a kind of "latent consciousness" that allowed itself to manifest creation of "all which exists or will come into being" (p. 292). What is truly radical about the idea of Nun, is that the ancient

Africans of Egypt, from the Old Kingdom (2780—2260 B.C.) were capable of conceiving and articulating a stratus that preceded the universe as we know it today; a stratus that was formless, the "non-created," that which is amorphous. It is out of Nun that all things proceed, proclaims pharaonic thought, "the gods, and the stars, the earth and the sky, the world of the living and the dwelling place of the dead," that all dimensions of human existence had a commencement, except the abyssal water which is placed in its own absoluteness (p. 292).

Of note also, Anta Diop (1991) and Obenga observe, is that Black African thought on primordial beginnings is centered around "water." Obenga emphasizes that "water" plays a seminal role in the cosmogonies of, for example, the Dogon of Mali, the Bambara, the Akan, and the Bantu-speaking peoples of Central, Eastern, and Southern Africa. Since a full explication of all these various African cosmogonies is beyond the scope of this work, a paraphrasing of Ogotemmeli Dogon's experience will serve as representative testimony for other cultures within Africa. Although Ogotemmeli used the words "Water" and "Nummo" interchangeably, he posited that "without Nummo...it was not even possible to create the earth, for the earth was molded clay and it is from water (that is, from Nummo) that its life is derived" (p. 298). In fact, in all African cultures (and Egypt is no exception), both ancient and modern water gods and water libation play an active part in religious proceedings. Hence the abyssal water about which the Egyptians wrote represents one of the many strands linking them to other parts of Africa, "the cultural unity" for which Anta Diop (1978) argued most convincingly.

Returning to the Pyramid Texts, Obenga notes that emerging from the primeval waters (Nun) is *Ma'at*. *Ma'at* represents "that which must be," a "part of the cosmic order, part of Truth and Justice... the Supreme Virtue... and a guide and measure of all human activity" (p. 317). In the hieroglyph, *Ma'at* is read as "the elevated notion of moral perfection." The ancient Africans of Egypt maintained that all men and things in society must conform to the cosmic order for Ma'at to retain balance in the universe. The *Ma'atian* ethics has manifested itself in the art, monuments, writing, social order, sciences, and religion of ancient Egypt. The awareness of "order and beauty" is especially exemplified in pharaonic art.

According to George James (1954), architects of the temples and pyramids had to be trained (at the temple school) in the sciences, in history, in the lore of the great Egyptian hierophants, in control of thought and action, in a life of virtue—in short, in the *Ma'atian* principles of Truth and Justice. Also trained in the *Ma'atian* principles, Obenga writes, was the Egyptian scribe, who was no mere recorder of events and experiences, but rather wrote in accordance with the precepts of Truth and Justice—in accordance with *Ma'at* (Obenga, in Van Sertima 1989: 317).

To bring precision to the concept of *Ma'at* outlined above, perhaps what is most germane to this discussion is what Maulanga Karenga (in Van Sertima 1989) refers to as the recognition and pursuit of a shared moral ecology "with the indispensable goal and standard for a righteous person and society" (p.373). The ancient Egyptians recognized that the cosmic order and social order had to be comprehended and practiced to maintain balance in the universe.

Among the various facets of the ancient Egyptian world-view emerging from the Pyramid Texts is the drama of creation. The creation myth of Isis (the first egg; mother and woman), Osiris (the first king, the dead man deified), and Horus (the falcon king), Budge (1969) acknowledges as wholly African in origin. The Trinity of Isis, Osiris, and Horus set the foundation for almost five thousand years of Egyptian religion. A paraphrasing of the Creation myth positions Isis as the virgin that gave birth to her brother and husband Osiris and from this union came their son, Horus. As the myth explains, Osiris was later slain by his envious brother, Set (known as the evil one, equivalent to Satan in Judaeo-Christian tradition), because of his great influence and dominion over many lands. The courageous and bereaved Isis searched for Osiris' body, which was dismembered into fourteen pieces and scattered over the earth. Upon recovery of his body, she resurrected him, and Osiris ascended to the netherworld. She raised her son Horus to avenge his father's death and ultimately take Osiris' place on earth.

In this abridged version of the creation myth, one can discern many cultural features of Africa, both ancient and modern. The female symbolism is most interesting on two counts: first, woman is seen as primary and not as an appendage of man (as she is in the "Adam and Eve" creation myth in the Bible); second, the concept of matriarchy is established in Egypt through this creation myth. Students of African history know that the female bloodline is all important when it comes to ascending the throne. Anta Diop (1990), in a brilliant study of the role and history of matriarchy in Africa, found that the seemingly all powerful presence of the pharaohs was tempered by that of the queen mother (see his *The Cultural Unity of Black Africa* for a detailed account of matriarchy). Also derived from this myth is the mother-and-child image and the subsequent madonna-and-child (Mary and Jesus) image which came to dominate Greek, Mediterranean, and later European religious practices. Thus, the African creation myth ultimately set the religious and social tenor for some four thousand years of civilization.

Brevity must temper the discussion of the much heralded religious and funerary literary texts, since no one piece of work can do justice to the existing corpus of writing that represents the Egyptian thinking on religion. For this reason I have refrained from any lengthy philological and religious discussions. My objective is simply to spur the interest of those who wish to investigate in greater detail.

The first translation of the Pyramid Texts in modern times is credited to Maspero (1882), but it was not until 1910 that Kurt Sethe's work became the major source for understanding the orthography, grammar, and vocabulary of the Pyramid Texts. To provide some system for understanding the literary character of the text, Sethe divides it into *Utterances*. These utterances, Faulkner (1969) points out, were clear instructive messages as to how certain hymns, rituals, and funerary procedures were to be executed. For example, Faulkner cites the recitation of the mummification of the corpse and presentation of food and water: "I give you your head, I fasten your head to the bones for you... I give him his eyes, that he may be content—a *htp*-offering"(p. 2). These two utterances are among several examples that one might find carved on the sarcophagus of the dead king. Another example illustrates The Ritual of the Opening of the Mouth": " O Osiris, I bring to you your son whom you love, who will split open your mouth"(p. 4). Other examples give directives for a libation spell, presentation of food to the dead, resurrection of the king, the king's ascension to the sky as a star, the king's union with the sun-god, his role in the beyond, and so forth. For those whose are interested in the mythology and religion of ancient Egypt, Wallis Budge's work *The Gods Of The Egyptians* (1969) is a good source.

The remarkable reflections of the ancient Egyptians were not restricted to the Pyramid Texts, but were also expressed in the so-called Ebers and Smith medical papyri. Charles Finch gives us some idea of the enormity of these papyri when he cites Homer as saying that the medical knowledge of the Egyptians was far in advance of any other people. Finch also dispels the false claim of Hippocrates to the title "Father of Medicine" (which will not be detailed here; see Finch's work on *The African Background in Medical Science)*. The medical procedures of diagnosis, prognosis, and treatment are numerous and complex. For example, there are written accounts of head injuries, and their examination, diagnosis, and treatment. But what is most interesting in the context of this research is the written language and medical vocabulary used to describe anatomy and pathology of the human organism almost 3,000 years before Hippocrates. Some of the Egyptian anatomical terms that have survived from the medical papyri are: *djnnt* = cranium; *djadja* = head; *wpt*=vertex, hat; *hr*=forehead; *hr*=face; *maa*=temporal region; and *ks*=bone. Finch's account of the procedures and nomenclature recorded in the medical papyri of the Nile Valley is yet another testimony to the important role writing played in documenting the findings of the ancient Africans of Egypt.

Literature

Literature was by no means a secondary concern in ancient Egypt. The monuments and the several art forms (which I have detailed earlier) are usually praised, while the corpus of literature is either omitted or marginalized. John Foster's (1992) translation attempts to address the reasons for the underestimation of the anthology of Egyptian poetics. He argues that the Western vision of Egyptian literature and culture is colored by two "major hindrances": the Bible, and the glorification of Greece above all other cultures. Foster believes that these two bastions of Western thinking contribute to the West's historical posturing toward Egypt — and, one suspects, to the rest of Africa as well. How else are we to account for the failure to ponder the mind of a civilization that excelled in architecture and the other visual arts? It would seem logical that that same mind was capable of producing literary masterpieces. Wiedemann (1902) and Foster confirm through their investigations that ancient Egyptian literature indeed paralleled the elegance and richness of the visual arts with its honored words in prayers and hymns, stories, and love songs. The poets in particular, cites Foster, "delighted in the working (or playing) with the nuances of words and meaning, and in the sounds of images of the language"(p. xv).

Some examples of Egyptian poetics will help illuminate the classical contributions, brilliance, imagination, and consciousness of the ancient Egyptians, whose works preceded those of Homer and Shakespeare. Foster's collection from some of the translated poems and hymns is a good starting point along the road to recovering the figurative language and many of the major devices that characterize good poetry: sound harmonies, the special imagery of the Nile Valley, eloquence, and above all, the art of skilled craftsmen with words. Here are a few samples of ancient Egyptian poetics.

"The Instruction for Merikare", in the format of a hymn, was for the son of a king in the twenty-first century B.C., probably Khety of the Tenth Dynasty. This hymn, about the Creator-God as supreme among all the gods, states that God was responsible for the creation of all humankind, and that man was created in God's image, in a universe founded upon justice (Ma'at). This hymn also confirms the fact of monotheism in Africa, which is often misunderstood because of the numerous deities. The author of the hymn insists:

> The generations come and go among mankind,
>   and God, who knows all natures, still lies hidden.
> None lift a hand against the powerful,
>   and everywhere the eye sees ruin;
> One worships whatever god is met upon the way
>   made of enduring stone or born of metal......
> It is you who create the new creature in Woman,
>   shape the life-giving drops into Man..
> Hark to the chick in the egg.... (Foster 1992, p. 3)

Among the many observations Foster makes about Egyptian literature, this genre stands out. He insists that the Egyptian corpus is almost entirely a verse literature, where most of the instructions, admonitions, laments, hymns, prayers, and an appreciable body of fiction, bear the marked characteristic of verse presentation. Notable also is the "couplet verse" composition where two lines are used to complete a verse sentence (p. xvii). (See Foster's *Echoes of Egyptian Voices* for a full account of this hymn and others that are similarly composed.)

Cogently, the example of "The Tale of Sinuhe" helps to dispel the inaccurate notion that all of Egyptian literature was formulaic religious text. This tale is considered by some scholars to be the finest piece of literature associated with Egypt. Foster identifies this narrative as salient for understanding ancient Egypt because it encapsulates many of the cornerstone values and principles that governed Egyptian social life. The story, told in the first person, chronicles the life of a trusted emissary who exiled himself before an attempted coup against his king. In exile, Sinuhue recounts the greatness of his king and laments his cowardly act of leaving his king in the time of greatest need. Sinhue subsequently returns to Egypt in his waning years and is greeted by his king and family whom he once served. A complete reading of this poem will lead one to realize that Shakespeare's forerunners had perfected their craft from as early as the Twelfth Dynasty in the twenty-first century B.C. (Foster 1992: 85).

Wiedmann (1902) also offers many examples of narratives from several papyri in which travel and adventure are the main subject. Like all people of ancient times, the Egyptians were fascinated by stories of foreign travel. Diplomats, as well as merchants, frequently left their homes to do business outside of Egypt. Among the many stories of foreign travel, the "Story of Saneha" and the "Shipwrecked Sailor" of 1250 B.C., are the most popular. Like other narratives, the "Shipwrecked Sailor" was told in the first person. While on a journey to the royal mines, the narrator's ship was embroiled in a storm, in which all his crew perished and he was the only survivor. On a plank, he managed to seek refuge on an island. The survivor was subsequently seized by a gigantic snake-like creature which took the sailor to its home and had him give an explanation of how he landed on the island. After an exchange of information between the sailor and the creature, the sailor was advised to remain on the island for four months and await the passing of a vessel that would rescue him. As predicted, the arriving ship brought the sailor many valuable gifts of gold, frankincense, jewelry, and other precious items which he took on his return to the pharaoh. This narrative, along with other similar stories, reminds us of the adventures of Sinbad the Sailor which was written much later.

Besides the stories mentioned above, Egyptian literature was punctuated by love songs, romance stories (remarkably similar to the

Western classic of Romeo and Juliet), ghost stories, tales of magic, lost jewels, foreign conquest, and stories of ordinary people's daily lives. It might be worthwhile to investigate how similar many of these stories are to the Greek epics and masterpieces.

This work does not pretend to chronicle all the various written texts of the ancient Egyptians. As a matter of fact, whole areas of writing have been omitted or merely mentioned in passing. For example, there is a large body of writing in the sciences that has not been addressed, such as the mathematics papyri, astronomy, geology, and psychiatry. Legal and civic journals in great numbers have also survived. However, what most urgently needs attention now is the fact that the body of written texts from ancient Egypt can be put on the continuum with the written tradition in Africa. In this regard, linguistic and typological material will be used as evidence to couch this position. The argument to be presented is not new.

Typology

The ancient testimonies of Herodotus, Diodorus, and Homer were some of the first evidence that identified authorship of the many ancient Egyptian texts as African in origin (see Chancellor Williams 1976; ben-Jochannan 1989; George M. James 1954; Anta Diop 1974). Unfortunately, over time their testimonies were challenged and relegated to the realm of hearsay and untruth. However, it was Gerald Massey's (1881) two-volume work, *Book of Beginnings* which forced modern scholars to rethink their position on the origin of the authors of the more than seven hundred thousand books seized by the invading Greek forces around 632 B.C. Massey argues that experts in philology, mythology, comparative religion, or Egyptology cannot be viewed as authentic if they neglect the study of phenomenology of types. He insists that typology is the foundation of all human symbolism, myth, language, and religion, and that by engaging in such an investigation one can illuminate the hidden development of man.

Massey presents examples which connect the ancient Egyptians to the southern reference, as the lands of their birth place and "land of the gods." Furthermore, in Egyptian the word *Af rui ka,* (the ultimate etymological root of the word *Africa*) signifies "birth place." More significantly, the many recorded customs that were celebrated by the Egyptians comprise yet another typological source to buttress the argument for the African origin of the ancient Egyptians. For example, the primacy given to the matrilinear order in ancient Egyptian mythology, where the paradigm of female goddesses (e.g.,Isis, Hathor) dominated, is unmistakably African. (Anta Diop's [1990] *Cultural Unity of Africa* offers a comprehensive discussion of matriarchy and its connection between Egypt and the rest of Africa.) The "Great Mother" (cited above by Massey, Rosalind Jefferies, and Obenga) is another example of the preeminence given to the female of the species in Egyptian thought, as in the rest of Africa, especially as she relates to the beginnings of primeval man—the motif of the "virgin mother."

With Great Mother as the primal creator, she gave birth, embodied and typified the elements such as darkness, light, air, fire, earth, water, and blood. Thus one sees in Egypt the obese water cow as an image of nature that represented the female principle. According to Finch (in Van Sertima 1989), the serpent—which was (and still is) a very common symbol both in Egypt and in the rest of Africa—represented, on the one hand, darkness and death, and on the other hand (when the serpent had its tail in its mouth) eternal life. In addition to the above attributes, since the snake is capable of shedding its skin, that act was used to symbolize renewal and resurrection, which dominated Egyptian religion and mythology. Significantly, the pharaohs of Egypt wore the serpent on their crowns and so did the ancient kings of Mali, Benin, and southern Africa. Another example which Massey used to demonstrate the typological connection between Egypt and the rest of Africa is the *hawk*. The *hawk* emblem personified the pharaoh as representative and protector of Egypt. In the remote past of Africa, as far back as prehistoric times, the *vulture* (which belongs to the same family tree as the *hawk*) of the cave paintings was also known as the "Mother Killer" who would do "whatever was necessary for her race to survive" (cited by Rosalind Jefferies in Van Sertima 1989: 98). One also sees a parallel between the use of the *falcon* in Egypt and a *bird of prey* in prehistoric Africa, as well as the paradox of the pharaoh who was usually male representing the dominant female paradigm of Africa. Other symbols such as the nocturnal cats and water are ties that bind the Egyptian image makers to their ancestral African past. Even though the inhabitants of the Nile Valley had advanced to a dynastic civilization, their use of symbols to elucidate a comprehensive world, both concrete and abstract ideas, was still grounded in the constellation of signs and symbols bequeathed by their predecessors. The hieroglyph, Massey argues, clearly shows the rich past of the ancient Egyptians.

Linguistic Comparisons

Equally persuasive, although by different methods, are the linguistic connections posited by Obenga, Massey, and Diop. Diop's findings will be highlighted here. In the context of language, the research of the African scholar Cheikh Anta Diop—*The Cultural Unity of Black Africa* (1990), *Civilization or Barbarism* (1991), and *The African Origin of Civilization: Myth or Reality* (1974)—argues convincingly that there are several unifying areas of cultural similarity throughout Africa, of which written language is the most striking. Diop presents an exhaustive number of philosophical terms from ancient Egypt that have survived in the Senegalese language, Wolof. For example, the Egyptian word *Nun,* which represents "the muddy and black primordial water," has its equivalent in Wolof *Nwl* = "black," *Ndoh um nwl* = "the water of 'Black,' of the black (river), of the Nile." Other examples include *Ta* (Egyptian)= "earth", *Ta* (Wolof) = "inundated earth, the very image of Egypt, of the Nile Valley," *Ta tenen* = "The earth that rises, the first mound that appeared within Nun," *Ten* (Wolof) = "a formed mound (in clay), as God made to create Adam; emergence, earth mound"; *Geb* (Egyptian) = "the earth, the divine," and *Gab* (Wolof) = "to dig the ground" (pp. 358-359). Such cases do not merely establish similarity of vocabulary, phonology, and meaning, but also clearly illustrate parallels between two African languages—one ancient and one relatively contemporary—and a more exact understanding of how Africans formulated their thoughts on the beginnings of the universe.

Similarly, in mathematics there are examples of parallel vocabulary in ancient Egyptian and in Wolof. For instance, *k(a)w* Egyptian ="height", *kaw* (Wolof)= "height; *s(e)k(e)d* Egyptian= "a slope" and *seggay* (Wolof)= "a slope"; *hsb/or/hsp* (Egyptian)= "simple cubit", *hasab* (Wolof) = "cubit"; and *pss* (Egyptian) = "to divide", *patt* (Wolof)= "to divide" (p. 277).

Other African languages also bear many similarities to Egyptian in terms of texts, vocabulary, and phonology, but they are too many to chronicle here. (See Diop, Massey, and Obenga for many such examples of cross-cultural and inter-cultural linguistics.) Earlier reference was made to the philosophical concept of water in Egyptian and in Wolof and how it is remarkably similar in meaning and usage across the two cultures. In addition to *"water"*, *Nun* (Egyptian), *Nommo* (Dogon), one can point to the similarities in the names *Amma* "water-god" (Dogon), and *Amon,* "water-god"(Egyptian). Ultimately, a much more in-depth study of the linguistic structure and world-view of ancient Africans would surely shed more light on the African beginnings of writing and the impact that had on other cultures.

Summary and Conclusion

This research has been an interdisciplinary intervention, scaffolded with arguments from history, philology, and linguistics. I believe that the approach taken here is useful for understanding a whole people's general world-view and specific motives for thinking and writing. If Egypt has now been recast in an African context, it is by virtue of its own thinking and writing. Our examination of the ancient Egyptian texts of mythology, philosophy, typology, religion, and popular literature (poems, love songs, epics, and everyday narratives), as well as the scientific papyri, reveals a corpus of work that is unmistakably African in origin and in nature. By examining the many facets of the Egyptian text, the old assumption that Egyptian writings were predominantly religious contemplations has given way to the broader and more complex basis of a grand African civilization. To build a convincing argument for the African character of the written record of ancient Egypt, a two-tier strategy was used: (1) a chronological continuity from the Africa of approximately 40,000 B.C. to the predynastic (4000 B.C.) and dynastic (3100 B.C.) cultures of ancient Egypt was traced; and (2) the southern cradle of Africa was taken to be the starting point for the journey of signs, symbols, ideas, beliefs, and social behavior that culminated in the "classic" Egyptian hieroglyph.

In the effort to place ancient Egypt on the continuum of the African tradition of writing, Gerald Massey's theory of the use of typology as a critical and essential tool was most instrumental in the illumination of the connectedness between the hieroglyph and other modes of sign-system communication in Africa. Obenga's exposition on ancient Egyptian thought and its kinship to currents of thought in other parts of Africa has also served to define the African stamp on the Egyptian text. While Diop's comparative linguistic study of the current Wolof and ancient Egyptian has also helped to cement my position, it must be noted that other scholars have presented and still are uncovering evidence linking other African languages from West and Central Africa with the pharaonic tongue. In the final analysis, to pursue an argument which orients Egypt towards any other geographical space but Africa would seem unpromising at best.

And yet, despite all the evidence presented above, and much more that could not be included here due to sheer volume, some scholars still insist that the ancient past of this seminal civilization was not African. There is a continual denial of the African nature and character of ancient Egypt, as well as an ongoing attempt to marginalize the voice of people of African ancestry from commenting upon the many important cultural contributions of Black Egypt, among which writing is paramount. It is important for the voice of all people to be heard. But it is impossible for people's voices to be heard if the echoes of the past are not known. Even more tragic, in the case of people of the African diaspora, disconnection from their ancestral roots has seriously impaired their ability to create texts that speak of their lives in the context of a long and connected past.

The working definition of language posited earlier in this work maintains that language is a construction of the shared matrix of all-encompassing communicative behaviors that help the participant convey information that is meaningful, shared, organized, and dynamic. The Egyptian hieroglyphs aptly exemplify this definition. In the spirit of Eco's theory of semiotics, one could anticipate an intensive study of the hieroglyph from the semiotic point of view of written languages, formalized languages, visual communication, and cultural codes (1976: 11).

Given such an understanding of language, wherever African peoples are found, especially among those aware of the ongoing efforts at assimilation and indoctrination into an absolute Western hegemony, there are efforts to create counter-hegemonic texts that are more representative of the "hyphenated" African experience. Unfortunately, the African-American and African-Caribbean texts, for example, are frequently relegated to folklore and therefore are not viewed as serious literature by comparison with works that represent the canon of Western civilization. However, African peoples need not feel inferior about their own culture's contribution to world literature. For it is now common knowledge that Homer and many other revered Greek writers were influenced by the Black people of Egypt. If African peoples are going to take full advantage of the rich body of works bequeathed to them—and to all mankind—by the ancient Egyptians, they must revisit the writings of their ancestors so that a substantive legacy can be left for future generations of African people to build upon.

Consciously, African-American and African-Caribbean people have made some attempts at constructing a core constellation of written texts, primarily in the area of literature. Also, a growing body of writings is becoming more pronounced in every aspect of the African experience, both on the continent and in the Diaspora, in recent times. However, writers and thinkers must be aware of two important landmarks: **(1)** The African tradition of writing goes back beyond Egypt, the Sudan, and Ethiopia. In fact, the written tradition of more recent times extends to East and West Africa and includes: Senegal and Mali's *Manding* script, Liberia's *Via* script, Sierre Leone's *Mende* script, Cameroon's *Bamoun* script and Nigeria's *Nsibidi* script. In addition, according to Williams (1976), the principal learning centers of West Africa (15th and 16th centuries A.D.) at Djenne, Gao, and Timbuktu/Sankore University have left behind a legacy of writing in medicine and surgery, letters, grammar, and so forth (p. 219). **(2)** Writing in ancient Africa was not restricted to mythology and religion but encompassed the full range of human experience.

In the final analysis, image makers from the African diaspora and the mother continent are fairly successful at keeping alive and developing the sense of the African mind. However, writers and thinkers must be charged with the responsibility of making available to people the optimistic and life-affirming philosophy that characterized the writing and thinking of Nile Valley cultures. I believe that the continuity of African peoples must be closely linked to an understanding of their past, if they are to contribute to the corpus of work started several thousand years ago. In this introductory study, the seeds for further research into the African literary tradition have only been planted.

ILLUSTRATIONS

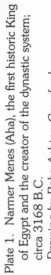

Plate 1. Narmer Menes (Aha), the first historic King of Egypt and the creator of the dynastic system; circa 3168 B.C.
Drawing by Reba Ashton-Crawford.

Plate 2. Khafre or Chephren, builder of the Second Great Pyramid of Gizeh. *Courtesy of the Museum of Fine Arts, Boston.*

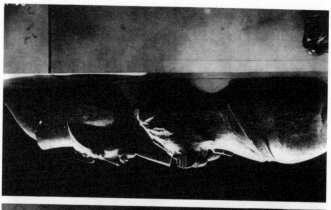

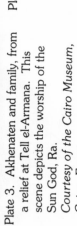

Plate 3. Akhenaten and family, from
a relief at Tell el-Armana. This
scene depicts the worship of the
Sun God, Ra.
*Courtesy of the Cairo Museum,
Cairo, Egypt.*

Plate 4. Portrait of Akhenaten, Pharaoh of the 18th Dynasty.
Courtesy of the Cairo Museum, Cairo, Egypt.

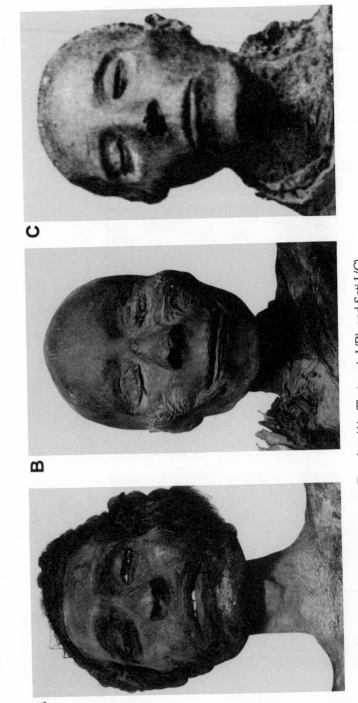

Plate 5. The Royal Mummies—Queen Taiouhrit (A); Thutmosis I (B); and Seti I (C). Courtesy of the Cairo Museum, Cairo, Egypt.

Plate 6. Palette of King Narmer Menes, obverse view; circa 3168 B.C.
Courtesy of the Cairo Museum, Cairo, Egypt.

Plate 7. Palette of King Narmer Menes, reverse view; circa 3168 B.C.
Courtesy of the Cairo Museum, Cairo, Egypt.

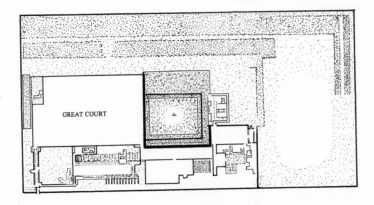

Plate 8. Step Pyramid and Complex at Saqqara.
Drawing by Reba Ashton-Crawford.

Plate 9. Step Pyramid of Djoser.
Drawing by Reba Ashton-Crawford.

Plate 10. Bent Pyramid at Dahshur, built by Seneferu
of the Fourth Dynasty.
Drawing by Reba Ashton-Crawford.

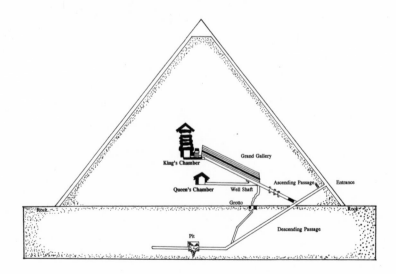

Plate 11. Diagram of the Great Pyramid passages.
Drawing by Reba Ashton-Crawford.

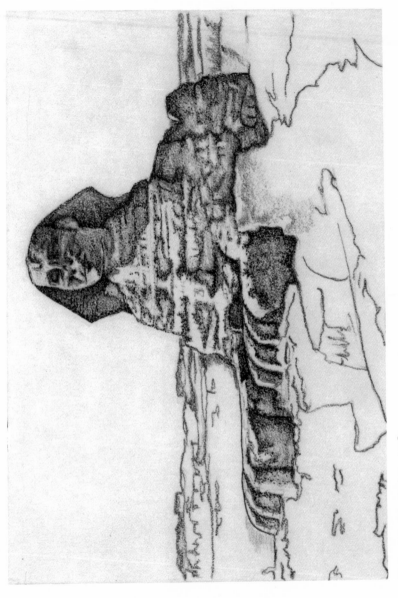

Plate 12. The Sphinx at Giza.
Drawing by Reba Ashton-Crawford.

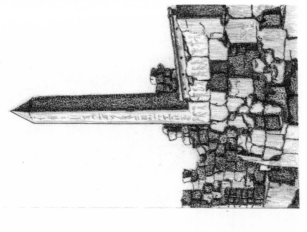

Plate 14. An Obelisk.
Drawing by Reba Ashton-Crawford.

Plate 13. The avenue of the ram-headed sphinxes at Karnak.
Drawing by Reba Ashton-Crawford.

Plate 15. The Egyptian Temple.
Drawing by Reba Ashton-Crawford.

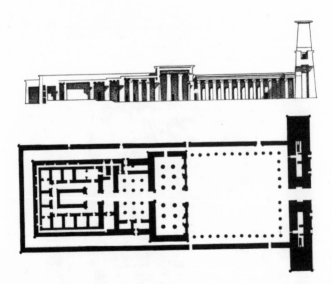

Plate 16. The Ptolemaic temple of Horus at Edfu.
Drawing by Reba Ashton-Crawford.

Plate 17. King Khephren.
   *Courtesy of the Metropolitan Museum of Art, New York,
   Rogers Fund, 1918.*

Plate 20. Painted Limestone Statue. *Courtesy of the Metropolitan Museum of Art, New York, Harris Brisbane Dick Fund, 1962.*

Plate 19. Triad of King Mykerinus. *Courtesy of the Cairo Museum, Cairo, Egypt.*

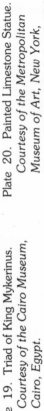

Plate 18. Mykerinus and his Queen. *Courtesy of the Museum of Fine Arts, Boston.*

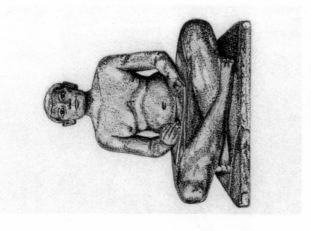

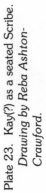

Plate 21. Limestone statue of Prince Hem-On, from Giza, 4th Dynasty. *Drawing by Reba Ashton-Crawford.*

Plate 22. Wooden statue from a tomb at Saqqara known as Sheikh-el-Beled, 5th Dynasty. *Courtesy of the Cairo Museum, Cairo, Egypt.*

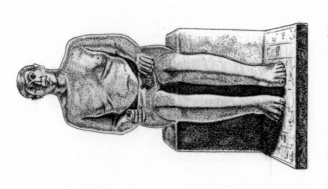

Plate 23. Kay(?) as a seated Scribe. *Drawing by Reba Ashton-Crawford.*

Plate 25. Tomb relief of two attendants leading bulls.
Courtesy of the Brooklyn Museum, Brooklyn, New York.

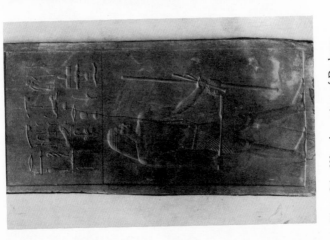

Plate 24. Wood carving of Ra-hesy.
Courtesy of the Cairo Museum,
Cairo, Egypt.

Plate 26. Hieroglyphic cartouches.
*Courtesy of the Metropolitan Museum of Art, New York,
Rogers Fund, 1908.*

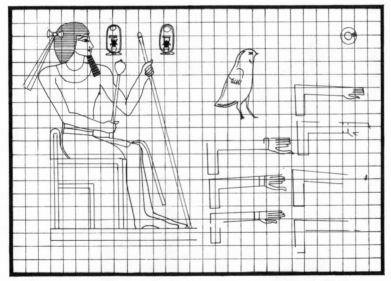

Plate 27. Grid and drawing showing the exact proportions prescribed for
rendering the King.
Drawing by Reba Ashton-Crawford.

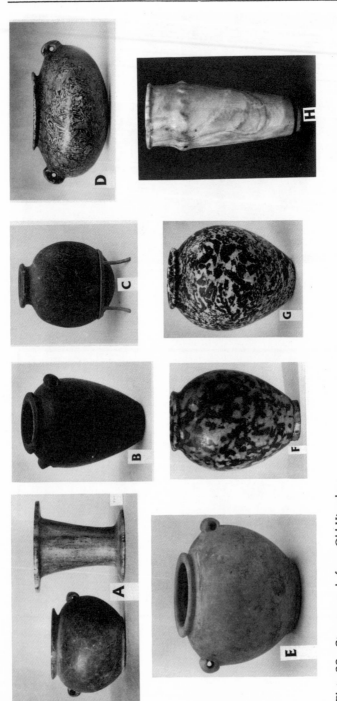

Plate 28. Stone vessels from Old Kingdom.
Courtesy of the Metropolitan Museum of Art, New York: (A) Rogers Fund, 1907; (B-C) Rogers Fund, 1910; (D) Rogers Fund, 1929; (E) Rogers Fund, 1938; (F) Purchase, Fletcher Fund and the Guide Foundation, Inc. Gift, 1966;(G) Theodore M. Davis Collection, bequest of Theodore M. Davis, 1915; (H) Gift of Mrs. Frederick F. Thompson, 1915.

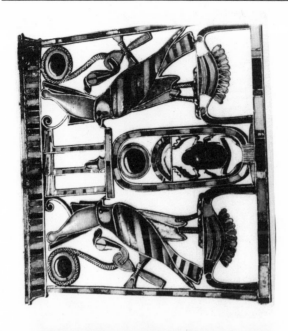

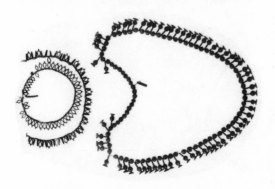

Plate 29. Jewelry from Old Kingdom.
Courtesy of the Cairo Museum, Cairo, Egypt.

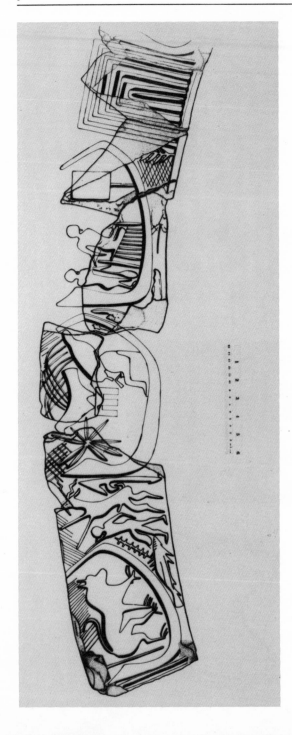

Plate 30. Archaic Horus incense burner.
Courtesy of the Oriental Institute, University of Chicago.

S

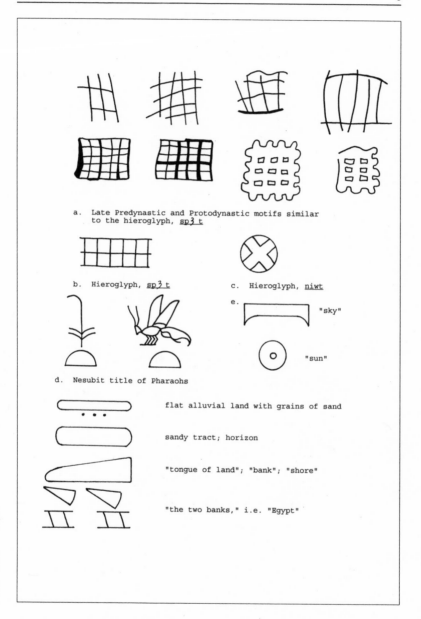

Plate 31. Predynastic symbols for geographical space.
Drawing by Reba Ashton-Crawford.

Plate 32. Hieroglyphic hawk development from predynastic to dynastic. *Drawing by Reba Ashton-Crawford.*

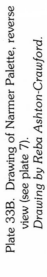

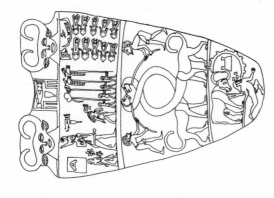

Plate 33A. Drawing of Narmer Palette, obverse view (see plate 6).
Drawing by Reba Ashton-Crawford.

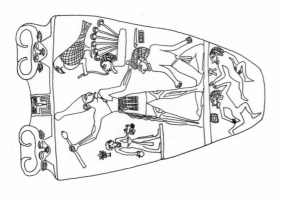

Plate 33B. Drawing of Narmer Palette, reverse view (see plate 7).
Drawing by Reba Ashton-Crawford.

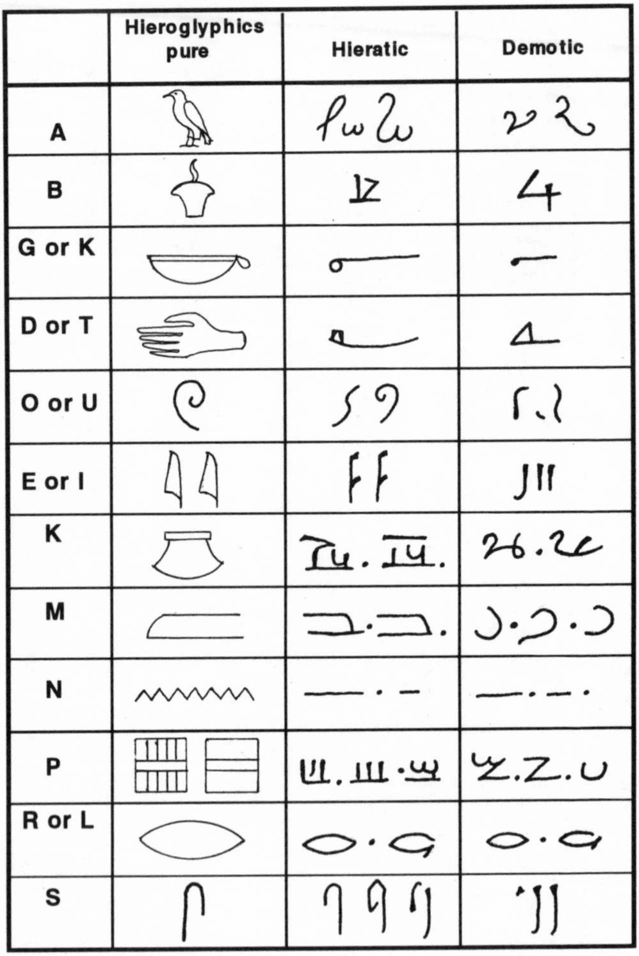

	Hieroglyphics pure	Hieratic	Demotic
A		ℓw ℓw	ν ℓ
B		ⱴ	4
G or K		σ ―	―
D or T		ᴀ ―	◿
O or U	ℚ	∫ 9	⌐.ℓ
E or I	ΛΛ	ƒ ƒ	ЈΙΙ
K		Ⱳ . Ⱳ .	26.2ℓ
M	⊂⊐	⊐.⊐.	Ɔ.Ɔ.Ɔ
N	ʌʌʌʌʌʌ	― . ―	― . ― .
P		Ⱳ.ΙΙΙ.ⱳ	Z.Z.∪
R or L	⬯	⊙ . ⊊	⊙.⊊
S	∩	9 9 ʃ	'ЈЈ

Plate 34. Hieroglyph script styles.
  Drawing by Reba Ashton-Crawford.

The Hieroglyph	What It Represents	Scholars Write It	How to Pronounce It
	vulture	ꜣ	a (father)
	arm & hand	ꜥ	broad a, as in palm
	foot	b	b (boot)
	basket with handle	k	k (king)
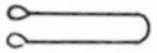	tethering rope	t̠	tj (reach)
	hand	d	d (dog)
	horned viper	f	f (feet)
	stand for a jar	g	g (go)
	reed shelter	h	h (house)
	twisted flax	ḥ	h (hat?)
	reed leaf	i	i (mill)
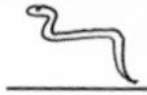	cobra	ḏ	dj (ledge)
	lion	l	l (light)
	owl	m	m (man))
	water	n	n (Nile)
	mat	p	p (pyramid)
	hill slope	ḳ	k (keen)
	mouth	r	r (right)
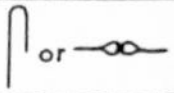	(1) folded cloth or (2) bolt	ś / s	s (sun) or s (zoo or rose)
	loaf	t	t (toe)
	quail chick	w	oo (too), also w (word)
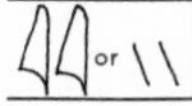	two reed leaves or two diagnal strokes	y	y (yet) or ee (city)

Plate 35. Hieroglyphic 24-consonant "alphabet."
Drawing by Reba Ashton-Crawford.

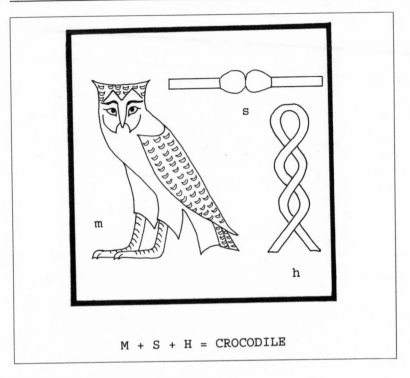

M + S + H = CROCODILE

Plate 36. Phonogram.
Drawing by Reba Ashton-Crawford.

Plate 37. Varying directions of writing in hieroglyphics: *upper panel*
    shows columnar inscriptions with both rightward and leftward
    orientations; *lower panel* shows horizontal inscriptions, again with both
    rightward and leftward orientations.
    Courtesy of the Metropolitan Museum of Art, New York:
    upper panel, *gift of J. Pierpont Morgan, 1912;*
    lower panel, *Rogers Fund, 1908.*

CHAPTER SEVEN

TOWARD A MODEL CURRICULUM

The Rationale

The curriculum advocated here would attempt to distill the content of the previous chapters.Most importantly, the curriculum cannot be constructed without an established understanding of the world-view and persona of the Egyptians, and all the cultural expressions examined above. The Egyptians had mastered an aesthetic which is the key to understanding their culture, for it is art and written language that constitute the material expression of the spirit and culture of a people.

Limits of the Model Curriculum

Optimally, the model curriculum will consist of a sequence of three courses. In addition, the proposed curriculum is planned with all racial groups in mind, although attention is focused specifically on the needs of African-American students.

First, students will be introduced to *the concept of culture,* using Nile Valley civilization of the first six pharaonic dynasties as the basis for their understanding. Important aspects relating to the definition of culture will include: geographical factors, history, myth, religion and philosophy, education, rituals, and social organization. Second, the sequence provides *an examination of the art* of the Old Kingdom, namely architecture, sculpture, painting, jewelry and pottery. Then, where possible, attention will be directed to *the aesthetics of the ancient Egyptians* that influenced the production of art and technique. Third, following the exposition on the visual art objects, the students will study *the development of the written text.*

Fourth, where possible, *museum trips* are recommended at least once per semester *to reinforce the classroom lessons.* In the New York area, for example, the Brooklyn Museum of Art, the Metropolitan Museum of Art, and the UNESCO Collection stand as the most organized sources of art from ancient Egypt in the United States because of the many significant pieces of art on display. In addition to "hands on" sources, the published field-work of egyptologist can supplement classroom instruction. From the standpoint of ancient Egyptian literary history, many written and pictorial sources are available in all the major libraries across the United States, and in many European countries, on the history and development of the hieroglyph and the voluminous literary texts, which include poetry, short stories, love songs, hymns, master epics, mythology, religion, philosophy, the sciences, and so forth. Ideally, the best educational aid for students who have completed this course of study in ancient Egyptian culture, art, and literature would be a visit to the ancient sites in Egypt themselves.

Present Situation in Art and Literary Education

The most compelling argument for implementing the teaching of ancient African art history, aesthetics, and written language into current curricula is the fact of our educational system's general failure to present authentic African studies, especially in connection with the study of art and written language. The fact that very little if any attempt has been made to correct this situation makes it all the more imperative that we address the problem now.

Given the lack of available informational and instructional material in the areas art and language, I have emphasized historical research in this work. In any event, taken together, my pedagogical philosophy represents the belief that a complete and inclusive approach to education will benefit all our students regardless of their respective cultural heritage. This proposal, then, is designed to provide educators with substantive information to fulfill an important mission—to educate *all* the citizens of this nation.

Value and Application to the Arts and Literature

The proposed curriculum provides the following:
(A) Students will learn that African art, writing, and civilizations flourished from approximately 10,000 B.C. (see: David Mac Ritchie (1890) *The Testimony of Tradition;* James (1954) *Stolen Legacy;* Diop (1974) *The African Origin of Civilization: Myth or Reality?;* Wallis Budge (1966) *Ancient Egyptian Language;* J. Cerny (1977) *Paper and Books in Ancient Egypt).* These authors and others examine

ancient and medieval African civilizations and their traditions of art and writing. For example, Kemet (present day Egypt), the Kushitic and Kiswahili empires (modern day Sudan), the West African empire of Timbuktu (modern Mali), Southern Africa (modern Zimbabwe), and North Africa, Mogadeshu and Bravis (modern Somalia), were some of the ancient and medieval African civilizations that possess rich but untapped histories of art and literature.

(B) Students will also be shown how ancient African art and writing made an impact far beyond the continent of Africa. For example, influences reached as far as Stonehenge, the pre-historic monument in Wiltshire, England, which many believe was constructed by Africans. According to Gommel (1908) and Squire (1905), the original inhabitants of what is now known as the British Isles were from Africa and played a highly visible role in "historical" times. Eyewitnesses like the Roman historians Pliny (who visited "Britannia" in the second century A.D.) and Claudius Maximus have described the early inhabitants in terms that can only mean Africans. The medieval chroniclers Godfrey of Monmouth and Giraldi Cambrensis also testify to the fact that Africans constructed Stonehenge. Modern-day scholars like Atkinson (1981) and the great Diop (who was most articulate and convincing on the point of African connection to Stonehenge) maintained unflinchingly that ground burial was a cultural practice of sedentary agricultural people, whereas Europeans were originally nomadic hunters and gatherers (and later seminomadic pastoralists), who practiced cremation. Diop and Atkinson have ascertained that Stonehenge and the other such megaliths in Europe were constructed by people who practiced ground burial, a tradition of Africa. Some research even suggests that some of the early inhabitants were African.

In connection with the Egyptian art and literary texts discussed in the earlier chapters, some significant examples of Egypt's influence on later civilizations are easily accessible. For example, Abydos has left a great legacy to the world in its City of the Dead. This city, where the building of temples was paramount, attained the zenith of ancient architectural structures—the Temple of Osiris. In general, several of the architectural features of the City of the Dead were later used by the city builders of Alexandria to erect what is now called Greco-Roman architecture.

It is well documented that Alexandria, the center of Greek civilization, was an off-shoot of Egypt (see James [1954] and Williams [1976] for an elaborate discussion of this topic). Egyptian philosophy was also the catalyst for the "Greek" ideas of democracy and humanism which permeated the legacies of art, storytelling, epic, and poetry that were handed down to the Greek, Roman, and the subsequent European societies.

Perhaps the best examples of the Egyptian influence on art lies in the early period of Greco-Roman civilization (335 B.C.—6 A.D.). The early Greek sculpture in the round was executed in ancient Egyptian poses (even if the faces, of course, were Greco-Roman). It is difficult to distinguish sculpture of the Egyptian New Kingdom and that of the early Greco-Roman period. In addition, replicas of the ancient Egyptian gods and the famous columns with papyrus crowns from Egypt are also common in Greece.

When one looks at the Americas, moreover, there is definite evidence that the ancient Egyptian culture, particularly the pharaohs of the Twenty-fifty Dynasty, had established a long relationship with the native people of the Americas, e.g., Central America and Mexico. Space does not permit here the detailed arguments and evidence which point to a strong Negro substratum manifested in urn figures executed in the manner of the Egyptian sphinx. Other examples include the bird-headed god, Ra, the step pyramid, temples, and the colossal, realistically rendered Negro head, which dominated the Olmec civilization. (For a complete discussion, see Van Sertima's *They Came Before Columbus* 1976.)

Briefly, we turn to similar and identical artforms that appeared in the Americas approximately 2,500 years after the beginning of dynastic Egypt. Van Sertima (1976) and Jairazbhoy (1974) cite glaring examples of the ancient African-Egyptian influence in the Americas at La Venta among the Olmecs of 814 B.C. to 680 B.C., which parallels the duration of the twenty-fifth dynasty of Black Egyptian kings. The Olmecs are known for their large representations of Negro faces in stone, while Tres Zapotes and San Lorenzo in Vera Cruz also carved such large heads from stone.

Let us now reconsider the pyramids. The pyramid (or *ziggurat*) is common to Africa and the Mediterranean region. Van Sertima (1976) and Paz (1990) both state that the step pyramid found in America can be traced to Babylon and Egypt. The first of such pyramids was built in the Americas at La Venta, which is also the site of the colossal Negro heads. No doubt, this pyramid represented a distinctive religious architectural form, whose significance parallels those structures in Egypt. In addition to the similarities between the Egyptian and American step pyramids, the bas-relief sculptures used in both are dominated by the "Mediterranean-type figure with beards and shoes" (Van Sertima 1976: 155). Other examples of the step pyramid found in the Americas are the Pyramid of Cholula, the Pyramid of the Sun near Mexico City and the Cerro Colorado Pyramid in the Chicama Valley of northern Peru.

Another notable and shared feature in the pyramids of both the ancient Americas and Egypt is the "fitted megalithic masonry" (Van Sertima 1976: 170). Van Sertima and Flinders Petrie refer to the finest examples of this technique, which requires considerable skill in fitting huge stone blocks together accurately without cement; the technique is abundant at Gizeh in Egypt and represented at Lixus in Morocco. Outside of Africa, the technique is utilized at Saccsachuaman and Cuzco in Peru and across the Pacific, especially at Easter Island. Of equal if not greater significance, A.B. Lloyd (cited in Van Sertima 1976) reveals that the methods of quarrying stone in both the Old and New Worlds are identical. Many more similar, if not identical, styles and techniques can be chronicled between ancient Egypt and the Americas, such as the lost wax technique, symbols like the sun and the falcon, astronomical science and its calendar, the temples, mummification, and writing on papyri.

The ancient Egyptian legacy of written text is astounding in its volume and influence on other cultures. For instance, many scholars who have studied the hieroglyph, including Davies (1987), conclude that our alphabet bears remarkable similarity to the Egyptian "alphabet." Similarly, in the context of popular literature, Wiedemann emphasizes the centrality of Egyptian stories and images and shows that travel and adventure were the subject of many papyri. Historical accounts tell us that many pharaohs were occupied by the desire to conquer foreign lands. Soldiers, sailors, and merchants often returned to Egypt with stories of their travels. The "Shipwrecked Sailor" narrative of 1250 B.C., which Wiedemann (1902) explicates, is similar to a certain Homeric tale told many years later. A review of the art and literature of ancient Egypt can only support the arguments for the African persona of ancient Egypt and for its influence on Greece and other cultures. Moreover, the abundance of evidence available presents a wealth of opportunities for cross-cultural investigation in the proposed model curriculum.

The Educational Philosophy Undergirding the Proposed Curriculum

According to Janice Hale-Benson (1986), the following three important components must be considered when designing a curriculum: political and cultural (ideology); relevant teaching methods (pedagogy); and academic rigor and content (excellence). Here are the views I propose on these matters.

Political/cultural

John Dewey's seminal work *Democracy and Education* (1916) is a pioneering and fundamental voice for the school's role in what has come to be termed democratic education. And in the case of education for all, this proposed curriculum addresses the specific concerns of students of African descent in the United States, especially as it relates to the political and historical background of African-Americans.

Dewey's vision for democratic education is summarized in his important argument that education should not exclude any group or groups of people who live within a democratic society. Dewey emphasizes the importance of education as an elemental tool in the continued advancement of a society. To maintain the continual growth of progressive ideologies, Dewey treats the school as the most important agent in the transmission of formal education. He held that if relevant educational experiences are not ensured for all people, the chances of their sharing and utilizing the knowledge and resources of a pluralistic society would be nil. In the past, and even more crucially now, the education of all Americans must take center-stage in the light of a rapidly growing, multi-racial population and the dawning of a competitive global society for the twenty-first century. A well-educated populace should lead to a more productive and harmonious society.

Unfortunately, Dewey's vision of democratic education is not yet a reality in America, especially for people of color. So argue Carter G. Woodson (1933), along with many contemporaries including Paulo Freire (1970;1987), Freire and Donaldo Macedo (1987), Jonathon Kozol (1991), Ira Shor (1987), and the New York State Board of Education (1989)—all of whom have helped to identify the historical shortcomings of the American educational system.

Woodson (1933) examines the legacy of education of Black people in the Americas and elsewhere, beginning with the system of colonialism. The colonial system of education ensures that the people who are colonized adopt the socialization process of the dominant culture's value system and history, which thus becomes the culture of its oppressed and repressed subjects. The labor force under a colonialist system of education thus becomes an aggregate of mere skilled commodities, pressed into whatever exploitation is profitable to the colonizer.

Speaking out against this inhumane treatment of Black people, Woodson calls upon the recipients of colonial education to re-educate themselves by joining the struggle for consciousness-raising and education-for-survival. Woodson declares that education-for-survival must struggle against the system that he terms "mis-education of the Negro" (p. 1). He describes the plight of Black people as "intellectual genocide" and says that "educated black people" should inspire race consciousness by embracing such expressions as "Negro literature, Negro poetry, African art, or thinking black" (p. 7). I must also add that greater focus on the African contribution to the sciences is equally important for consciousness-raising, education-for-liberation, and education-for-survival. (Ivan Van Sertima's *Blacks in Science: Ancient to Modern* [1989] is a good starting point for such an investigation.) My earlier discussion on the sciences involved in art-making also attempts some outlines that could be further investigated.

Generally speaking, Woodson declares that people of African ancestry must become intellectually aware through the "new" education he proposes. People of African descent must know that they hail from illustrious civilizations of the past and that they are linked to a long history that precedes slavery.

In essence, Woodson argues, to get beyond "education-for-survival" and to succeed in the struggle of "education-for-liberation," African peoples must be taught how to function in their own best interests and stop "begging the question" of their own humanity.

Indeed, since Woodson's treatise of 1933, significant changes have occurred in the education of African-American people, but much more still needs to be accomplished. Concerning the residues of colonial education, Freire (1970) in *Pedagogy of the Oppressed* warns against the certain danger of "mis-educated" people who can only envision themselves as adopting the roles of the oppressors they despise in speech. Mis-educated people are individualistic, thus they separate themselves from the oppressed and from the struggle for "liberation education." Thus, they become co-tyrants and fellow guardians of the very system that oppresses their comrades.

In an attempt to foster education that is meaningful and liberating, Freire and Macedo (1987) identify literacy as crucial. They have moved literacy beyond the common and narrow definition of one's ability to read and write. Literacy, in its "recast" role, is extended to the widest scope of education. The critical context for education is identified as *public schools and all places where educational functions are learned and contested.* In substance, Freire and Macedo argue that literacy is part of the battleground whereon people locate their respective histories and cultures and thereby become active agents "in the struggle to expand the possibilities of human life and freedom"(p. 11). Hence literacy becomes part of the political dimension in human life wherein meaning and relationships of power are determined. Significantly, this "radical" theory of literacy does encompass the definition of illiteracy as a complementary and crucial component of the politics of literacy. For example, if one is unable to identify with the prescribed experiences of the dominant social group, then that individual is deemed illiterate. In such instances, the label of illiteracy is used as a manipulative tool by those who determine the dimensions of literacy. Illiteracy is therefore relative to a particular political ideological construct and set of interests (Freire and Macedo 1987: 12).

At a time when literacy, multiculturalism, education-for-liberation, and the Commissioner's Task Force on Minorities report on *A Curriculum of Inclusion* (1989) occupy center stage of our education debate, it would be unwise to exclude considerations from the educational philosophy in a model curriculum. In particular, *A Curriculum of Inclusion* (1989) espouses a pedagogical approach that features the cultural contributions of *all* Americans. The advocates of this model propose that the experiences and voices of all ethnic groups be recounted and heard in hopes of confirming, legitimizing, and encouraging every student's own experience and voice. Then the ultimate goals of the educational environment will be built upon the student's culture and thus add meaning and importance to the student's life.

The broadening of the present education curriculum to include the study of ancient African art, language, and literature would show African-American children that their ancestral culture has made significant contributions to the world. It must be understood that the idea is not to promote African and African-American art and literary education to the exclusion of the art and literary histories of all other cultures. (Children of African ancestry need to learn about the rest of the world, too! Actually, the African experience is most effectively grasped when seen in relationship to all others.) A fundamental educational objective of this curriculum is simply to give African and African-American children the opportunity to frame positive images of themselves and commit themselves to a positive African identity.

Pedagogical Relevance

The issue to be addressed here is the method that will be used to teach African-American students and others of African ancestry. Much current available research shows that black students have distinctive learning styles, and teachers need to know of these peculiarities. For example, it is now widely accepted that African-Americans are influenced by the oral tradition; hence teachers should adjust their "talk" around an approximation of the students' "talking time." In other words, equal "talking time" should be considered when teaching students of African ancestry. Ideally, all students need to be heard and validated in the classroom. Furthermore, the teacher should encourage the learners to express themselves creatively through "raps," poems, and songs. Also, students of all ages learn best in small communities which emphasize "hands-on" and "experiential" learning in a variety of situations. Their education, then, need not be boring "talk and chalk," since music, environment arts, fashion arts, and folklore are already familiar pastimes to students of African ancestry. For example, most African-American homes, even when poor, have a deliberate sense of decor, furniture style, arrangement, books on various subjects, and the practice of story telling. Thus, even the mere description of the student's own home environment can be used as a reference and a resource when designing learning activities.

Academic Excellence/Content

Given the recent efforts to improve the standard of education in America, all disciplines must maintain the integrity of high academic standards. There is no place for mediocrity in our schools. Although art and literature might seem to be alien disciplines to most students of African ancestry, their teachers must encourage and require that they perform as well as their "Euro-American" counterparts. The extension of the definitions of art and literature to accommodate diverse cultural interests does not mean that disciplined learning must be relaxed for "newcomers."

Jerome Hausman (cited in Burton et al., 1988) makes a similar point as to how art education and education in general should work with respect to diversity. Perhaps, Hausman's most convincing argument is made when he contends that "the teaching of art in our schools has not been exempt from charges of relativity and failure" (p. 105). Our schools need to move away from the "relativized" standards that have emerged in response to diversity, toward more clearly delineated standards comprising the unity of all areas of knowledge that should be learned by all students.

In addition to the responsibility of art education to recognize and include diverse cultural perspectives, Hausman contends that if art education is to be taken seriously and become a meaningful part of the school curriculum, "its content must be broadened and its requirements made more rigorous" (p. 106). Moreover, if art education is going to seize this moment and join in the vanguard of educational reform, "then its content needs to be expanded to include attention to the disciplines that contribute to understanding art" (ibid.)—namely, anthropology, archaeology, art history, literature, and aesthetics.

The academic rigor and excellence which this model curriculum proposes should set itself the following two important goals: (1) to help remove art education from the periphery of serious academic discourse (as recommended by the Getty Program of Discipline-Based Art Education); and (2) to expand art education to include the use of the published research of pertinent scholarly disciplines (without which, the first goal will remain thwarthed). Of equal importance is the threat of what D'Souza (1991) calls "closed-minded, 'anything goes' liberalism" employed by some opponents of the sweeping changes in education. Some schools, he observes, are diluting their curricula in order to accommodate non-Western cultures and, by so doing, are actually minimizing the importance of multicultural education. Such an approach cannot be encouraged in our schools as it undermines the very progress of education which America needs to secure its future in a competitive world. Although educators must be allowed to argue their philosophical differences, accommodation to such differences should not occur uncritically and at the expense of the important question of serious curricular changes.

Application of Information about Ancient Egyptian Art and Literature

In order for the information provided in earlier chapters about ancient Egyptian art, writing, and literature to be taught to students, dedicated teacher participation is crucial; thus, a word about the teacher is in order here. The teacher associated with this model curriculum should understand and believe that the school can transmit and influence democracy. It would be most beneficial if the teacher were a member of the community and the culture of the students. Since such an ideal situation might be the exception rather than the norm, the teacher should at least be *familiar* with the Black student's culture, particularly the "African-American Vernacular" or "Black English". Equally important, argues Hale-Benson (1986), is "duality of socialization," which ensures that the Black student can participate in and contribute to the larger society. In other words, the teacher should serve as the mediator between the mainstream culture and the Black student. The sense of balance required on the part of the teacher is indeed delicate, thus the need for professional training is important. Such balance is crucial, since African-American students are quick to judge whether a teacher of African ancestry has or has not betrayed his or her culture. There is little or no redemption for those people of African ancestry who are perceived by their peers as "White" or "sellouts" of the culture. However, great respect and admiration is paid to those who can function as a Black person in the mainstream culture. Hitherto, the responsibilities of the teacher in this model curriculum are exacting (Hale-Benson 1986: 167).

In response to the demands of the proposed curriculum, formal pedagogical training is equally important for the teacher, regardless of his or her racial origin. Like Philip Jackson (1986), I am aware of the different arguments about "knowing how to teach"(p. 1). According to Jackson, a sampling of the views currently voiced argue that content is easily learned; others say the task of imparting knowledge is difficult. Some contend that teaching can be learned "on the job" while others maintain that much must be learned beforehand. Clearly, a definitive answer as to which faction is correct will not be provided here, nor do I believe that a universally correct answer is possible. In the instance of this curriculum, however, it is advocated that the teacher receive adequate training in pedagogy at a teacher-training institution. At the very least, teachers should have training in child development, learning theories, and curriculum development, as well as studies in African and African-American cultures. In practically all instances a knowledge of the psychological development of the group with which the teacher is working and a substantive understanding of the students' culture are essential prerequisites to the success of the proposed curriculum.

Aims and Rationale of the Model Curriculum

A pedagogical rationale is an explicit statement of the educational values and expectations of what students will learn in a curriculum of study. The goals, objectives, learning activities, educational philosophy, teaching approaches, assessment procedure, evaluation, materials, and all instructional aids are organized to facilitate the accomplishment of the general statement of the curriculum (Robert Zais 1976).

Definition of Goals and Objectives of the Model Curriculum

Goals and objectives of a curriculum are the expectations for behavioral changes that students should experience in a curriculum of study. Thus, instructional material should be organized and developed consistently with the stated goals and objectives.

One of the main goals of the model curriculum is to promote students' understanding of how people in other cultures express themselves using visual communication forms (namely the plastic arts and writing) and to learn that these forms are an integral expression of the social, political, religious, mythological, philosophical, and general world-view of a culture. Hence the purpose here is to help develop students' capacities for perception, comprehension, and evaluation of the written and visual statements made by a culture.

The emphasis of this program is to challenge educators to reverse the general trend of exclusion of ancient African studies today in our schools' education curricula. The evidence, for example, in the New York State Board's *A Curriculum of Inclusion* (1989) shows that schools are promulgating the values and ideals of the dominant culture exclusively; by doing so, all students—irrespective of ethnic origin— become victims of cultural arrogance and ignorance.

The philosophy of the model curriculum purports that an education in the arts and language should draw upon principles of learning and common sense to produce a framework for improving instruction, enriching and enhancing the background of all students for future study. In this instance, Thomas Brown's (1986) model of variables becomes invaluable in the design and implementation of the proposed curriculum. These variables include: motivation, classroom climate, student-teacher interaction, and evaluation. The learning activities are developed around subject areas in which these variables may be manipulated for the benefit of all students. For example, motivation, an important concept in conventional learning theory, is separated into two components: interest and transfer. In particular, interest (characterized by relevance and awareness of purpose) must come from a source other than those reflective of the values and ideals of the dominant culture. In other words, the teacher of ancient African art and literature, irrespective of his or her ethnic origin, should be interested in and, if possible, have a strong desire to put forth a point of view that is not influenced by the Western persuasion.

The model curriculum envisions a balance in which a major ancient African culture is explored and legitimized, while students are shown its connection with European/American and other cultures. Although the curriculum content addresses specific issues of art and the literary text of ancient Egypt, there is also the need to exercise some basic academic skills. Hale-Benson's recommendation for the acquisition of some basic skills in all the disciplines becomes important here. She argues that the acquisition of basic skills is crucial to all students, particularly students of African ancestry, whose scores are consistently behind those students from other racial groups. Among the basic skills to be emphasized, *language/communication* skills are critical to an education in art and language, since a substantial amount of reading is required. Brown, Hale-Benson, and others agree that students of African ancestry show distinctive difficulties in reading and mastering the language of the school, which still is "Standard Main Stream American Dialect." In keeping with the multidisciplinary approach and all-around development of the student, the proposed curriculum's emphases on appropriate speech patterns, listening, imitating, reciting, and writing are crucial.

Equally relevant, at least, is the fact that in the proposed curriculum students will be faced with a wide range of *mathematical concepts,* since these concepts are important and integral to the making of art in ancient and traditional Africa. Here, for example, is one such problem: Given that a pyramid in Egypt is a wedge, then, if one were to add a number of pyramids of similar dimensions to an existing one, joining the apexes and bases appropriately, what geometrical figure would one construct? Could it be that the Egyptians understood that the earth was of a similar shape? In addition, many features of the structure and development of language—both written and spoken—must be emphasized.

Here is an example of language structure that students can be encouraged to examine: Given that ancient Egyptian sentences generally began with a verb followed by the subject or person performing the act, and then by the received action of the person or object, write a passage using such formations of structure and compare it with the way you speak.

Along with the linguistic and mathematical skills development, a positive self-image and positive attitude towards school and learning will be emphasized. While students do need specific cognitive skills, those skills cannot be divorced from how the learners feel about themselves, the content, the learning process, the teacher, and the school. In Hale-

Benson's (1988) view, educators must be aware of the many reasons—including those that have not yet been fully identified—why students of African ancestry are uninterested in school. In the case of an art and literary education, we need to tread lightly by making sure that the material presented is relevant and that Africa is the focal point. Then the integration of other cultures follows throughout the curriculum. With their exposure to the history, cosmology, social order, and world-view of African peoples, it is hoped that a lasting interest and pride in learning about art, literature, language in general and their own racial heritage will be gained by young people of African ancestry.

Instructional Objectives of the Model Curriculum

The objectives of the proposed curriculum are the carrying out of the two major concerns and trends impacting the future of educational development into the next century, which Arthur Costa (1989) identifies as: (1) knowledge; and (2) thinking. He cautions that polarization of these two educational necessities would be counterproductive to their natural integration.

With the integration of knowledge and thinking in view, Vincent Ryan Ruggiero's (1988) *Teaching Thinking Across The Curriculum* is very useful to the approach adapted by the proposed curriculum. He sets forth a number of objectives which educators in any discipline can select. Appropriately, then, here are the important dispositions that should be encouraged in students.

Curiosity about their mental processes and eagerness to develop them further. Many students know very little about their own mental processes simply because they have never taken note of or asked crucial questions about them. For example: How keen is my judgement between what is hearsay and what can be proven?

Sensitivity to problems and issues. By becoming more aware of problems and issues, one becomes alert and therefore able to make intelligent connections between problems and everyday life experiences. For example, after studying Egyptian architecture, students should make the connection between the Washington monument and its forerunner the obelisk. (In other words the roots of the Washington monument are African!)

A positive attitude towards novelty. Creative ideas become possible when one shows the willingness to experiment with the new or unknown. Conversely, those who are unwilling to venture into the unknown are more likely to feel uncomfortable in situations which challenge their interest.

Interest in widening their experience. The wider a person's experience, the more resourceful he or she will be when it comes to problem solving. There are many ways of stimulating students' interest. For example, if a curriculum of study does not insist on dismantling the barriers of each academic discipline which separate and disconnect it from all other disciplines, but instead establishes connections, then students will be aware of the possibilities of applying what they learn in one subject to others.

The desire to reason well and to base judgements on evidence. On one level, all human beings want to reason well and base judgements on evidence. But on another level there is a very different dynamic at work. Carol Tarvis (cited, Ruggiero 1988) believes that "the very organization of our faculties seems designed to screen out information we don't want to hear, information that is at odds with our basic beliefs" (p. 72). This phenomenon, she argues, links human beings to the elementary need for order and meaning in life's experiences. To encourage students to reason well, Ruggiero contends, will require educators to demonstrate the difference between "right reasoning" and flawed reasoning—i.e., that "right reasoning" makes a genuine difference, while a flawed approach can result in faulty solutions and unreasonable beliefs which can in turn engender frustration, disappointment, and anguish.

Willingness to subject their ideas to scrutiny. A truly critical thinker not only exercises his ability to scrutinize others; he is also ready to subject himself to the scrutiny of others. Essentially, self-criticism cannot be neglected, as it is the ultimate test of one's strength. This stage of development in critical thinking should be guided through the process of being able to evaluate and prove or disprove one's own ideas.

Curiosity about the relationship among ideas. Simply put, students must be encouraged to ask many questions. In turn, teachers must be willing to take time to answer these questions or lead students to the sources that may best answer their questions. Most importantly, students must learn the cause-and-effect relationship that permeates all dimensions of life.

A passion for truth. This objective implies, on the one hand, a "philosophical attitude," which is usually associated with the humanities and, on the other hand, a "scientific attitude" common to the empirical sciences. If we acknowledge that both the humanities and the sciences are in pursuit of the truth, and that only their approaches differ, then the common denominator is the desire for truth. One's position should not merely be, "I agree or disagree," but rather, "Let me find out why." Of course, students must be persuaded against the popular and erroneous notion that "each person makes his own truth" or that being entitled to an opinion constitutes immediate access to truth. Unquestionably, uninformed opinions are not equal to informed ones (Ruggiero, 1988, pp. 68-76).

Finally, the goals and objectives should also seek to engage the four categories which Eisner (1972) identifies: intellectual skills, cognitive strategies, verbal information, and attitudes. Above all, the overriding goal this curriculum hopes to achieve is the merging of convention and innovation.

Design of the Model Curriculum

The pattern of knowledge to be acquired by students who participate in the proposed curriculum will be fundamentally triadic. To establish my proposed approach, Daniel Bell's (1967) triadic division (cited, Conrad 1990) will be used. It suggests that a "crosshatching" arrangement may be necessary, wherein a student in art and literature, for example, would study the history of art and literary texts from various cultures through general history, archaeology, and aesthetics. The purpose of this approach is not to argue for interdisciplinary courses but rather to give students access to the vast and varied body of knowledge to be tapped, and the various disciplines that can be employed to gather the information. The argument here is that students at an early stage— early secondary school or early college—need to be aware that one's education can be and in fact is informed by many disciplines.

To achieve an integration of knowledge, the proposed curriculum model is organized in the following steps:

1.*History and tradition.* This first step involves providing a comprehensive background about the history, world-view, traditions, social order, education, philosophy, religion, and mythology, which in effect made up the culture of ancient African Egyptians. Through such an introduction, the stage will be set for an understanding of how cultural institutions and ideas are reflected in the art and literature to be examined.

2. *Introduction of other disciplines into art and literature.* This second step introduces students to the disciplines that inform an education in art and literature. Through the proposed curriculum all students will have the opportunity of learning how another culture organizes its perspective on documenting ideas—i.e., namely the art and written language of that culture. For example, students will learn how a specific science (such as anthropology) acquires, utilizes, and revises its findings to arrive at conclusions about art and culture. In effect, students will have the opportunity to learn that they can understand the art of a civilization by studying the social norms, world-view, system of beliefs, rituals, and so forth. The immediate benefit of forging links between an education in art and literature and other disciplines such as anthropology, archaeology, linguistics and history is that it affords the student the opportunity of learning to analyze art and literature from varied points of view. It is important to note that Daniel Bell advocates that students be introduced to how the various disciplines function first before they are used in an interdisciplinary approach. In the case of the proposed model curriculum, the disciplines of anthropology, archaeology, linguistics, history, and aesthetics should be addressed so that students can learn the respective function of each discipline. He suggests that a grounding in these disciplines through their "conceptual framework and analytical techniques should be a prerequisite for inter-disciplinary work" (p. 342).

3. The extension of art and literary education to other Subject areas. The organization of the major program is essentially the application of the discipline to different subject matter in the field. For example, students may investigate the differences or similarities between Egyptian freestanding sculpture of the twenty-fifth dynasty and Greco-Roman sculpture of the fifth and sixth centuries B.C. In such an exercise, analytical techniques will occupy center stage in the student's education. They must also be able to make similar analyses and connections between, "the highly poetic phraseology" of the Egyptian poet (which Wiedemann identifies in his analysis in the "Story of the Peasant") and that of Homer and other Greek poets of later times, or between the romantic stories of ancient Egyptian and those of the Hellenistic period, Shakespearean times, and beyond.

In the final analysis, the following approaches will combine to comprise the main characteristics of the model curriculum:

* General historical and cultural foundations of the art and language development of ancient Egyptian culture.
* The methodological and philosophical presuppositions of the disciplines chosen.
* The application of appropriate disciplines to problem-solving in art and literature.
* Comparative artistic and literary studies, particularly between Western and non-Western cultures.

Teaching Strategies

Anyone who is familiar with teaching, argues Brown (1986), knows that there is always more content to impart than time will allow. One can imagine then, how complex the task of teaching becomes when the selection of strategies for instruction are considered in the curriculum. However, if the goals and objectives of the curriculum are to be achieved, different approaches should be used. In the proposed model curriculum, small group learning is one of the preferred teaching strategies. Recent research in psychology and educational practices, report Lauren Resnick (1987) and Brown (1986), have found that small group learning (or "social communities") play an important role in shaping learners' disposition toward thinking. The research has observed, for example, that through cooperation and social interaction, problem-solving and meaning-construction show a remarkable improvement over many other pedagogical approaches that focus on individualistic achievement. Through student participation in social communities, Resnick and Klopfer argue, students come "to expect thinking all the time, to view themselves as able, even obligated, to engage in critical analysis and problem solving"(p. 6). Significantly, the group approach is most appropriate since one of the major goals of the model curriculum is joining skill and content in the thinking curriculum (Resnick and Klopfer 1989: 6-9).

Other teaching strategies will include a variety of learning activities, some of which are prescribed by Ruggerio, such as: field trips to museums; the use of self-regulated computer programs; encouraging students to generate questions of their own about issues in art; written language development; analyzing and evaluating their own questions; students attempting to provide answers to their own questions; requiring journal entries that would aid in the development of thinking skills; posing problems for students to solve as assignments or for students' personal satisfaction; and having students debate important issues arising out of the course or from local and national debate. Of course, the teacher's role as model is very important: one has to practice what he or she preaches.

Finally, it must be emphasized that in order for these teaching strategies to be successful, students must know that they are viewed seriously by others. Again the teacher's role is essential. He or she must not show partiality for a particular position. In effect, the classroom should be a place that encourages openmindedness.

Evaluation Procedures

First, an attempt must be made to distinguish between assessment and evaluation, since the two terms are often confused and used interchangeably. According to Stanley S.Madeja (1977), evaluation is a methodological activity used to measure the student's achievement. A compilation of the information gathered can be used later by educators to make general conclusions about the success or failure of a program of study. He summarizes the nature of evaluation as having two major purposes in a school: one is "to determine the effectiveness of the instructional program and all its components," the other "to assess students' progress and to diagnose their problems" (p. 376).

Equally important, evaluation falls into two categories, namely, formative and summative. The formative method evaluates student work in progress; summative evaluation gives an overall progress report of a student's work and the teaching effectiveness, after the completion of a unit or a semester of work.

Assessment is a very precise form of evaluation procedure, commonly associated with letter grades or numerical grades. Stufflebeam (1985) defines the main function of assessment as the evidence which describes a student's demonstrated abilities and achievements. This information tells the student, teacher, and parents about the current levels of achievement.

Given the above definitions, evaluation is a broad description of the circumstances of progress and problems that surround learning and teaching, whereas assessment serves as a more immediate and precise evaluative tool. However, even though each has a different purpose, they are complementary and equally important in education.

The proposed model curriculum views assessment and evaluation as very important tools to monitor and measure the achievement of cognitive and affective goals by all students. Like Hale-Benson's model, the proposed model curriculum espouses that the evaluative procedures used, formative and summative, should be instrumental not only to identify the outstanding individuals, but also to collect data on those students who are not doing as well. Strengths and weaknesses of a curriculum are important information when considerations of curricular improvement and development are discussed.

Since this curriculum aims at merging convention and innovation, other evaluative procedures are also to be encouraged. For example, teachers can use written observations and/or personal notes, at their discretion, and include peers as evaluators, as they tend to have a more intimate knowledge of each other's progress. To win parental involvement in student education, it might be a good idea to have parents do observations at home and in the classroom.

Finally, although it is not possible to prescribe precise approaches for all situations, the evaluative procedures chosen should be used to measure how well the stated goals and behavioral objectives are reflected in students' progress with respect to achieving the basic minimum standards of the curriculum.

CHAPTER EIGHT

CONCLUSIONS AND IMPLICATIONS

This work is the first of many studies which will propose offering an education in art, literature, and linguistics to all students, particularly those of African-American descent. The content, goals, and objectives of the proposed curriculum are all aimed at shifting art, literature, and linguistics to the center of the present debate in education calling for "excellence" among all American students in all subjects. More particularly, the proposed curriculum is also aimed at moving art and language study beyond the traditional approach in a few ways. For example, by employing an interdisciplinary approach, the promise of enhancing one's acquisition of information will be improved. It also departs from tradition by focusing on the art, writing, and literature of Egypt in the "recast" context of Black Africa. In an attempt to secure a broad and accurate view of ancient Egyptian art, written language, and aesthetics, the proposed curriculum content takes the student on a brief journey through the ancient Egyptians' origin, development, and culture. Particular emphasis is placed on the epoch of the Old Kingdom, which laid the foundation for the later periods of Egyptian civilization.

Another notable feature of the proposed model curriculum is its alignment with a current development in curricular planning—*The Thinking* Curriculum, in which the goal is to integrate mastery of content and mastery of thinking.

Generally speaking, it is hoped that, through the learning activities of the proposed curriculum, the students will become more aware of the differences and similarities between their own environing artistic and literary traditions and those of another culture. As a consequence of such an awareness, it is expected that students will acquire informed influences on their ideas, their artistic and literary perception, and their appreciation-response to great works of art, visual, written, and oral.

Although the proposed model curriculum is a medium to achieve a series of carefully planned goals and objectives closely related to the components of art and language, the curriculum also has other important aims. Foremost among these is cultural literacy. The present work argues that all cultures in a pluralistic society should be adequately represented. When this is achieved, African-American students, for example, can learn about the great contributions ancient Africa has made to the world. Providing information about an ancient African culture will not only positively affect the African-American student's sense of self and pride in his or her own heritage, but students of other cultural extractions will grow to understand and respect the African contribution to the Americas and to the rest of the world. Consequently, it is hoped more African-Americans will then be persuaded to view art and literature more seriously and thereafter resume the African tradition of contributing to the world's masterpieces in art and literature.

To put all dimensions of the proposed curriculum into perspective, approach toward a model curriculum hopes to affect an education in art, literature, and language, mainly in the following areas: relevance and appropriateness; "interdisciplinariness" and academic seriousness; and the integration of knowledge and thinking (as envisioned in *The Thinking Curriculum*). Then education in art, literature, and language may become serious and progressive disciplines. According to Paulo Freire (in Schor 1987), *progressive teaching* is more than the transmission of knowledge about an object or about some subject; in the latter, the acquisition of knowledge is usually characterized by rote memorization on the part of the student. Instead, *progressive teaching,* among others things, teaches the "student-learner" how to apply analysis in order to find and extrapolate for him or herself the deeper meaning in whatever is being studied. In other words, the learner actively enters or penetrates the pedagogic discourse, so the content and thinking are integrated, while inventiveness and curiosity become part of the process of learning and teaching.

Freire concludes that to teach content in a way that allows the student to appropriate something personally meaningful from the subject matter "implies the creation and exercise of serious intellectual discipline"(p. 213). The effectiveness of an intellectual discipline is possible only when a learner's critical abilities are constantly being engaged and challenged.

The ideas for the model curriculum herein proposed imply that there is need for some radical changes in our schools' approach to and assumptions about an education in art, literature, and written language for all students. More specifically, the ideas for the proposed curriculum may prove very important with respect to further investigation of the teaching and learning strategies of African-American children. According to Hakkim Rashid (in Hale-Benson) and *A Curriculum of Inclusion,* if African-American and other so-called "minorities" are to become culturally literate, then their education must prepare them to participate as members of a culture that is characteristically diversified. Hale argues that the question of whether America needs a separate or special educational process for every ethnic group is not a necessary one to answer. (That question might be best answered *within* each ethnic group itself.) When a well-articulated pedagogy is established for African-Americans, she believes, it can be implemented in a multicultural setting (Hale-Benson, 1986, p.196; New York State Board of Education Task Force on Equity and Excellence, 1989, p.6).

Although an education in art, literature, and written language lends itself quite naturally to an interdisciplinary approach to learning and teaching, it is hoped that other content areas can adopt a similar approach, which allows one discipline to interface with other appropriate ones. An education in ancient African Egyptian art and literary development can also play an important role in modeling multiculturalism for the general education system in the United States, through its *practical* inclusion of all cultures' contributions in the actual *study* of art, language, and literature.

A final implication of the proposed curriculum for an education in art, language, and literature takes into consideration my forthcoming Teachers' Guide, which will outline a synthesis of content, goals, objectives, and learning units suggested for students in art production, art history, aesthetics, art criticism, literary criticism, philology, and linguistics. The compilation of the Teachers' Guide will include a team of teachers working toward strategies which are appropriate to their particular schools.

With my holisitc outlook on knowledge, the proposed model curriculum was conceived with the intention of providing a flexible structure in which the introduction of ancient African art and writings can become an integral part of a student's education at the secondary school level and college level in the United States. I am aware, however, that the success of the proposed curriculum will depend largely upon the willingness and competence of the teachers who choose to implement these ideas through thoughtful, skillful, motivating, and innovative pedagogy.

BIBLIOGRAPHY

A. Curriculum

Brown, Thomas J. *Teaching Minorities Effectively*. Lanham, Md.:
    University Press of America, 1986.

Bullough, Robert, Stanley L. Goldstein, and Ladd Holt, eds. *Human Interest
    in the Curriculum:Teaching and Learning in a Technological
    Society*. New York and London: Teachers College Press, Columbia
    University, 1984.

Burton, Judith, Arlene Lederman, and Peter London,eds. *Beyond DBAE:
    The Case for Multiple Visions of Art Education*. University Council
    on Art Education, Summer 1988.

Chapman, Laura. *Approaches to Art in Education*. San Diego Calif.:
    Harcourt Brace Jovanovich, 1978.

Conrad, Clifton J. F., ed. *ASH Reader on Academic Programs in Colleges
    and University*. Madison: Department of Education Administration,
    University of Wisconsin Madison,1990.

Costa, Arthur L. *Techniques for Teaching Thinking*. Pacific Grove, Calif.:
    Midwest Publications, 1989.

D'Souza, Dinesh. "Illiberal Education." *Atlantic Monthly*. March 1991: 52-
    78.

Dewey, John. *Democracy and Education*. New York:The Free Press,
    MacMillan Publishing Inc., 1916.

Eisner, Elliot. *Confronting Curriculum Reform*. Boston: Little, Brown and
    Co., 1971

Eisner, Elliot and Elizabeth Vallace.*Conflicting Conceptions of Curriculum*.
    Berkeley, Ca.: Mc Cutchan Publishing Corp.,1974.

Freire, Paulo and Donaldo Macedo. *Literacy:Reading the Word and the
    World*. South Hadley, Mass.: Bergin and Garvey Publishers,Inc., 1987.

Freire, Paulo. *Pedagogy of the Oppressed*. New York: Herder & Herder,
    1970

Goslin, D., ed. *Stage and Sequence:The Cognitive-developmental
    Approach to Socialization. Handbook of Socialization Theory*. New
    York: Rand Mc Nally,1969.

Greer, Dwaine. *A Structure of Discipline Concepts for DBAE. Studies in
    Art Education*. Summer 1987.

Hale-Benson, Janice. *Black Children:Their Roots, Culture and Learning
    Styles*. Baltimore and London: The Johns Hopkins University Press,
    1986.

Jackson, Philip. *The Practice of Teaching.* New York and London:
    Teachers College Press, Columbia University, 1986.
Kelly, A.V. *Curriculum Context.* London: Harper and Row, 1980.
Kozol, Jonathan. *Savage Inequalities: Children in America's Schools.*
    New York: Crown Publ., 1991.
Madeja, Stanley, ed. *Arts and Aesthetics:An Agenda for the Future.*
    St Louis, Missouri: Cermel, Inc., 1977.
Mattil, Edward. *A Seminar in Art Education for Research and Curriculum
    Development.* Penn State University, University Park, Pa., 1966.
McFee, June King. *Art, Culture, and Environment:A Catalyst for
    Teaching.* Belmont, Calif.: Wadsworth Publishing Co.,1977.
New York State Board of Education Task Force on Equity and Excellence.
    A Curriculum of Inclusion. Albany: New York State Board of
    Education, 1989.
Phenix, Philip. *Philosophy of Education.* New York:Holt, 1958.
Pratt, David. *Curriculum Design and Development.* New York: Harcourt
    Brace Jovanovich,1980.
Rayala, Martin. *A Guide to Curriculum Planning in Art Education.*
    Madison: Wisconsin Department of Public Instruction, 1986.
Resnick, Lauren and Leopold E. Klopfer eds. *Toward the Thinking
    Curriculum: Current Cognitive Research.* ASCD publications, 1989.
Robinson, Ken, ed. *The Arts and Higher Education.* Guildford, England:
    The Society for Research into Higher Education, University of
    Guildford, 1982.
Ruggerio, Vincent. *Teaching Thinking Across the Curriculum.* London:
    Harper and Row Publishers, Inc., 1988.
Shor, Ira, ed. *Classroom: A Source for Liberatory Teaching.* Portsmouth,
    N.H.: Hein Educational Books Inc., 1987.
Shor, Ira and Paulo Freire.*A Pedagogy for Liberation: Dialogues on
    Transforming Education.* South Hadley, Mass.: Bergin and Garvey
    Publishers, 1986
Stufflebeam, Daniel. *Conducting Educational Needs Assessment.* Boston:
    Kluwer Nijhoff, 1985.
Woodson, Carter.G., *Mis-education of the Negro.* Washington, D.C.:
    Associate Publishers,Inc., 1933.
Zais, Robert. *Curriculum: Principles and Foundation.* London and New
    York: Harper and Row, Publishers, Inc., 1976.

B. Archaeology, Anthroplogy, History

Atkinson, R.S.C. *Stonehenge and Neighboring Monuments.* London:
    H.M.S.O., 1981.
—. *The Prehistoric Temples of Stonehenge and Aveburg.* Crawley:
    Garrod and Lofthouse International Ltd., 1980.
ben-Jochannan, Yosef. *Black Man of the Nile and His Family.* Baltimore,
    Md.: Black Classic Press,1989.

Bernal, Martin. *Black Athena. Vol.I.* New Brunswick: Rutgers University Press, 1987.

—. *Black Athena. Vol. II.* New Brunswick: Rutgers University Press, 1991.

Blavastky, H.P. *Isis Unveiled: A Master Key to the Mysteries of Ancient and Modern Science and Theology.* Pasadena, Calif.: Theosophical University Press, 1976.

Bryan, C.P. *The Papryus Eberus.* London: London Press, 1930

Budge, Ernest A., trans. *The Book of the Dead. The Papyrus of Ani in the British Museum.* London: British Museum, Longmans and Co., 1895.

Casson, Lionel. *Ancient Egypt.* New York:Time Incorporated,1965.

Crowley, Daniel. *African Folklore in the New World.* Austin: University of Texas Press, 1977.

David, Rosalie A. *The Egyptian Kingdoms.* New York and London: Elsevier Phaiddon Press Ltd., 1975.

Davidson, Basil. *The Story of Africa.* London: Mitchell Beazley Publishers, 1984.

—. *The African Past:Chronicles from Antiquity to Modern Times.* New York:The Universal Library, Grosset and Dunlap, 1969.

Diop, Cheikh Anta. *The African Origin of Civilization: Myth or Reality.* Chicago: Lawrence Hill Books, 1974.

—. *The Cultural Unity of Black Africa: The Domains of Patriarchy and of Matriarchy in Classical Antiquity.* Chicago: Third World Press, 1978: and London: Karnak House, 1989.

—. *Civilization or Barbarism:An Authentic Anthropology.* Brooklyn, N.Y.: Lawrance Hill Books, 1991.

Eliade, Mircea. *A History of Ideas.* Vol. 1. Chicago: The University of Chicago Press, 1978.

Emery, W.B. *Archaic Egypt.* New York, N.Y.: Penguin Books, 1961.

Fernandez, James. *On Symbols in Anthropology.* Malibu, Calif.: Unbena Publication, 1982.

Fryer, Peter. *Staying Power: The History of Black People in Britain.* London: Pluto Press, 1984.

Geertz, Clifford. *The Interpretation of Cultures.* New York: Basic Books Inc., 1973.

Gommel, George. *Folklore a Historical Science.* London and Detroit: Singing Free Press, 1908.

Herodotus. *History of Herodotus.* Trans by George Rawlinson. New York:Tudor, 1928.

Honour, Flemming J. *A World History of Art.* London: Book Club Associates, 1983.

Jackson, John G. *Introduction to African Civilization.* New York: University Books, 1970.

Jairzbhoy, Rafia Ali. *Ancient Egyptians and Chinese in America.* Totowa, N.J.: Rowman & Littlefield, 1974.

James, T.G.H. *Ancient Egypt:The Land and Its Legacy.* Austin, Tx.: University of Texas Press, 1988.

James, George G.M. *Stolen Legacy.* San Francisco: Julian Richardson

Association, 1954.

Kamalu, Chukwunynere. *Foundations of African Thought.* London: Karnak House, 1990.

Leakey, Louis. *The Stone Age Culture of Kenya Colony.* London: Flass, 1971.

Levi-Strauss,Claude. *Structural Anthropology.* New York:Basic Books, 1963.

Lofland, John. *Analyzing Social Settings.* Belmont Calif.: Wadworth Publishing Company Inc., 1971.

Mac Ritchie, David. *The Testimony of Tradition* . London: Kegan Paul, Trenel Tripner and Co. Ltd., 1890.

Mbiti, John.S. *African Religions and Philosophy.* New York: Anchor Books, Doubleday and Company, Inc., 1969.

O'Connor, David. *A Short History of Ancient Egypt.* Pittsburg, Pa: The Carnegie Museum of Natural History, 1990.

Petrie, Flinders. W.M. *The Pyramids and Temples of Gizeh.* London: Field and Tuer, 1885.

—. *The Making of Ancient Egypt.* London: Sheldon Press; New York: The Universal Library, Grosset and Dunlap, 1969.

Sarton, George. *The Life of Science.* Freeport, N.Y.: Books for Libraries Press, 1971.

Silverman, David. *Religion in Ancient Egypt: Gods, Myths, and Personal Practice.* Ithica, N.Y.: Cornell University Press, 1991.

Snowden, Frank Jr. *Blacks in Antiquity.* Cambridge, Mass.: Nelson, 1970.

Squire, Charles. *Celtic Myth and Legend.* New Castle: Van Nuys. 1905;1975.

Tompkins, Peter. *The Magic of the Obelisks.* New York: Harper and Row, 1981.

—. *Secrets of the Great Pyramid.* New York: Harper and Row, 1971.

Turnbull, Colin. *The Human Cycle.* New York: Simon and Schuster,Inc., 1983.

Van Sertima, Ivan. ed. *Blacks in Science: Ancient and Modern.* New Brunswick and London: Transaction Books, 1989.

—. *Egypt Revisited.* New Brunswick and London: Transaction Books, 1990.

—. *Black Women in Antiquity.* New Brunswick and London: Transaction Books, 1988.

—. *The African Presence in Ancient America:They Came Before Columbus.* New York: Random House, 1976.

Volney, C.F. *The Ruins, or, Meditation on the Revolutions of Empires: and the Law of Nature.* Baltimore, Md.: Black Classic Press, 1991. [Reprint of 1890 (New York: Peter Eckler) edition].

Williams, Chancellor. *The Destruction of Black Civilization.* Chicago,: Third World Press, 1976.

Wilson, John. *The Culture of Ancient Egypt.* Chicago and London: The University of Chicago Press, 1956.

C. Art

Aldred, Cyril. *The Development of Ancient Egyptian Art*. London: Alec Tiranti Ltd., 1962.

— . *Egyptian Art in the Days of the Pharaohs*. New York and Toronto: Oxford University Press, 1980.

—. *Middle Kingdom Art in Ancient Egypt*. London: Alec Tiranti Ltd., 1956.

—. *New Kingdom Art in Ancient Egypt*. London: Alec Tiranti Ltd., 1961.

—. *Old Kingdom in Art in Ancient Egypt*. London: Alec Tiranti, Ltd., 1949

Badawy, Alexander. *A History of Egyptian Architecture*. Los Angeles and Berkeley: University of California Press, 1966.

Dewey, John. *Art as Experince*. New York: Capricorn Books, 1958.

Maspero, Gaston. *Art in Egypt*. New York:Charles Scribner's Sons, 1960.

Otten, Charlotte. *Anthropology and Art*. Austin and London: University of Texas Press, 1971.

Otto, Eberhard. *Egyptian Art*. New York: Harry N.Abrams, 1967.

Paz, Octavio. *Mexico Splendors of Thirty Centuries*. New York: The Metropolitian Museum of Art, 1990.

Petrie,Flinders. *The Arts and Crafts of Ancient Egypt*. London: T.N. Foulis, 1923.

Ross, E. Denison, ed *The Art of Egypt through the Ages*. London: Studio Ltd., 1931.

Smith, Baldwin. *Egyptian Architecture as Cultural Expression*. New York and London: Appleton-Century Company Incorporated, 1938.

Stewart, Desmond. *The Pyramids and Sphinx*. New York: Newsweek Book Division, 1971.

Wingert, Paul. *Primitive Art: Traditions and Styles*. New York: Meridan Books, The World Publishing Company, 1965.

D. Written Language

Arnett, William. *The Predynastic Origin of Egyptian Hieroglyphs*. Tacoma, Wash.: University Press of America Inc; 1982.

Budge, E.A. Wallis. *Ancient Egyptian Language*. Chicago: Arts Publishers Inc., 1966.

— (trans) . *Egyptian Book of the Dead*. New York: University Books, 1960.

— . *The Gods of the Egyptians. Vol 1*. London: Constable and Company, Ltd., 1969.

Callender, John. *Middle Egyptian*. Malibu, Calif.: Undena Publications, 1975.

Cerny, J. "Language and Writing." in: J.R Harris, ed. *The Legacy of Egypt*. London: Oxford University Press. 1971: 197-219.

— . *Paper and Books in Ancient Egypt*. Chicago: Ares, 1977.

Davies, W. *Reading the Past Egyptian Hieroglyphs*. London: British

Museum Publications, 1987.

Depuydt, Leo. *Conjunction, Contiguity, Contingency*. London: Oxford University Press, 1933.

Eco, Umberto. *A Theory of Semiotics*. Bloomington: Indiana University Press, 1976.

Englund, Gertie Frandsen. *Crossroads*. The Carsten Neibuhr Institute of Ancient Near East Studies—Papers from the conference on Egyptian Grammar, Helsingor, May 1986.

Faulkner, R. O. *The Ancient Egyptian Pyramid Texts*. London: Oxford University Press, 1969.

Foster, John. *Echoes of Egyptian Voices*. Oklahoma City: University of Oklahoma Press, 1992.

Gardiner, A. *Egyptian Grammar*. London: Oxford University Press, 1973.

Groll, Sarah. *Non-Verbal Sentence Patterns in Late Egyptian*. London: Oxford University Press, 1967.

Hoffman,Michael. *Egypt Before the Pharaohs*. London: Michael O'Mara Books, 1991.

Massey, Gerald. *Book of the Beginnings. Vols. I and II* London: Williams and Norgate, 1881.

Scott, Joseph. *Egyptian Hieroglyphs for Everyone*. N.Y.: Funk & Wagnalls, 1968.

Wiedemann, A. *Popular Literature in Ancient Egypt*. London: David Nutt Longacre, 1902.

INDEX